Dedicated to God—I can only do these things through the gifts you've given me.

} Acknowledgments

First and foremost, I'd like to thank God for keeping me in the game and helping me to get this finished.

Second, I'd like to thank Matt Piper for an already amazing book. Having such a solid legacy was wonderful to build from.

Major thanks to Mark Garvey for giving me the opportunity and also just being a swell guy. Best of luck with your future projects!

Also, major, major thanks to Cathleen Small. I wouldn't be able to tie my shoes without your help and attention to detail. Your cheery demeanor and cool-headedness kept me on track as usual.

Big thanks to Mike Prager for committing the little bit of time that you have to keeping me legit. Also, thanks again for getting me involved in the whole writing world in the first place!

Thanks to the Propellerheads for allowing me to work on such an amazing program and for just being one of the coolest companies out there. This book literally wouldn't exist without your amazing work. My best to Ernst, Leo, Tage, Marcus, Michael, James, Ludvig, Mats, Kristoffer, and the whole family.

Also, thanks to Rodney Orpheus for getting me my first copy of Reason. I still have the same box.

Also, big thanks to the Bitplant crew: Thomas and Wolfgang. I've stared at so much of your amazing work for hours on end. I never get to tell you guys how amazing I think your work is. I'm telling you now.

Oh, and Kurt Kurasaki: You've been a great friend to me and such an inspiration at the same time. Every visit's always a pleasure.

Thanks to Magnus Lidström: I love the Malström and all of your work. I'm proud to say I'm your groupie. www.soniccharge.com

Great thanks to my family for putting up with me while I was frantically running around trying to finish this. This consists of: Bill, Suzanne, Alex, Jennifer, and Will Childs. Allison, Tommy, Haley, and Lexi Parchman. Amy, Warren, Caleb, Collin, and Caroline. Cynthia and Tim Sweeney, Ruby Briscoe, Judy Briscoe, Andrew Mamaliga, Shelby Briscoe...miss ya, man.

Thanks to my friends: Christian Petke, Ashley Horstman, Jay Tye, Amrita Soni, Ozzie Ozkay-Villa, Brick Pursely, Baron Pursely, Shane Grey, Mikey Riley and family, Kate Luce, Sera. Also, Hope Works, Avoca Coffee, The Usual—Brad Henstarling—thanks for providing me a place to cool my heels while my brain was fried.

About the Author

Starting off as a small boy on a farm in a galaxy far, far away, **G.W. Childs IV** dreamed of sound and music. As he grew, he learned synthesis, sound design, songwriting, and remixing. As a soldier in Psychological Operations, G.W. learned ways to creatively use sound. As a touring musician performing with the likes of Soil & Eclipse, Deathline Int'l, and Razed in Black, he learned to bring music to the masses.

Still listening to his inner child, G.W. decided to work in videogames as well, and he *really* stepped into a galaxy far, far away doing sound design on *Star Wars: Knights of the Old Republic II: The Sith Lords*, acting in *Star Wars: Battlefront*, and composing music for MTV's *I Woo You*.

But the call of synthesis never fully left his ears, so G.W. did a lot of sound design on the popular music applications Reason 3 and Reason 4 and the amazing Rapture plug-in from Cakewalk.

Excited to share knowledge from these wonderful adventures, he has written books such as *Creating Music and Sound for Games, Using Reason Onstage: Skill Pack, Making Music with Mobile Devices,* and *Your Free Open Source Music Studio,* in the hopes of inspiring other people in galaxies far, far away.

} Contents

❊ ❊ ❊

CONTENTS }

CONTENTS }

Introduction

There has never been a better time to start learning Reason. The manufacturers themselves have mentioned that the current version, Reason 5, is the one they've always wanted to do.

Why is this version so important? What makes it so different from previous versions that have garnered awards upon awards? How could it be better?

Reason's history is one of amazing fame. Nearly everyone who has worked on music even in a minor way knows about this program. Even non-musicians know about it. I can't count the number of times I've had a relative, a girlfriend, or a best friend mention that he or she has heard of Reason because "so-and-so uses it."

But, again, if Reason is so well known already, how could it be better? Why is right now the best time to start learning it?

First, the creators of Reason have added the amazing new Kong drum module, which complements every device within Reason in amazing ways.

Yeah, that's great, another drum module.... No, seriously—it's huge.

Second, blocks, blocks, blocks... These are an amazing way to create and organize your songs. They're part marker, part step sequencing. They're a real game-changer.

But, here's the biggest reason (pun intended) of all: sampling. For every version of Reason up until now, you had to import audio files for use with modules such as Redrum, NN-XT, and NN-19. Reason did not record audio, period. But with version 5, you can now record audio into individual instruments such as Redrum and all the other modules listed.

But what's even more incredible is that it's really easy.

But this book won't talk to you only about the features I've been raving about here. *Reason 5 Ignite!* covers all of it! All the instruments up until now, all the instruments that are new, and all the features that you must know about if you are to learn Reason—everything that makes Reason a complete package.

Throughout this book, you won't hear, "You can't do that, but you can do this." That's what you would've heard in earlier books on Reason 3 and 4. But now you can do it all! And, I'm happy to say that this book will show you it all.

This book is organized so that every module gets its own chapter. It gets into the thick of each module—just like Reason gets really thick in general.

Reason 5 Ignite! is also organized so that you can jump around if there's a particular instrument that you just *have* to know about now! However, I suggest covering the first couple of chapters before you start bouncing around if you're completely new to the program. They'll at least get you familiar with Reason basics.

All right, I can hardly contain my excitement as I write this. So, rather than exploding, I'm going to use a phrase that I say often when it comes to Reason: Let's get started!

1 } Getting to Know Reason 5

Congratulations. You've gotten yourself some top-notch music production software, and it's not hard to learn. You have a book in your hands that will give you a substantial head start and really save you some time in the learning process. To that end, Chapters 2 through 9 will focus on particular bits of Reason and will go pretty deep into each area.

The purpose of this first chapter is much like the purpose of the practice mode on a videogame, where you can get used to controlling the vehicle without anyone shooting at you. I'd like to help you get a feel for the basic functions in Reason that you'll be using for the rest of the book and also point out a couple of important settings that you should be aware of to get the most out of Reason 5 (and have the best experience possible with this book).

In this chapter you will learn how to:

※ Set your Reason Preferences so that you can get the most out of this book
※ Add devices to the Reason rack
※ Use the 14-channel Reason Mixer
※ Use the Reason Sequencer

Don't Install from the Reason 5.0 DVD

What? Don't install from this beautiful DVD that I just took out of the pretty black box? That's right. Why? Because by the time you read this, Propellerhead will have already released an update for registered users, and the update will work better than version 5.0. Trust me: No matter how awesome the software company is (and Propellerhead is a very cool company), the original release version usually has some bugs or bits that weren't quite ready when the software first came out. So please register yourself and your software at www.propellerheads.se. Then log in and download the latest update for Reason 5. After you run the installer you downloaded and launch Reason for the first time, it will ask you to put in the pretty black DVD, and it will install your Reason Factory sound bank and Orkester ReFills from the DVD. By the way, if you already installed from the disc, don't worry. All you have to do is uninstall and then download and install the latest version from www.propellerheads.se.

Important General Settings

Here are a few settings that will help you as you use Reason. They are also settings that I used when creating the tutorials in this book, so if you set them the same way, we can both be on the same page and avoid unnecessary confusion.

1 **Open** the **Reason Preferences** (from the Edit menu if you're using Windows or from the Reason menu if you're using a Mac) and make sure you're on the General page.

2 **Set Editing: Mouse Knob Range** to Very Precise. That way you can select very specific values when you move knobs and faders on the Reason devices.

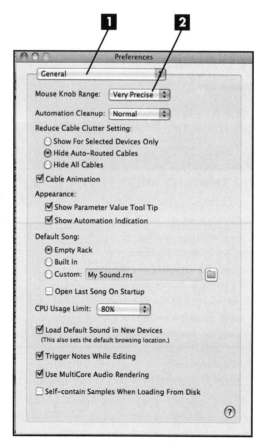

3 **Check** the box next to **Show Parameter Value Tool Tip** if it is not already selected. That way, when you let your cursor rest over a control on a Reason device, a red text box will appear, telling you the full name of the control and the exact value it is set to.

4 **Check** the box next to **Show Automation Indication** if it is not already selected, so that if you record automation on a knob, fader, or other control, there will be a green outline around it to show that it is automated (and will move by itself at some point during song playback).

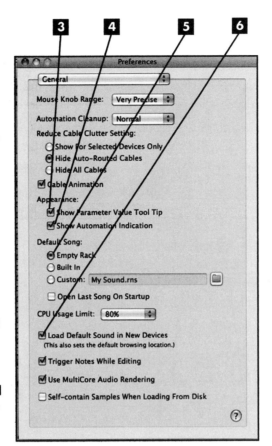

5 **Set Default Song** for Empty Rack, because nearly all the exercises in this book will start with an empty rack.

6 **Check Load Default Sound in New Devices** while you are using this book, because that's the way I had it set as I constructed the exercises.

For information regarding settings on the rest of the Preferences pages (including Audio Preferences and Keyboards and Control Surfaces), consult the Reason Operation Manual and the manual for your specific audio interface or MIDI device. There are just too many possible configurations to try to cover them all in this book.

Getting to Know the Reason Rack

One great thing about Reason is the way devices are arranged and connected the same way they would be in a real studio rack. This makes the logic simple to understand and very familiar to anyone who has worked in a recording studio or who has connected guitar pedals or modular synthesizers, for that matter.

Rack Front and Back

In the demo song you are about to open, you will see that several of the devices in the Reason rack are folded. This means their size is minimized so that you can see as many devices as possible at one time on the screen. You will unfold a few of them in the following exercise.

1 From the File menu, **select Open** and **browse** to **Reason (Program/ Application Folder) > Demo Songs > More Demo Songs> eXode – Radiant Emission.rps** and then **open** that **song**.

2 **Click OK** to close the Song Information window.

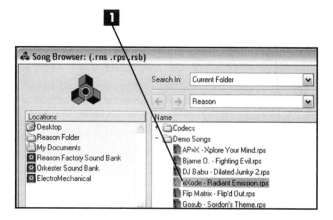

3 **Click** the **triangle/arrow** on the left of the Reason hardware device to unfold it. This device represents the connection between the rest of the rack and your sound-card and MIDI devices.

4 **Unfold** the **MClass Mastering Suite Combinator** to see all the fancy gold devices being used to put the final audio processing on this song.

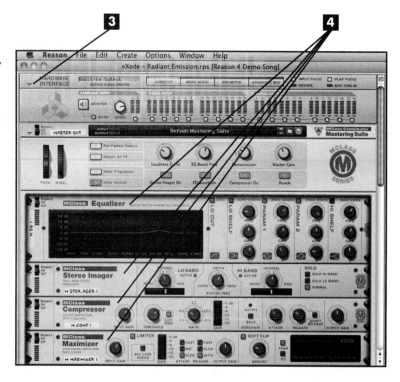

5 Press the **Tab key** on your computer keyboard to flip the Reason rack around and enjoy the hot cable-swinging action. Then **drag** the **vertical scrollbar** down until you see Remix. Remix is also referred to as Mixer 14:2.

6 **Unfold Mixer 14:2 (Remix).**

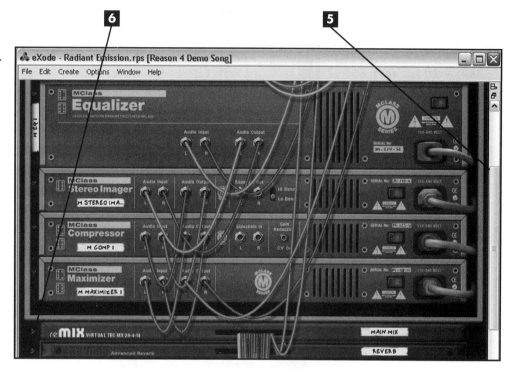

7 **Click** on the **cable** plugged into the Channel 8 Left Audio input, and **drag** and **connect it** to the Channel 9 Left Audio input. This is how you make connections on the back of the Reason rack.

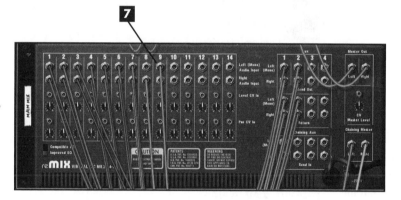

Before moving on, here's one last word about folding. You will notice that to the left of each track in the Reason Sequencer, there is a fold/unfold triangle as well. It serves the same purpose as in the rack. It allows you to fold an item to save space when you are not editing it or unfold it when you need to see the details. But before getting into the Reason Sequencer, let's create some devices in the rack.

Creating Devices

For the next exercise, you will want to start with an empty rack, either by launching Reason or by selecting New (Ctrl+N) from the File menu. If you have Default Song set for Empty Rack on the General page of your Reason Preferences as instructed in the "Important General Settings" section at the start of this chapter, you should be good to go. The purpose of this exercise is to show you the different ways to create devices in the Reason rack.

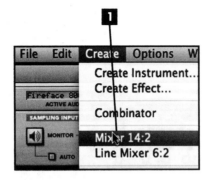

1 From the Create menu, **select Mixer 14:2**.

2 **Right-click** on **Mixer 14:2**, and a context menu will pop up. From that menu, **mouse over Create** and **select Subtractor Analog Synthesizer**.

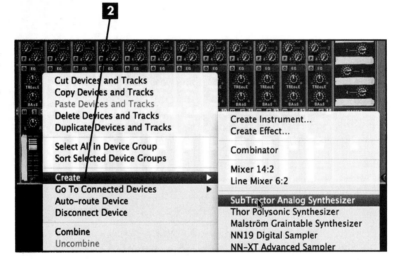

3 From the Window menu, select **Show Tool Window**. (Or you could use the F8 key, which is the keyboard shortcut for this same function.)

4 **Drag** a **Malström Graintable Synthesizer** from the Tool window and **drop it** under the Subtractor in the rack.

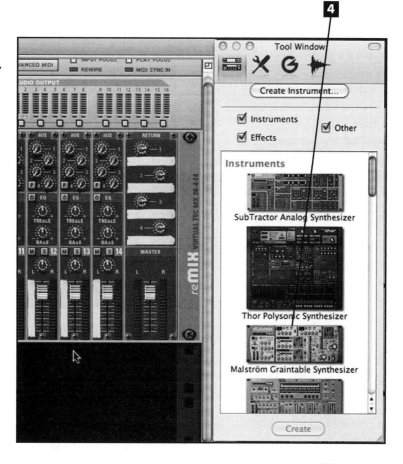

5 From the Create menu, **select Create Instrument**.

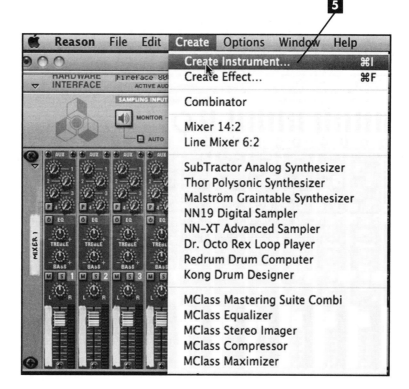

6 Now instead of choosing a specific device, you will be choosing a specific sound from the Patch Browser (which could come from any instrument). **Expand** the **Bass folder** and then **double-click** on **Attack Bass.zyp**.

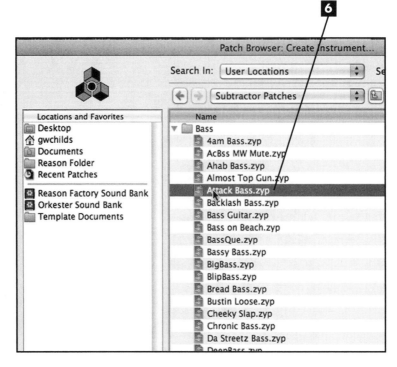

7 Now that you have created an instance of Thor, **drag** the **vertical scrollbar** up to the top of the page, and you will see that all three devices you created have been automatically routed to the first three channels on Mixer 14:2.

8 **Click** the **Tab key** on your computer keyboard to flip your rack around.

The reason why I wanted you to flip the rack around in Step 8 is so that you could see the cables connecting the three instruments to the Mixer, as well as the cables connecting the master outputs of the Mixer to Outputs 1 and 2 of your soundcard by way of the Reason hardware device.

Mixer 14:2 (Remix)

The Mixer 14:2 is the 14-channel mixer you will be using at least one instance of in all of your Reason songs. It is laid out like a pretty standard analog mixer. In the next exercise, you will get a feel for its various functions.

Mute, Solo, Pan, and Volume

1 From the File menu, **select Open** and **browse** to **Reason (Program/ Application folder) > Demo Songs > Turbotito – Sydney Heat.rps. Open** that **song**. Then **click OK** to close the Song Browser window with the nice photo of Filip Nikolic in his techno-color dream coat.

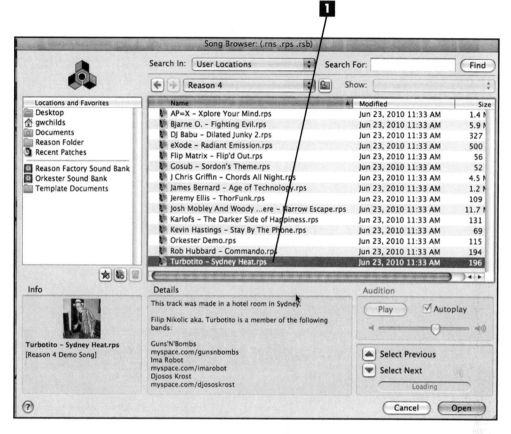

2 **Click** the **Play button** on the Reason Transport, and you will hear the song start playing.

3 **Click** the **Mute button** on Channel 2. This will mute the drums, and you will not hear them anymore. When you are satisfied that this works, **click** the **Mute button** again to unmute the drums.

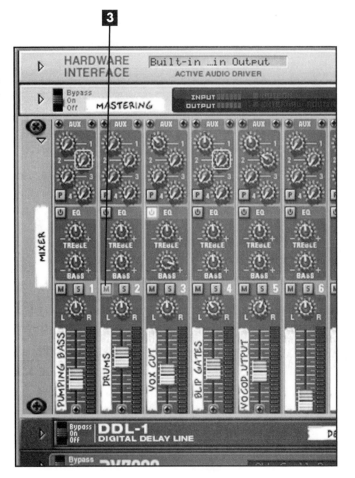

4 **Turn** the **Channel 1 Pan knob** all the way to the left, then all the way to the right, and then back to center. You should hear the synth bass move from left to right and then back to center in the stereo field.

5 **Turn up** the **Channel 1 fader** to a value of 80, exactly even with the Channel 2 (drums) Level slider. Now the pumping bass track is overpowering.

6 On your computer keyboard, **press Ctrl+Z** to undo that last step. The Channel 1 Level slider should return to its original, lower position. Although it's faster to use Ctrl+Z, you could also choose Undo Change Channel 1 Level from the Edit menu.

7 Slowly **turn** the **Master Fader** all the way down and then back up again. The whole mix should come down and then back up again.

EQ and Auxiliary Send/Return

Of course, EQ stands for *equalizer* and refers to the Bass and Treble knobs on each channel. Anyone who has ever owned a home stereo is familiar with that. However, if you've never used a professional mixing console, you may not be familiar with auxiliary sends and returns. Each of the four Auxiliary Send knobs on each channel allows you to send the audio signal from that channel into an effects device, such as a reverb or delay. Those Aux Send knobs control how loud of a signal you are sending to the effects device. The signal coming back from the effects device comes through the auxiliary return, and the four Auxiliary Return knobs control how much audio signal from the effects device will be sent to the Master Output L/R of the Mixer. The next exercise picks up where the previous one left off, still using the Turbotito - Sydney Heat demo song.

1 With the Turbotito - Sydney Heat demo song playing, **turn** the **Channel 2 Treble knob** all the way down. Nothing will happen.

2 Now **click** the **Channel 2 EQ On/Off knob**. Now the treble is turned down.

3 **Turn** the **Channel 2 Treble knob** all the way up and then back to center.

4 **Click** the **Channel 2 Solo button**. Now every track except for Channel 2 is muted.

5 **Turn** the **Channel 2 Aux (Auxiliary) Send 1 knob** all the way up. Because Aux Return 1 is coming from the RV7000 Reverb, you will hear reverb applied to the drums.

Sequencing in Reason/Reason Transport Controls

Because there are so many facets to the Sequencer and what it can do, rather than going into exhaustive detail in a single chapter, I am taking the approach of introducing a new slice of Sequencer functionality in each chapter. I think this will be a more fun and natural way to learn, and my expectation is that by the end of the book you will be quite comfortable with Reason 5's Sequencer.

Loop On/Off, Click, and Left/Right Locators

1 From the File menu, **select Open** and **browse** to **Reason (Program/Application folder) > Demo Songs > eXode – Radiant Emission.rps. Open** that **song**. Then click OK to close the Song Browser window.

2 **Click Play** on the Reason Transport and let the song play until about Bar 17.

3 **Click Stop twice** (once to stop playback and once to return the song position marker to Bar 1).

4 **Click** the **Loop On/Off button** to turn on looping and then **click Play**.

5 As the playback loops the bars between the left and right locators, **activate** the **Click button**.

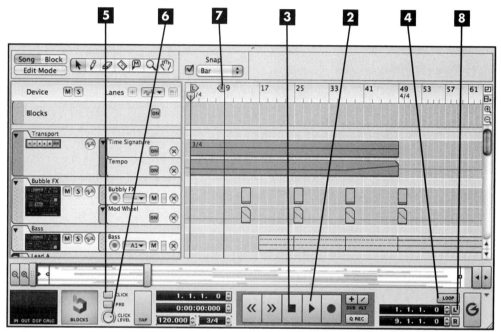

6 **Turn** the **volume** of the click up and down using the Click Level knob.

7 **Drag** the **right locator** over to Bar 17. Now your loop is twice as long as it was.

8 **Click** the **Go to Left Locator button** (labeled L), and the song position marker will jump to the left locator, continuing playback from that point.

9 **Click** on the **first number** (17) in the right locator window, **type** in **57**, and **press Enter** on your computer keyboard. Now the right locator is at Bar 57.

10 **Listen** to the **song** all the way from Bar 1 through Bar 57. Notice that the first Sequencer track is labeled Transport and contains a lane labeled Time Signature and another labeled Tempo.

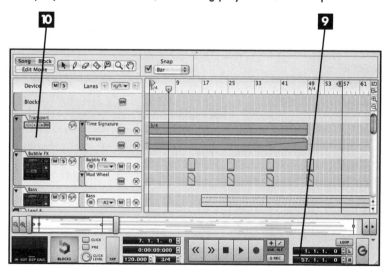

11 Also **notice** the **green outlines** around the Tempo and Time Signature display windows in the Reason Transport. This indicates that these parameters have had automation recorded for them so that they will automatically change during the song.

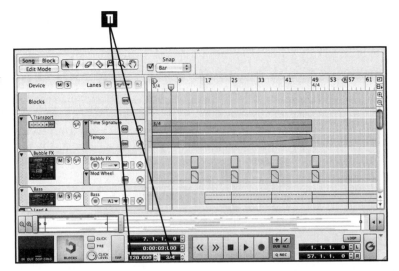

As you listen to the Radiant Emissions demo song for this exercise, you will hear the tempo ramp up as you watch the upward line at the end of the Tempo lane in the Transport track. You will also hear the time signature change from 3/4 to 4/4 at Bar 49. You will see these changes displayed in the Tempo and Time Signature windows in the Reason Transport. In Reason 5, it is very easy to do tempo and time signature changes.

Zooming, Scrolling, Hand Tool, and Magnifying Glass Tool

The next exercise should help you get comfortable with the tools you will use to view just what you need to see in the Reason Sequencer. This exercise picks up where the previous exercise left off.

1 With the Radiant Emissions demo song still loaded and playback stopped, **drag** the **horizontal scrollbar** all the way to the right (Bar 217), and you will see the end marker. The end marker determines the actual end point when you export your song as an audio file.

2 Slowly **drag** the **vertical scrollbar** all the way to the bottom, and you will see that there is a whole lot of this sequence you haven't seen yet.

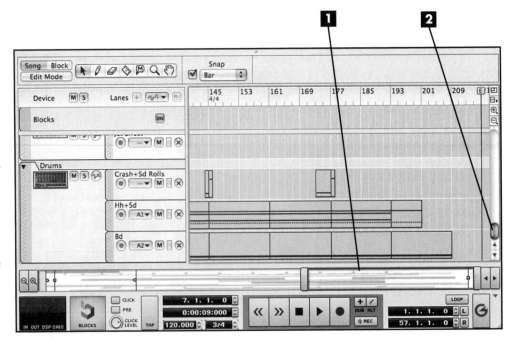

3 To see more of the sequence, **drag** the **top** of the Reason Sequencer upward, almost all the way to the top of the window, just under the first RV7000 Advanced Reverb.

4 **Click** the **Vertical Zoom In button** a few times, and you will see the Sequencer tracks get taller, so you can see more vertical detail.

5 **Click** the **Horizontal Zoom In button** a few times to see more horizontal detail.

6 **Select** the **Hand tool**.

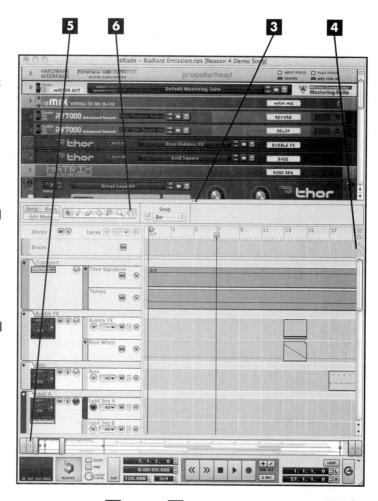

7 **Click (and hold)** in the **middle** of the Sequencer window, and you will be able to drag the entire sequence up and down, left and right, and round and round. It's like controlling the horizontal and vertical scrollbars at the same time.

8 **Select** the **Magnifying Glass tool**.

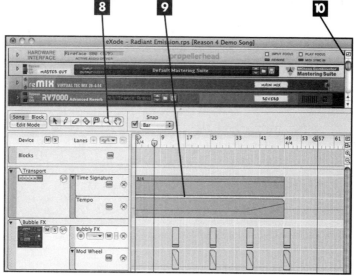

9 **Ctrl-click** in the **middle** of the Sequencer window several times until you can see all the tracks again. (Without holding down Ctrl, clicking with the Magnifying Glass tool zooms in both horizontally and vertically; Ctrl-click zooms out.)

10 This next trick is where it's really nice to have two LCD computer monitors: **Click** the **button** in the upper-right corner of the Reason rack.

In Step 10, after you click the button, you will have two windows: a separate Sequencer window and a separate rack window. It's really helpful to have two LCD monitors, so you can have the Sequencer on one monitor and the rack on the other.

Time Signature and Snap to Grid

The Radiant Emission demo song starts off with a time signature of 3/4 and eventually changes to a time signature of 4/4. If the time signature is 4/4, the first number in the time signature means that there are four beats in a bar (or measure), and the second number means that a 1/4 note equals one beat. With a time signature of 3/4, the first number means that there are three beats in a bar (or measure), and the second number again means that a 1/4 note equals one beat. If you chose a time signature of 6/8, that would mean that there are six beats per bar, and a 1/8 note equals one beat.

The following exercise picks up where the previous exercise left off. You will be focusing on the Sequencer window.

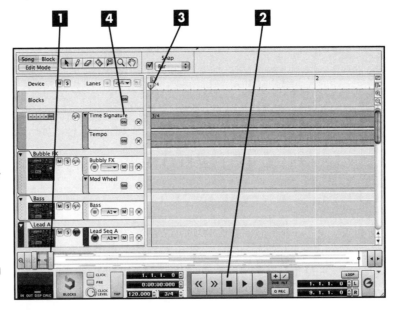

1 Drag the **horizontal magnification slider** all the way to the left for maximum magnification.

2 Click the **Stop button** on the Reason Transport until the song position marker is at Bar 1.

3 Drag the **song position marker** to Bar 2. Since Snap is set to Bar, you will not be able to leave the song position marker anywhere between Bars 1 and 2.

4 Turn off the **Time Signature lane**. Since the Time Signature lane had set the time for 3/4, and you turned it off, now the song is at its default time signature of 4/4.

5 Set the **Snap value** to 1/2. Then **drag** the **song position marker** between Bars 1 and 2, and you will see that it stops at the 1/2 note as well.

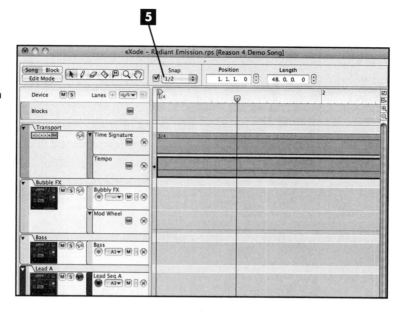

6 **Turn off Snap to Grid.** Now you can leave the song position marker at any point between Bars 1 and 2.

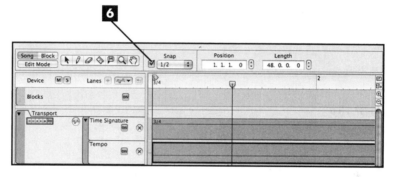

7 **Click** the **Snap to Grid button** to turn it back on and **set** the **Snap** value to 1/16. Then **move** the **song position marker** back and forth, and you will see that it can be left at any 1/16 note.

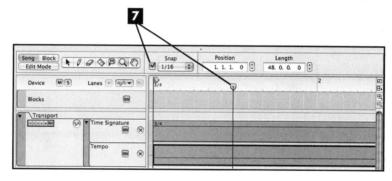

Editing Tools: Selection, Pencil, Razor, Eraser, and Mute

The following exercise picks up where the previous exercise left off and again focuses on the Sequencer window.

1 With Snap to Grid still activated, **set** the **Snap value** for 1/16 and **select** the **Pencil tool**.

2 **Click** once at **Bar 1** on the Sequencer track labeled Bass. You have just created a clip with a duration of 1/16 note.

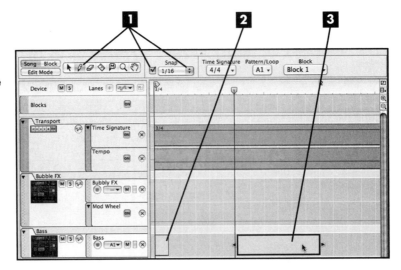

3 Starting at the second 1/4 note from Bar 1 (that's three 1/16 notes from the end of the clip you drew), **draw** a **clip** that is one 1/4 note long.

4 **Choose** your **Selection tool**.

5 **Click** once on the **first clip** you drew to select it. Then **click** on the **arrow** on its right side and **drag** it to the **right** so that the end of the first clip touches the beginning of the second clip. Now you have two clips that each last a 1/4 note.

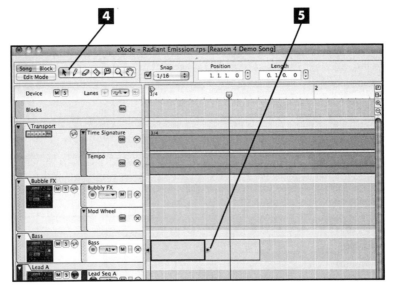

6 **Select** your **Razor tool**.

7 **Slice** each **clip** in its middle. Now you have four 1/8-note clips.

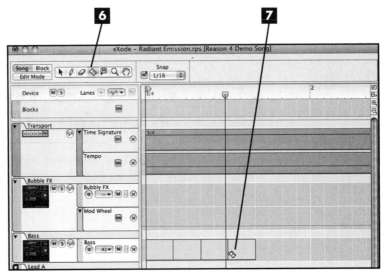

8 **Choose** the **Selection tool**. Then, while **holding** down the **Ctrl** button, **click** on each **clip** so that all four are selected.

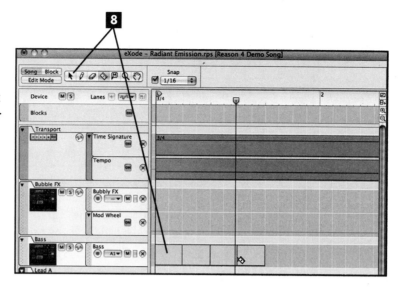

9 **Right-click** on one of the **clips** and **choose Join Clips** from the context menu.

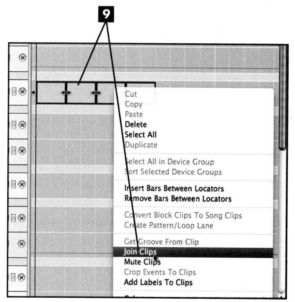

10 **Double-click** on the **clip**, and now you can **see** the Key Edit window, where you can draw in notes with your Pencil tool if you want.

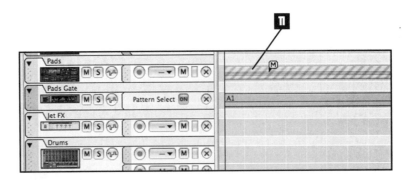

11 Next, **scroll down** to the **Pads track** and **select** the **Mute tool**, which simply looks like an M with a circle around it. **Click** the **clip** located within the Pads lane. This will cause gray lines to appear in the middle. If you press the spacebar to play the song from the beginning, this clip will now be muted. **Click** the **clip** again to Unmute.

12 **Click** the **Arrange/Edit Mode button** to go back to the Arrange mode.

13 **Select** the **Erase tool**.

14 **Click** on your **clip**, and it will be erased.

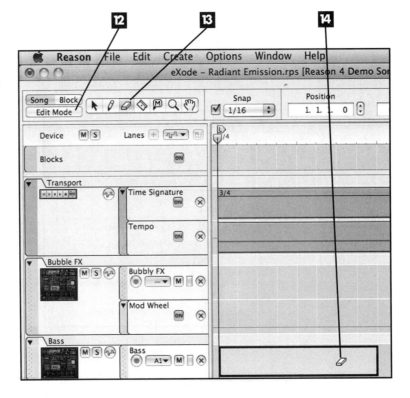

You will get plenty of practice with the Key Edit window later in this book, but for now I just wanted to show it to you. Now you can see that Snap to Grid affects how the song position marker can be moved, how clips can be resized, as well as how the Pencil tool works. It also affects how you move the left and right locators, and it makes it easy to move clips and drop them exactly on the bar or beat you want.

Blocks

One of my favorite features in Reason 5 is the new Blocks mode. Blocks are essentially a cross between markers and pattern-based sequencing. Pattern-based sequencing is awesome because you can throw together some cool loops, one at a time, and then later come back and chain all of the loops together to form a song. Because Reason's blocks are exhibited at the top of the Sequencer window, you can easily see where you are in your current song when all of the blocks have been chained together.

Let's take a look at how blocks work by going to the File menu and choosing Open. Select the Reason folder from your Locations and then double-click Demo Songs. Choose Sharooz – Polyform.rps.

When Polyform is open, you'll notice that the Reason 5 demo looks slightly different from some of the Reason 4 demos that we've looked at. For one thing, having Kong (see Chapter 10 for more on Kong) present within the rack is a huge difference, but also the Sequencer looks a little different because of the colored blocks at the top. Listen to the song before you begin. Double-click the Stop button on the Transport when you are finished to return the playhead to the beginning of the song.

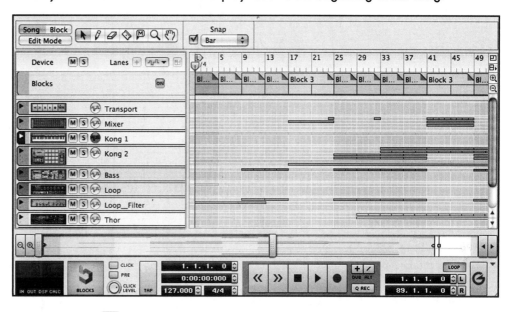

1 Notice the **blocks** right above the Transport track within their own lane simply called Blocks. **Click** the **Magnifying Glass** from the toolbar or simply **press Y**. Once the Magnifying Glass is selected, **click** in the **Sequencer area** once or twice. Suddenly, you should be able to read the name of each block.

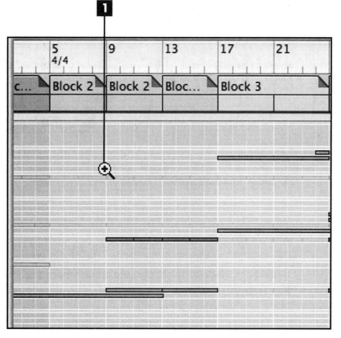

2 Now that the blocks are totally visible, **press** the **Q button** to bring up your cursor again. If you click on Block 2, you'll notice that an arrow appears next to the title Block 2. If you click the small down arrow, a menu will appear, allowing you to select other blocks. **Scroll** through the **menu** and **select Block 3**.

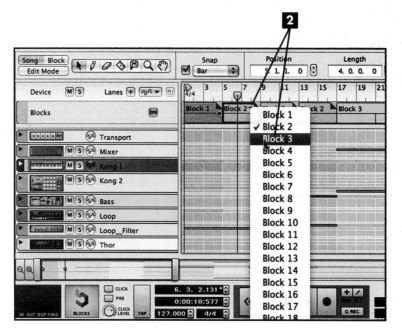

3 **Double-click** the **Stop button** on the Transport, which we talked about earlier in this chapter. This will move the playhead to the beginning of the song. **Press** the **Play button** to hear the change you made. Notice that there is indeed a new drumbeat being played, much earlier than before. This is how easy it is to work with blocks! You can change whole portions of a song within the linear timeline of a Sequencer by simply selecting your premade parts from a list. Now, **double-click** on **Block 3** at the top.

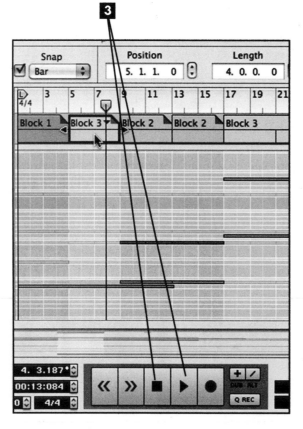

When you double-click a block from the Sequencer, you actually go into the Block mode, where you can edit the block that you double-clicked. You can also enter Block mode at any time by pressing B or by clicking the Blocks button in the upper-left corner of the Sequencer window. This is also the mode where you create blocks of your own. The Blocks drop-down menu in the upper-left corner allows you to move to a different block. We'll stick with this one for the moment.

4 **Select** the **Thor Sequencer lane** so that a keyboard appears under it and then **press** the **Record button**. Play some keys; it doesn't have to be pretty.

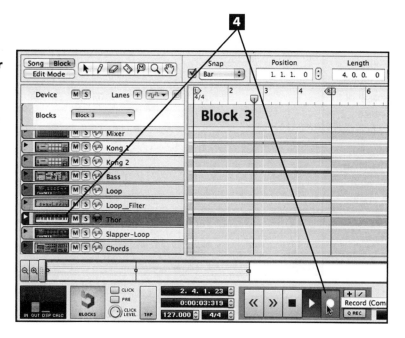

Congratulations, you've just recorded part of your first block! Note that any block you make will need to be kept between the L and R loop locators at the top. Also, the E marker (End) has to be at the beginning of the loop as well. If you don't observe these steps, the block will not cue properly from within the Sequencer.

5 Now, **click** the **B button** again to leave Blocks mode.

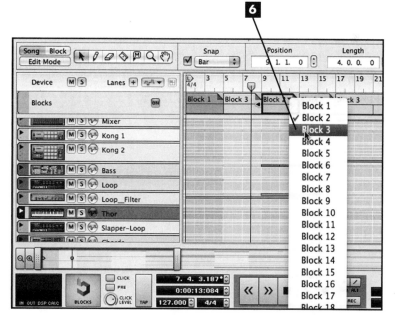

6 In the Sequencer, let's try out our handiwork. **Select Block 2 at Measure 9** and then **change it** from the drop-down menu to Block 3. **Double-click Stop** again and start it from the top. Notice how the whole intro is different now. While it's playing, try changing around some more blocks.

7 Because you're starting to get comfortable with blocks, let me throw a curveball at you. **Delete** all **blocks** from Measure 1 to Measure 7. Simply select them and **press** the **Delete button**. If you hold down the Shift button as you select each one of the blocks, you can select multiple blocks and then press Delete.

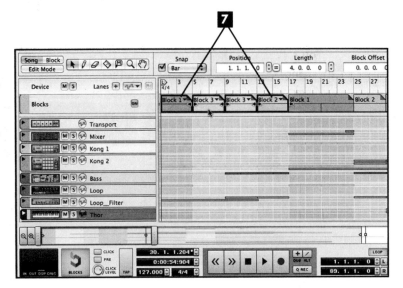

8 We have some wiggle room now. **Select** the **Pencil tool** from the toolbar. **Draw** a **block** at Measure 1. This is how you draw a block into your sequence. You can also use the arrows on the side of the block to extend it. No matter how far you extend it, it will continually stretch into more instances of the same block.

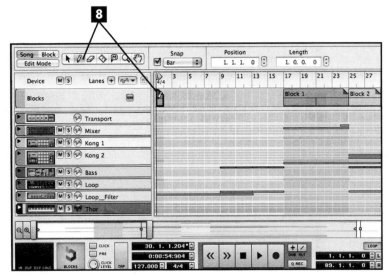

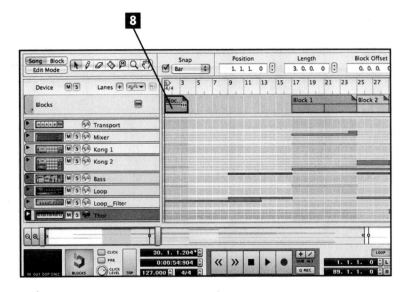

Imagine the possibilities when it comes to working with blocks. You can basically create a song by painting in colored blocks and then rearrange whenever you want to. You can also sequence over blocks. These clips will appear in color, and the block-arranged material will appear subdued in the background. If you want to turn off Block mode, simply click the big Block button on the Transport bar.

Now that we have a better understanding of blocks, let's move on to automation!

Recording Automation in the Reason Sequencer

This sounds very fancy, but it's really quite easy. Almost every little move you can make in Reason can be automated, which means that the move can be recorded and then played back automatically. You will see multiple examples of this throughout this book. Right now, here's an easy one. You're going to automate a Solo button on the Mixer 14:2.

1 From the File menu, **select Open** and **browse** to **Reason (Program/ Application folder) > Demo Songs > Turbotito – Sydney Heat.rps. Open** that **song** and then **click OK** to close the Song Information window.

2 **Move** the **left locator** to Bar 41.

3 **Click** the **Go to Left Locator button**.

4 **Click** the little **triangle** to the left of the Mixer track in the Reason Sequencer (to unfold the track).

5 **Right-click** on the **Channel 4 Solo button** and **choose Edit Automation** from the context menu. A Channel 4 Solo lane will appear on the top of the Mixer Sequencer track. Channel 4 is labeled Blip Gates.

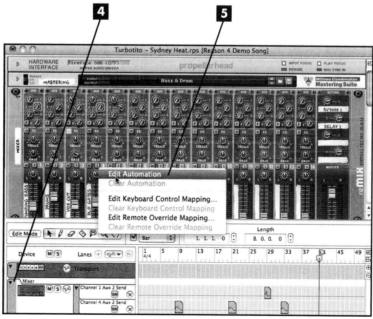

6 **Select** the **Pencil tool**.

7 **Draw** a **clip** on the Channel 4 Solo automation lane, from Bar 41 to Bar 45, and then **hold down** the **Alt key** (to temporarily turn your Pencil back into a Selection tool) and **double-click** on the **clip**.

8 **Set** the **Snap value** to Bar.

9 **Click** once in the **upper-left corner** of your clip to create an automation point. This will turn on the Channel 4 Solo button.

10 **Click** once in the **lower-right corner** of your clip to make another automation point. This will turn off the Channel 4 Solo button.

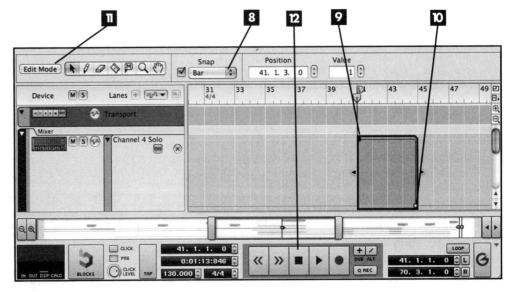

11 **Click** the **Arrange/Edit Mode button** twice to change back to Arrange mode.

12 **Click** the **Stop button** so that the song position marker returns to Bar 1. Then **click** the **Play button** and listen.

When you listen to the song, you should hear everything except the Blip Gates drop out right at Bar 41 and then come back in dramatically at Bar 45. The way we did this was very precise and efficient. Another way you could have done this (instead of drawing in the automation) would've been to select the Mixer Sequencer track, click Record, and then hit the Channel 4 Solo button at the appropriate moments and record the automation live.

Picking up where the previous exercise left off, let's automate a fade-out.

1 **Right-click** on the **Master Fader** and **select Edit Automation** from the context menu.

2 **Draw** a **clip** with your Pencil tool starting at Bar 61 and ending at Bar 73 and then **hold down** the **Alt key** (to temporarily turn your Pencil back into a Selection tool) and **double-click** on the **clip**.

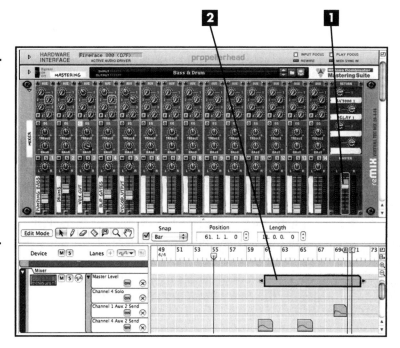

3 **Click** once in the **upper-left corner** of your clip (at Bar 61) to create an automation point.

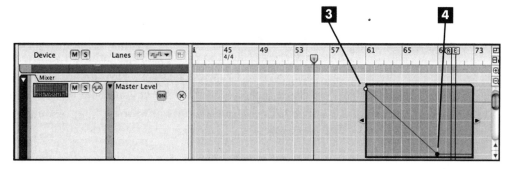

4 **Click** once at the **bottom** of the clip at Bar 69 (a little bit to the left of the right locator and end marker) to create another automation point.

5 **Click** the **Arrange/Edit Mode button** twice to change back to Arrange mode.

6 **Click** the **Stop button** once or twice so that the song position marker returns to Bar 1. Then **click** the **Play button** and listen.

Again, you could have simply moved the Master Fader with your mouse while recording the automation on the Mixer track in the Sequencer, but drawing it in is smoother and more precise. If you wanted to get fancy and make a fade that's tapered at the end, you could add an extra automation point or two toward the bottom of the clip in the second half of the fade, so that the first half of the fade is faster while the second half fades more gradually.

You could automate a tempo change the exact same way as you created the fade in the previous exercise, by right-clicking on the Tempo window and choosing Edit Automation. In fact, you can easily automate nearly anything that can be done in Reason.

Read the Fabulous Manual (RTFM)

If you get stuck anywhere in this book, and something you are trying to do isn't working even though you have reviewed my steps, please refer to the Reason Operation Manual. It is a PDF file found in the Documentation folder in your Reason program folder. The Operation Manual is a very helpful resource. It is your friend in time of need. It will get you unstuck. Find the chapter dealing with the device that is giving you trouble or look up a key word in the index. The Help manual, which is accessible from the Help menu inside Reason, is the same thing as the Operation Manual but without pictures. I am a big fan of PDF manuals. They allow me to use the Search function. I just type in a word related to my problem and generally find my answer very easily by clicking the little binoculars icon in my PDF viewer (Adobe Acrobat or Foxit Reader) and typing in my search term. If somehow you don't have a PDF viewer (and your computer doesn't know what program to use to open PDF files), both the viewers I mentioned are available for free download. Just do a Google search and download directly from the Adobe or Foxit website.

Propellerhead Online Support

Another helpful resource is the Propellerhead website. It is a good idea to register your copy of Reason at www.propellerheads.se. Then you can access all the helpful articles in their Support section. I have found answers there to the most odd and specialized technical problems that you could imagine. I have been surprised more than once to find a specific answer to something I thought was a very strange or difficult problem.

As a last resort, I've had good results emailing their tech support through the support section of the Propellerhead website. You may have to wait a day or two for a response (due to different time zones), but the responses I have received have been very thoughtful, detailed, and helpful.

All right. Now that you've got your feet wet, it's time to jump into learning the big gun in Reason's beat-production arsenal: Dr.Rex.

2 } Dr. Octo Rex

No other instrument in Reason 5 has been overhauled as much as Propellerhead's proprietary loop player, Dr.Rex. In fact, it's been given a full name now, to make it a little more personal. Dr.Rex is now called Dr. Octo Rex, and he has a much bigger bag of tricks than before.

If you are unfamiliar with the loop format that Propellerhead introduced years ago, in the form of Rex files, let me explain how they work. Propellerhead makes a program called ReCycle that does something unique to rhythmic audio. Well, it was once unique; many people have copied it now. But, ReCycle was the first—trust me. ReCycle analyzes a drum loop, for example, and assigns a unique identifier to each drum "hit" within the loop. In a sense, it's cutting up the loop into small chunks based on different drum hits—but at the same time, keeping all of the audio in one complete audio file. These audio files are referred to as *Rex files*.

Why does it break things into pieces? That is part of the magic! If you break a rhythm into small chunks, it's easier to change the speed of the rhythm without changing the pitch. Also, these chunks are mapped to different keys on a MIDI controller, allowing you to trigger different hits within the loop. In a sense, any drum loop or rhythmic loop suddenly becomes a new drum kit.

What makes having a dedicated Rex loop player within Reason so much fun is that you can at any point drop into a song any of the large number of Rex files that come with Reason. Or, you can use your own Rex files that you make, if you own ReCycle. When you drop in these files, they will automatically play in beat with your current song. And, if the loop is melodic, you can change the pitch on the fly, without changing the rhythm.

If this seems confusing now, don't worry; it will make more sense as we move along. For now, let's start getting acquainted with Dr. Octo Rex and see, step by step, what it can do.

In this chapter, you'll learn how to:

* Load loops
* Apply loops to a sequence
* Work with the Filter and LFO sections
* Modify Rex files

Loading Your First Loop

Loading up a loop into ol' Dr. Octo couldn't be easier. And once it's in there, it couldn't be more fun. Let's get started by putting in a simple drum loop.

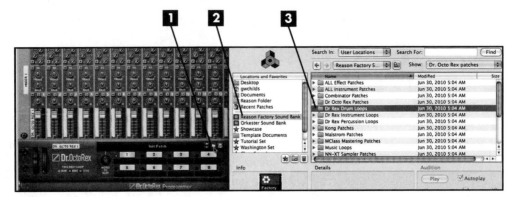

1 Click the **Browse Patch button**.

2 **Select** the **Reason Factory Sound Bank** under Locations and Favorites.

3 Within the Reason Factory Sound Bank, **double-click Dr Rex Drum Loops**. This is the loop folder for the original Dr.Rex player.

4 **Select** the **Acs01_StrghtAhead_130.rx2 drum loop** within the Dr Rex Drum Loops folder.

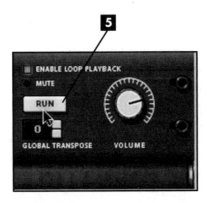

5 Congratulations, you've just loaded your first drum loop! To hear the drum loop, simply **click** the **Run button** on the front of Dr. Octo Rex. The loop will start playing.

Of course, after you click the Run button a few times, the novelty will wear off, and this won't seem to interesting anymore. Thankfully, Dr. Octo Rex does quite a bit more. In fact, Dr. Octo Rex—unlike its former incarnation, Dr.Rex—actually can hold more than one loop. Seriously!

In the next section, we'll look at how to add additional loops to Dr. Octo Rex.

Loading Multiple Loops

Why would you want multiple loops within Dr. Octo Rex? What is the advantage of this? Glad you asked! When there are multiple loops within Dr. Octo Rex, you have the ability to trigger different loops within Dr. Octo Rex at will. You can do this either with the numbered buttons on the front of Dr. Octo Rex or with your MIDI controller.

In the previous exercise, I showed you the quick, easy way to load a single loop. In this section, I'll show you how to load a multi-loop patch and how to change out a specific loop within the patch.

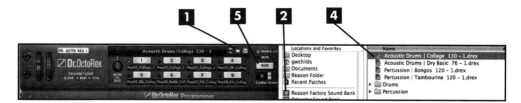

1 Click the Browse Patch button.

2 Select Reason Factory Sound Bank from the Locations and Favorites section of the browser.

3 Double-click Dr Octo Rex Patches.

4 Select Acoustic Drums | College 130 - 1.drex.

5 Click the Run button and then try pushing the different numbered buttons to change the loops within this patch. You can also trigger the loops via your MIDI controller by playing keys E-0 to B-0.

6 To change out a loop within this patch, right-click (or Control-click) on the small display window above the loop that you want to change and select Open Browser. You may use any of the loops within the Dr Rex Drum Loops folder or the Dr Octo Rex Patches folder. The loops just need to have .rex at the end of the name.

Pretty simple, eh? And think of how powerful what we just covered is! Not only can you load and trigger a single loop, but you can also trigger multiple loops, as well as individual parts of each loop in the upper register of the keyboard (yeah, you can—try it). You really *do* have a real drummer now, ready and at your disposal.

If you like triggering loops via either the buttons or the MIDI controller while they are running with the internal Reason Sequencer, you also should notice the Trig Next Loop buttons on the left of Dr. Octo.

These buttons let you trigger by:

❄ **Bar.** The next loop will only start with the next bar—not too early, not too soon.

❄ **Beat.** Trigger by the beat! Instead of being rigidly stuck between whole bars in your song, cut between each beat of the sequence.

❄ **1/16.** There are 16 notes available within one beat when you're using sixteenth-note quantization. Switch between any of those 16 notes.

To experiment with these settings, try running the Reason Sequencer and then try changing loops with the different settings by using either the numbered-loop triggers or your MIDI controller, using the keys I mentioned previously.

Applying Loops to Sequence

Now you know how to trigger loops within the sequence. But what if you want to apply these loops to the sequence? Maybe you want to modify parts of the beats within a Dr.Rex loop. (Yes, you can do this. Keep reading!) What if you aren't into triggering the loops in real time? Maybe you just want a couple of static loops available to you.

Let me show you how to drop these loops into your sequence.

1 Click the **small arrow** in the lower-left corner of Dr. Octo Rex.

2 Set your **loop locators** to where you want the loop and all of its repetitions to begin and end. Make sure to **press** the **number 1 button** on Dr. Octo Rex, too.

3 Click the **Copy Loop to Track button**. You will see loop regions appear automatically within your sequence.

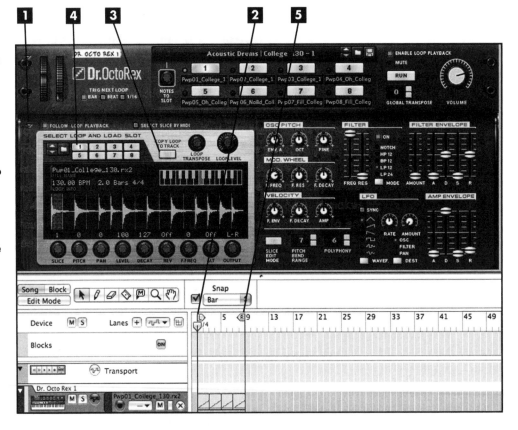

4 To apply another loop within the patch to your sequence, **click** the appropriate **numbered loop trigger button** to bring up another loop within your Dr. Octo Rex patch. **Press number 3**.

5 **Reposition** your **loop locators** to a different section of your song. Do not place them in the same section as before, or you will write over another loop.

6 Click the **Copy Loop to Track button** again.

A different loop region will appear between the repositioned loop locaters.

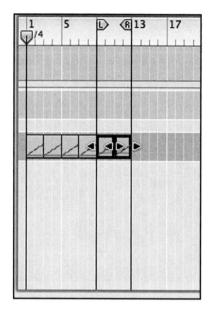

There you go! You now know how to use Dr. Octo Rex to paint in audio loops as if you were painting in Photoshop. Drop loops all over your song, wherever appropriate. Also, make sure you keep these loops in the Sequencer for the upcoming tutorials. They are needed! If you need to quit right now, be sure to save your work.

❄ **NOTE**

Out of all of the different percussive instruments in Reason 5, Dr. Octo Rex (and Nurse REX in Kong; see Chapter 10, "Kong") is the only device that uses real drum loops generated by real drummers with a real drummer feel. Take advantage of this. Loops created by real drummers using real kits add an organic feel to your songs that you can't duplicate easily with a computer. This is also true of the instrument loops found within the Dr Rex folder of the Reason Factory Sound Bank, and so on.

Filter Section

There may be situations in which you want to sonically mold the overall frequency of your loops to quickly and easily fit into a song.

For example, suppose you're using Kong for your main drums, but you also like how the drum loop you were playing around with works with your other drums. Because both of the drum sections are very thick, and the Kong drums are already working best as your main drums, you need to make the loop less thick.

This is where you would use your filter section. By applying a band-pass or high-pass filter, you can remove lower frequencies from your loops, allowing them to sit in your mix without sonically competing with the other drums already present.

Now let me show you how to apply a filter to a loop. For this exercise, just make sure you are on the same Dr. Octo Rex patch as the previous exercise. If you forgot which one it was or you've already moved on, refer to the previous section.

1 **Click** the **Run button** on Dr.Rex and keep the main Sequencer off. Do not click Play on the main Sequencer or press the spacebar.

2 **Move** the **Filter Freq slider** down and notice how the high end is being cut as you do this. This is because it's set to LP 12 by default. LP stands for *low-pass*, and it cuts all high end according to how it's applied.

3 Now, **change** the **Filter mode** to BP 12. This puts your filter into band-pass mode. This cuts the highs *and* the lows around the slider. Essentially, it makes your loop very midrange, which is good if you're trying to get it to sit in your mix. There's no competing with the high end of the vocals or hi-hats, and there's no competing with the low end of your main drums.

4 **Move** the **slider** around in BP 12. Notice how it works. Try some of the other settings, too.

You can also use filters as effects. By sweeping the Freq slider up and down, along with the Res (or *Resonance*) slider, you can achieve the DJ effects that have been prevalent in pop music for years.

When using the Filter section with the accompanying Filter Envelope, you can also sculpt new behaviors for each drum strike within your loop. Try turning up the Amount slider in the Filter Envelope section and then modifying the settings while your loop is playing. Neat, eh?

Indeed, the Filter section is a mighty tool for all of your looping endeavors. It gives you great and easy power over how your loops sound, where they sit, and even their sonic behaviors.

There may be situations where you want to program the Freq slider to go up and down throughout the song or with a more intricate pattern. You can program this with automation; however, it would be intricate and exhausting. But there is another portion of Dr. Octo Rex that makes this endeavor really easy. Read on, and I'll show you more.

LFO Section

LFOs, or *low-frequency oscillators*, are strange things. They are essentially waveforms that oscillate specific parameters of different parts of an instrument. You have to decide the function that will be oscillated, of course, but once it's set and active, an LFO can add a lot of excitement and coolness to a drum loop.

What are some of the parameters to which you can apply an LFO? You can see on Dr. Octo Rex. The Dest button allows you to choose which function will be oscillated by the LFO.

You can choose from:

- ※ **OSC (Oscillator).** The oscillator in this case would be the audio loop. So, basically, you would be oscillating the pitch of the audio.
- ※ **Filter.** This causes the LFO to open and close the filter.
- ※ **Pan.** This causes the LFO to control the pan of a specific loop. Or, to better explain, it causes the loop to oscillate between different speakers.

This probably sounds like a bunch of geeky, techno-gibberish at this point. However, after you've completed the following exercise (setting up an LFO to modulate the filter of Dr.Rex), it might make more sense. So, think about going back and reading the previous section again later...or don't. For now, let's get started.

1 **Click** the **Dest button** on Dr. Octo Rex until the red light lands on Filter.

2 **Raise** the **Amount** to about 12:00.

3 Your filter should still be set to band-pass, or BP 12, from the previous exercise. **Lower** the **Freq slider** to halfway.

4 **Click Run** to hear the loop with the LFO.

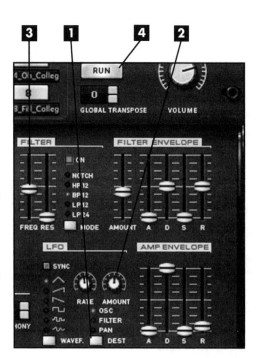

While running Dr. Octo Rex with the LFO, try adjusting the Freq and Res sliders. You can get some crazy effects doing this with your loop. Also, try adjusting the rate of the LFO with and without sync.

Sync actually sets the rate to a note value or quantize value that syncs with the main Sequencer in Reason 5. When sync is off, the LFO is free-floating. Each setting allows a different effect. But if you want the LFO to be rhythmic, go with Sync.

All right, so we've had some fun with the basic functions on Dr. Octo Rex. Now let's go back to working with Rex files in the Sequencer, as we did earlier. This time, let's modify the loops themselves.

Modifying Rex Files

As I mentioned earlier in this chapter, Rex files are audio files that have been sliced up and mapped to different MIDI notes. This may seem a bit strange at first, but when you see it in action, it's quite magnificent.

What's also really exciting about Rex files is that while the portions of the loops are cut into pieces, the original performance is kept intact with MIDI as well. The audio literally becomes sequenced material for your use!

In this section, let's try modifying a loop and see how it works. For this exercise, simply continue where you left off from the previous section. If you've moved on and played around since then, refer to the first four steps in the "Loading Multiple Loops" section earlier in this chapter and then follow the "Applying Loops to Sequence" section.

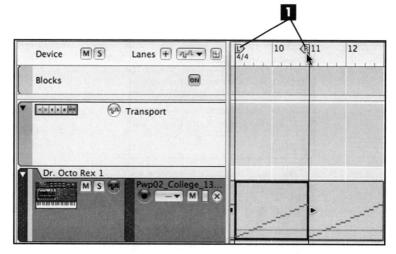

1 **Set** your **loop locators** so that the left loop locator is at Measure 9 and the right loop locator is at Measure 11.

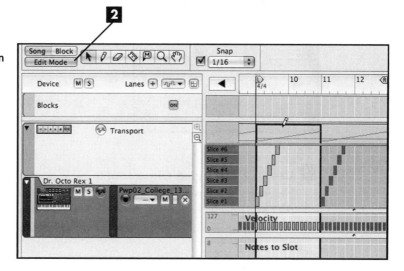

2 **Click** the **Edit Mode** button to go into Edit mode or **double-click** on the **clip**.

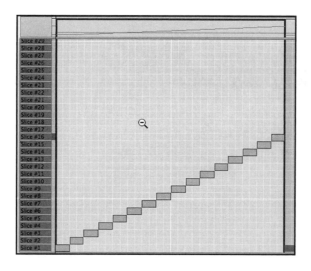

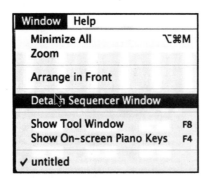

3 **Use** the **Magnifying Glass tool** to get yourself into a closer view of the Loop Sequence. You can also increase the Sequencer view by detaching it from the Reason rack or by simply raising the divider between the Sequencer and the rack to give you more Sequencer visibility.

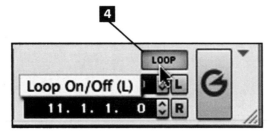

4 **Turn on** the Sequencer **Loop button** or **press L** on your computer keyboard.

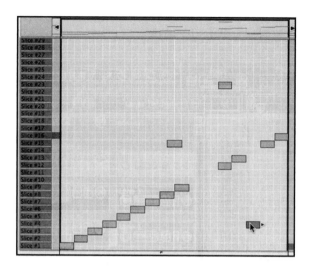

5 **Press** the **spacebar** on your keyboard so that the loop starts playing in between the loop locators. While this is going on, try moving around the different notes within the loop that make up the loop as a whole. Notice how the overall loop changes as you move these notes around. Note: You can also use the Pencil tool to draw in more loop notes.

See? A Rex file or a Dr. Octo Rex loop is completely malleable in terms of how a loop can be edited, and you can use it to create an entirely different drum loop if you want. Using a MIDI controller with Dr. Octo Rex also means that you can actually use any Dr. Octo Rex loop as a drum kit, a palette of sounds, and more.

Conclusion

As you can see, Dr. Octo Rex is more of a mad scientist than a general practitioner. He comes across as smooth and sophisticated, but once you really jump into it with him, he's crazy.

In the next chapter, we'll experiment with a little Murder...er, Redrum. See you there!

3 } Redrum

In Chapter 2, you learned about using Dr.Rex to add preexisting drum loops and musical grooves to your music. Now you are about to learn how to make your own beats from scratch with Redrum!

Redrum has a familiar look reminiscent of classic drum machines, such as the Roland TR-808 or 909. Like those classic drum machines, Redrum offers step programming, with a row of 16 Step buttons. Unlike those old drum machines, Redrum is infinitely flexible, allowing you to load as many different sounds as there are WAV and AIFF files in the world (well, not all at the same time). You can mix and match samples to create your own drum kits, which you can then save as Redrum patches, and even sample your own sounds from within Redrum. You can instantly create fully random drum patterns that can serve as starting points for your creative process. Once you get into Redrum, you will find it is easy to use and an essential tool for producing electronic music with Reason.

In this chapter, you will learn how to:

* Program your own beats using Redrum's internal pattern-based sequencer
* Automate pattern changes so that all the drum patterns you use in a song will automatically start at the correct time as your song plays
* Use the Reason Sequencer to control Redrum
* Customize your Redrum drum kits by swapping out individual samples and by adjusting various parameters on each drum channel
* Learn to sample your own sounds in Redrum

❋ PLEASE SAVE YOUR WORK

When dealing with multiple interfaces, you can really start adding up channels of I/O. But is there any limitation? Actually, yes. With Pro Tools 9 (the basic standalone software version), you'll have up to 32 channels of inputs and outputs. That's often just fine for smaller facilities, but if you need more, consider Pro Tools | HD Native, which supports up to 64 channels of I/O, or Pro Tools | HD, which maxes out at a whopping 160 channels of I/O!

Making Beats with Redrum's Pattern Section

Although Redrum can be played with a MIDI controller or the Reason Sequencer, just like any of the other Reason instruments, part of the real fun of Redrum is using it like a classic drum machine, and that means creating beats using Redrum's built-in pattern-based sequencer. When creating patterns this way, each step in the pattern is represented by one of Redrum's 16 Step buttons.

Programming Your First Redrum Pattern

This exercise should demonstrate how easy it is to program a beat inside of Redrum. Let's try it!

1 In an empty Reason rack, **drag** in a **Mixer 14:2** and an instance of **Redrum** underneath. Then **click** on Redrum's **Patch Browser button** and **select Reason Factory Sound Bank > Redrum Drum Kits > RnB Kits > RnB Kit 02.drp**.

2 Turn the **Tempo** down to 80 in the Reason Transport panel.

3 **Click** the **Select button** on Channel 8 of Redrum. As you can see by looking at the top of the channel, a hi-hat cymbal sample is loaded into this channel. (The name displayed in the sample display window is Hh_Sexy.wav.)

4 **Click** on **Step buttons** 1, 3, 5, 7, 9, 11, 13, and 15. This will create an eighth-note hi-hat pattern, since every other sixteenth-note is played.

5 **Click Run** to hear what you are doing. If you count your hi-hat pattern out loud, it will sound like "1 and 2 and 3 and 4 and...."

6 **Click** the **Select button** on Channel 2 of Redrum, so that you can create a snare drum part. Then **click Step button 5** and **Step button 13**. This actually puts a snare drum on Beats 2 and 4 of your drum pattern.

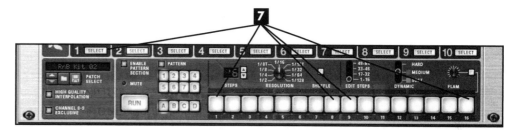

7 Now let's add the bass drum (or kick drum). **Click the Select button** on Channel 1 of Redrum and then **click Step buttons** 1, 8, 9, and 16.

If your beat sounds right, click File > Save As and name the Reason song Redrum_Ignite. We'll be using this beat later. In fact, if you are moving on to the next exercise right now, you can just leave it open.

Shuffle

Adding shuffle gives your rhythms a "swing" feel. The specific way this works is that when the Shuffle feature is activated, all sixteenth notes that fall between eighth notes are delayed to a degree determined by the Global Shuffle Amount knob to the far left of the ReGroove Mixer. A couple of famous (older) examples of shuffles used in popular music are "Rosanna" by Toto and "Fool in the Rain" by Led Zeppelin. By the end of this short, easy exercise, it will be very clear how you can use Shuffle in a hip-hop groove.

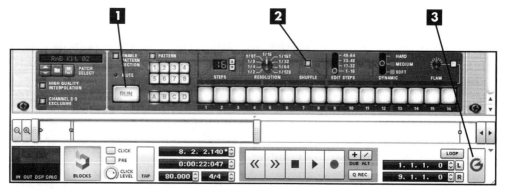

1 **Open** the Redrum_Ignite **song** you saved in the last exercise, or if you still have the last exercise open, just pick up where you left off. **Click Run** so you can hear your beat.

2 **Click** the **Shuffle button**. You now should hear a little bit of shuffle applied to the bass drum.

3 In the Reason Transport panel, **click** the **ReGroove Mixer button**. The ReGroove Mixer will open.

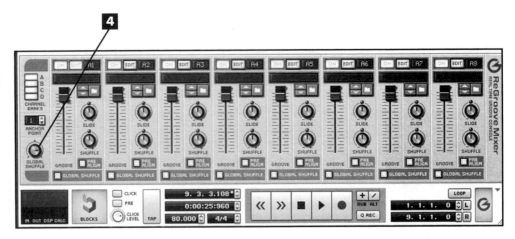

4 Slowly **turn up** the **Global Shuffle Amount knob** all the way, and you will hear Steps 9, 12, and 16 of the bass drum pattern played later and later. Then **turn** the **knob** back to about 3 o'clock (70%), which I think is a good amount of shuffle for this beat.

Steps 9, 12, and 16 of the bass drum pattern are sixteenth notes that fall between eighth notes. This is easy to see if you click on the Select button on Redrum's Channel 1. Those three notes are being played a little later now than they were before they got shuffled. Click File > Save if you want to have this beat shuffled next time you open the song.

The full name for the Shuffle button is Pattern Shuffle. This is because it will apply shuffle only to patterns being played back in Redrum's Pattern section. It will not affect any MIDI information already in the Sequencer (such as if you have used Copy Pattern to Track or otherwise recorded something in the Sequencer that is playing through Redrum). If you do use Copy Pattern to Track to copy a Redrum pattern to the Reason Sequencer while the Shuffle button is engaged, the information copied to the Sequencer will be "shuffled." So when you look at the MIDI notes in the Sequencer in Edit mode, you will see that any sixteenth notes that fall between eighth notes are delayed to a degree determined by the Global Shuffle Amount knob. Also, be aware that ReGroove's Global Shuffle Amount knob only affects Redrum's Pattern section. It does not "shuffle" anything in the Reason Sequencer, even if the track in the Sequencer is playing Redrum.

Auditioning Redrum Patches (Drum Kits)

The next short exercise will show you a nice way to find the perfect drum kit for your beat.

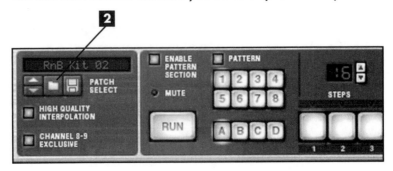

1 **Open** the Redrum_Ignite **song** you saved in the last exercise and click Run so you can hear the beat.

2 **Click** Redrum's **Browse Patch button**.

3 **Click** on various **drum kits** in any folder you like within Factory Sound Bank > Redrum Drum Kits. Some of the kits may take a few seconds to load, but once a kit is loaded, you will automatically hear it playing the current pattern.

4 If you agree that I have already selected the perfect pattern for this beat (ha ha!), then **click Cancel**, and no changes will be made.

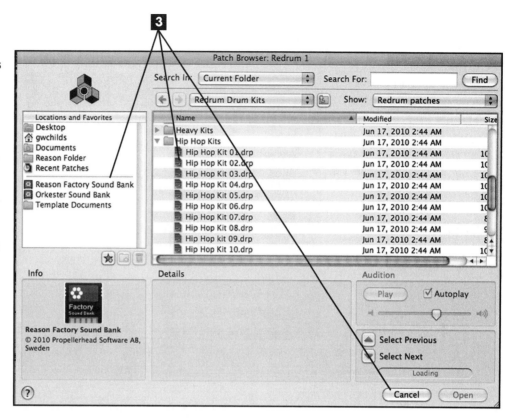

Loading Individual Samples on a Channel

What if you like the sound of your kit, except that one drum is not quite right? Redrum has got you covered. You can load samples on individual Redrum channels by clicking the Browse Sample button with the folder icon on it.

1 With your Redrum_Ignite song still open, **click** the **Trigger Drum button** on the top of Channel 3. You will hear some sort of weird snare drum (which almost sounds like a hand clap to me).

2 **Click** the **up/down arrows** to the left of the Browse Sample button on Channel 3 to scroll up and down through samples in the current folder. Each time you click the up or down arrow, click the Trigger Drum button to hear the new sample.

3 To see all of the available samples currently loaded into memory, **click** in the **Sample Display window** (3a). Notice the Open Browser selection at the top of the context menu that appears. It has the same function as clicking the Browse Sample button. **Click** on any **drum sample** in the list to select it (3b).

4 **Click** Channel 3's **Browse Sample button**. From here, you can select any sample from any of your Reason ReFills (or from anywhere in your hard drive, for that matter).

Adding Dynamics to Your Patterns

See that little Dynamics switch on the bottom right of Redrum? By default (that is, when a new Redrum is first dragged into the Reason rack), that switch is set to its Medium position. So every Step button you click on plays its sound at medium volume and lights up amber. If you had it in the Soft position and clicked a Step button, it would light up yellow and play a little softer. In the next exercise, you'll see some pads light up rosy red (or is it pink?) as we make those drum hits loud.

1 **Open** the Redrum_Ignite **song** you saved in the last exercise and click Run so you can hear the beat.

2 **Click** the **Select button** on Redrum Channel 2 so that you can edit the snare drum.

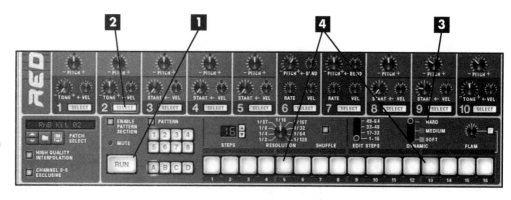

3 **Move** the **Dynamics switch** into the Hard position.

4 **Click** once on **Steps 5 and 13**. The Step buttons should change color from amber to red, and you will hear the snare drum get louder.

5 **Click** the **Select button** on Channel 1 so that you can edit the bass drum.

6 **Click** once on each of **Steps 1, 8, 9, and 16**. The bass drum will get louder.

You can save again when you are finished with this. Of course, you could have made any of these steps softer by moving the Dynamics switch to the Soft position and then clicking on the Step buttons. If you accidentally clicked an extra time on any of the Step buttons, you probably saw the light go off altogether. You activate as well as deactivate the Step buttons by clicking on them.

Stringing Patterns Together

You've been working with this pattern for a while, and if you're like me, you might be thinking it could use a little something extra. In the next exercise, you will make a new pattern that complements this pattern.

1 **Open** the Redrum_Ignite **song** you saved in the last exercise. **Right-click** anywhere on **Redrum** and **select Copy Pattern** from the menu that pops up. (This is known as a *context menu*.) This copies the pattern to the Clipboard, just like copying something to the Clipboard in Microsoft Word, Adobe Photoshop, or any other similar program.

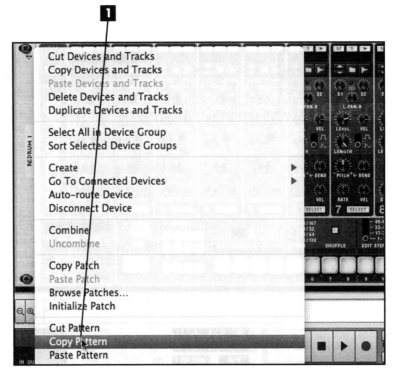

2 **Click** on the number 2 **Pattern Select button**. This is an empty pattern.

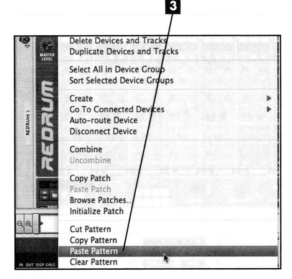

3 **Right-click** anywhere on **Redrum** and **choose Paste Pattern** from the context menu. The pattern that was already saved as pattern number 1 will be copied to pattern number 2 as well.

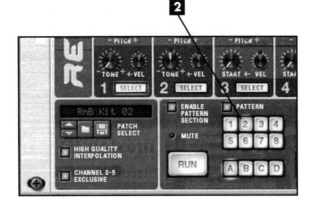

4 **Click** the **Select button** on Channel 2 so that you can edit the snare drum. Then click once on **Step button 13** to deactivate that step.

5 **Click** the **Select button** on Channel 1 to edit the bass drum. Then **click** on **Step buttons 12 and 13**.

6 **Click** on the number 1 **Pattern Select button**. Then **click Run**, and as soon as the beat starts, **click Pattern Select button** number 2. As soon as that pattern starts, **click** on **Pattern 1** again, and so on.

If you get the timing right, you should hear each pattern once before it switches to the other pattern, and the beat should make sense. Save the song.

If you had clicked Record on the Reason Transport during the previous exercise, you could have recorded yourself making those pattern changes. Then, when you played back the sequence, the pattern changes would happen automatically just as you recorded them. Personally, I get confused by switching those patterns manually while the track plays, and I usually mess it up. So next, I'm going to show you a much easier way to make the patterns switch back and forth in perfect time.

Automating Pattern Changes

Before you start the next exercise, I want to mention that even though you see only eight Pattern Select buttons, below those Pattern Select buttons are four Bank Select buttons (A, B, C, and D). So you actually have eight patterns for Bank A, eight patterns for Bank B, and so on, for a total of 32 patterns in just one instance of Redrum. In the next exercise, we will continue to stick with Bank A, since we are still dealing with only two patterns and do not really need any other banks.

1 **Open** the Redrum_Ignite **song** you saved in the last exercise. Then, in the Reason Sequencer, **click** the **Horizontal Zoom-In button** a few times until you have a nice big display. **Drag** the **horizontal scrollbar** all the way to the left, so you can see Bar 1.

2 **Drag** the **right locator** over to Bar 3.

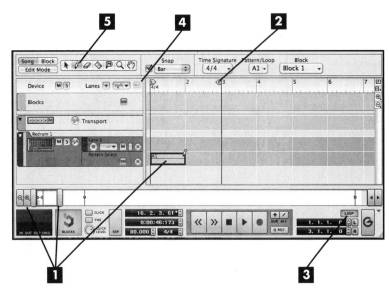

3 **Click** the **Loop On/Off button** to turn on looping. (It should be lit up blue.)

4 **Click** the **Create Pattern Lane button**.

5 **Select** the **Pencil tool**. Then **click** once inside **Bar 1** in the Pattern Select lane. You have just drawn in Redrum pattern selection for Bank A, Pattern 1.

6 **Choose Bank A, Pattern 2** from the Pattern Select drop-down menu.

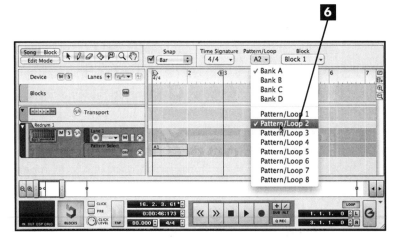

7 With your Pencil tool still selected, **click** inside of **Bar 2** in the Pattern Select lane. Redrum should switch to Pattern A2 when the Sequencer plays Bar 2. **Click Play** to hear your loop and the automated pattern change.

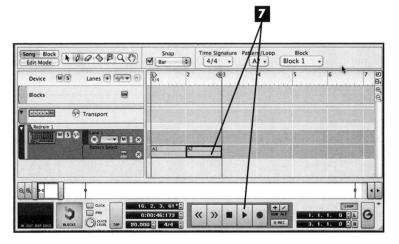

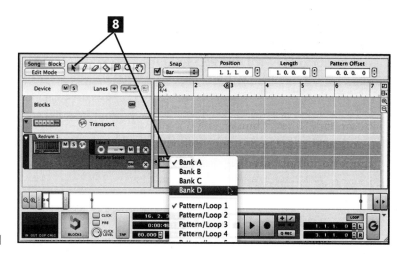

8 **Choose** your **Selection tool** (which looks like a cursor). **Click** inside **Bar 1** in the Pattern Select lane and then **click** the **drop-down arrow** next to where it says A1. Notice that you can select any pattern here, the same way you could in the Pattern Select drop-down menu you saw when you had the Pencil tool selected. Don't make any change, though.

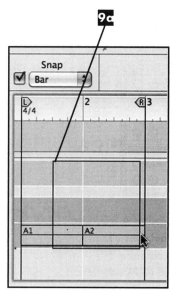

9 Now, just to practice copy/paste in the Reason Sequencer, **click and drag** your **mouse** to create a square covering Bars 1 and 2 (9a). (Alternatively, you could **hold** the **Shift key** while clicking on both **bars**.) Now that both bars are selected, **hold down Ctrl** and **click and drag** the **two bars** of information over onto Bars 3 and 4 (9b). Don't let go of Ctrl until you have released the mouse button.

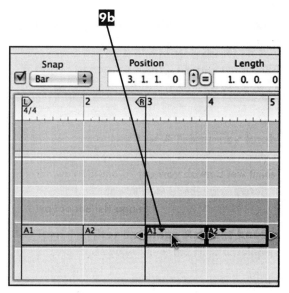

What you did in Step 9 is something you will be doing with all your Sequencer tracks, no matter what instrument they are controlling. As in a Microsoft Word document, you can cut, copy, and paste to save time. Because your songs will usually last more than three minutes (instead of only two bars!), you will do this to extend drum beats and bass lines through your songs. Also, you can copy and paste anything that repeats (such as a verse or chorus section) throughout the song.

The exercise you just finished is the last one I will ask you to save for this chapter. You will not have to refer back to your Redrum_Ignite song from here on out. The other exercises are standalone exercises.

Making Patterns with More Than 16 Steps

In the previous exercise, we put together two one-bar patterns to make a two-bar loop. Each pattern had the default 16 steps and used a resolution of 1/16, so each step equaled a sixteenth note. In the following exercise, you will make a single pattern that lasts two bars (32 steps at 1/16 resolution).

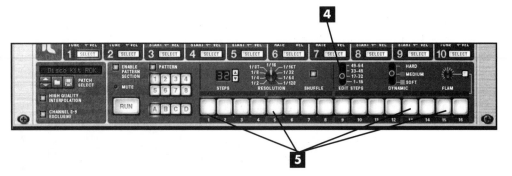

1 Start with an empty rack. **Create** an instance of the **reMix Mixer** and then **create** an instance of **Redrum. Click** the **Run button** on Redrum.

2 By default, Disco Kit RDK should be loaded, and the Channel 1 Select button should be lit so that you can edit the bass drum. **Turn up** the **pattern length** to 32 steps (either by using the up/down arrows or by clicking and dragging inside the display window).

3 **Click** on **Step buttons 1, 5, 9, and 13**. You will hear the kick drum on those four beats and then silence for the next four beats.

4 **Move** the **Edit Steps switch** into the 17–32 position. Previously, you were editing the first group of 16 steps. Now you will work with the second group of 16 steps.

5 **Click** on **Step buttons 1, 5, 9, 13, and 15**. Now you will hear a four-on-the-floor bass drum pattern with a little pickup beat at the end of Bar 2.

Electro-Fun: Randomize Pattern

Redrum's Randomize Pattern function is truly one of my very favorite parts of working with Redrum. It is so cool that we simply must play with it right now!

1 Start with an empty rack. **Create** an **instance** of the reMix Mixer 14:2 and then **create** an **instance** of Redrum. **Turn up** the **song tempo** to 133 in the Reason Transport panel.

2 **Open** Redrum's **Patch Browser** and **select Patch Browser and select Reason Factory Sound Bank > Redrum Drum Kits > Electronic Kits > Electronic Kit 6.drp.**

3 **Turn up** the **bass drum volume** by turning the Channel 1 Level knob up to 86 (about 2 o'clock).

4 **Right-click** on **Redrum** (Ctrl-click if you're on a Mac) and then **select Randomize Pattern** from the pop-up menu. Note that Randomize Pattern is also available in the Edit menu.

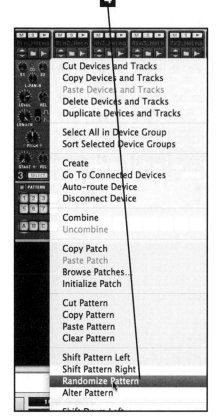

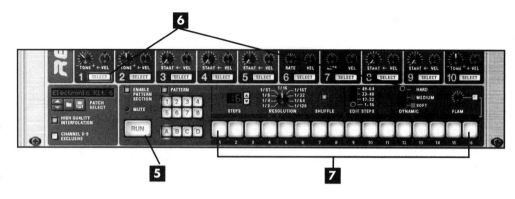

5 **Click Run** to hear the pattern.

6 **Make sure** the **Select button** on Channel 1 is lit. This is, of course, the bass drum. Then move the **Dynamic switch** into the Hard position.

7 **Click and drag** across all 16 **Step buttons** twice so they are all white (inactive). You should not hear the kick drum anymore.

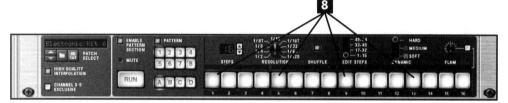

8 Now **click** on **Step buttons 1, 5, 9, and 13** so that you have a four-on-the-floor bass drum pattern.

What can make this exercise extra fun and useful is to select Pattern 2 on Redrum and then repeat Steps 4 through 8. You can easily create a whole bank (eight patterns) of intelligent-sounding (but actually random!) patterns this way, with a four-on-the-floor bass drum pattern holding it all together. You could also add other elements, such as a steady hi-hat pattern, while leaving the complexity of the random pattern for the rest of the drums in the kit.

The next short exercise picks up where the previous exercise left off (so you should already have Redrum in your rack, with a randomized pattern and a four-on-the-floor bass drum pattern).

1 **Right-click** on **Redrum** and **select Copy Pattern** from the context menu.

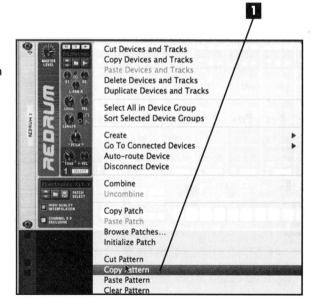

2 **Select Pattern 2** and then **right-click** on **Redrum** and **select Paste Pattern** from the context menu.

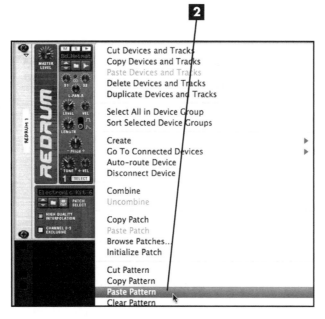

3 With Channel 1 selected (bass drum), **click** on the **number 15 Step** button to create a little pickup note on the bass drum.

4 **Select Pattern 1** and **click Run**. As Redrum plays, alternate between Pattern 1 and Pattern 2 by using the Pattern Select buttons. You will hear the same rhythm but without the bass drum pickup note on Pattern 1 and with the pickup note on Pattern 2.

Randomize Pattern is a great way to experiment. If you don't like the first random pattern you hear, simply roll the dice again by selecting Randomize Pattern again. It's a great way to stimulate the creative process, and it can result in many happy accidents! And if you want to tweak these random beats in the Reason Sequencer, you can always choose Copy Pattern to Track from Redrum's Edit or context menu, similar to what you did with Dr.Rex (Copy REX Loop to Track). Finally, please note that Randomize Drum is also available from the Edit and context menus. As the name suggests, Randomize Drum merely randomizes the currently selected drum channel, instead of randomizing the whole pattern.

Flam

When you double-strike a drum, this is known as a *flam*. In Redrum, applying flam to a step entry will add a second hit to the drum beat, very soon after the first hit. The delay between these two hits is determined by the Flam Amount knob. The Flam Amount knob is a global control that affects the amount of flam for all drums in all patterns to which flam is applied.

55

✳ ✳ ✳

1 In an empty Reason rack, **drag** in a **Mixer 14:2** and an instance of **Redrum** underneath. **Click Run**.

2 **Click** the **Select button** on Channel 2. **Click Step buttons 3 and 7**. You will hear two snare hits.

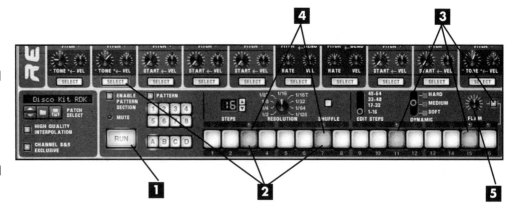

3 **Click** the **Edit Flam button**, which will light up red. Then **click** on **Step buttons 11 and 15**. You will hear the flam effect on these two hits and notice that the red LED above these steps is lit constantly to indicate flam.

4 **Click** the **red LED** above Step button 3, as well as the one above Step button 7. Now flam is applied to all four snare hits. (Note that clicking directly on the LEDs adds flam even if the Edit Flam button is turned off.)

5 Now slowly **turn** the **Flam knob** all the way to the right to hear the delay between the initial drum hit and the flam hit increase and then slowly **turn it** all the way to the left to hear the delay decrease.

You can use flam to accent certain notes and to create drum rolls (or cymbal rolls). You will also do a little trick with it in the Pattern Resolution exercise that follows.

Pattern Resolution

The length (or note value) of each step is determined by the Pattern Resolution setting. The default is 1/16, meaning that each step is one sixteenth note. You can program different Pattern Resolution settings for each pattern within a single instance of Redrum. Although changing this setting while playing back a pattern will cause the pattern to play back more rapidly or more slowly, it has no effect on the Reason song tempo. You could use lower resolutions, such as 1/8 or 1/4, for simple patterns. In the following exercise, you will use a very high resolution to make a snare roll that might be suitable for certain brands of electronic music (though the particular snare sound we will use may not be the hippest for this!).

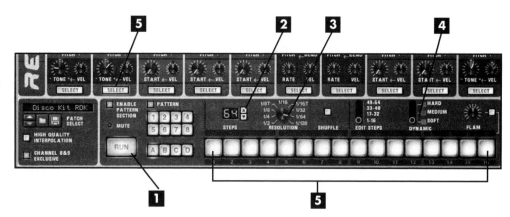

1 In an empty Reason rack, **drag** in a **Mixer 14:2** and an instance of **Redrum** underneath. **Click Run**.

2 **Turn up** the **Pattern Length** to 64 steps.

3 **Turn up** the **Pattern Resolution** to 1/64.

4 **Set** the **Dynamic switch** to the Soft position.

5 **Click** the **Channel 2 Select button** and then **click and drag** across all 16 **steps**. They should all be lit up yellow.

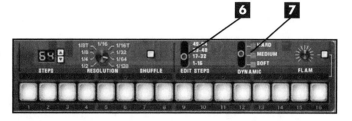

6 **Move** the **Edit Steps button** to the 17–32 position.

7 **Set** the **Dynamic switch** to the Medium position. Then **click and drag** across all 16 **Step buttons** to activate them.

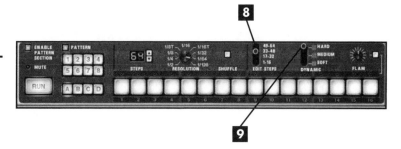

8 **Move** the **Edit Steps button** to the 33–48 position.

9 **Set** the **Dynamic switch** to the Hard position. Then **click and drag** across all 16 **Step buttons** to activate them.

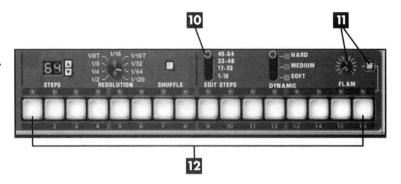

10 Move the **Edit Steps button** to the 49–64 position.

11 Click the **Edit Flam button** and **turn flam** almost all the way to the left, to a value of 6 or so.

12 Click and drag across all 16 **Step buttons** to activate them.

Of course, unless you are some kind of deviant, you probably wouldn't want to let this pattern loop over and over. Rather, it would be a one-bar roll that you could throw in once, leading into another pattern. And as I have stated, that other pattern could be of any resolution you want.

> **⁂ RUN / ENABLE PATTERN SECTION / PATTERN ENABLE**
>
> The Run button is used to start and stop playback of Redrum's Pattern section. When the Enable Pattern Section button is engaged, the Run button will automatically engage whenever you press Play on the Reason Transport panel. You can also click the Run button at any time, regardless of whether your Reason song is playing. In either case, when Run is engaged, you will see the step lights move from left to right. If the sounds in Redrum are going to be triggered by note info from the Reason Sequencer, a MIDI controller, or a CV device (instead of using the Pattern section), then you will want to turn off Enable Pattern Section. If Enable Pattern Section is turned off, clicking the Run button will have no effect.
>
> To actually hear any patterns you have created, you must also engage the Pattern Enable button. This button (merely labeled Pattern) mutes and unmutes pattern playback starting on the next downbeat according to the time signature selected in the Reason Transport panel. This is a useful feature when you have more than one Redrum in your rack and you wish to bring them in and out of the mix alternately.

Using the Reason Sequencer with Redrum

We have already used the Pattern Lane in the Reason Sequencer to control pattern changes. What we have not done yet is to turn off Redrum's Pattern section entirely and sequence purely in the Reason Sequencer. I think a big part of the fun of Redrum is using its built-in pattern-based sequencer, but playing on pads (such as an Akai MPC or an M-Audio Axiom) or playing on a MIDI keyboard comes quite naturally to many people, and Redrum can do that as well. Also, with the Reason Sequencer, you can draw in your notes in Drum Edit mode with the Pencil tool, which is another variety of workflow that you may find comfortable. In the following exercise, I am using a MIDI keyboard, but if you are advanced enough to have set up some trigger pads instead, and it's all working for you, then that's great, too!

1 In an empty Reason rack, **drag** in a **Mixer 14:2** and an instance of **Redrum** underneath. **Click** the **Enable Pattern Section switch** to turn it off. Now Redrum will not start its pattern section when you click Play on the Reason Transport.

2 In the Reason Sequencer, **click** the **Edit/Arrange Mode selector button** to change to Edit mode. You will see the Drum Editor. **Click** the **small magnifying-glass buttons** at the bottom left of the Sequencer to zoom so that Bar 1 fills up almost the entire window.

3 **Click** the **Loop On/off button** to turn on looping and then **make sure** the **Click button** is on (lit blue).

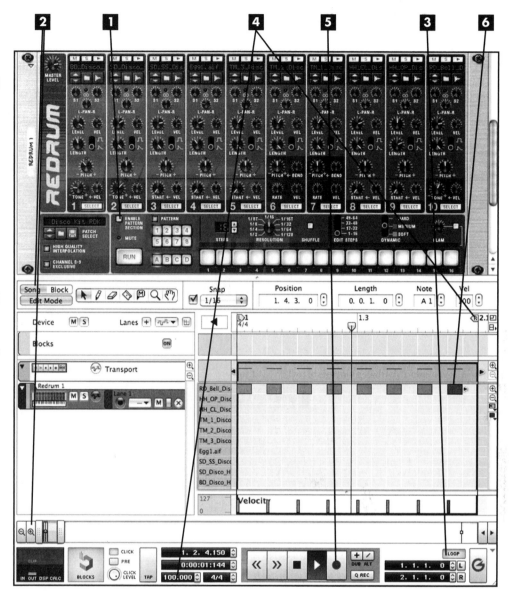

4 **Turn down** the **Tempo** to 100 (so you won't feel rushed!). Then **hold down** the **Alt key** while you **click** on the **Bar 2 marker**. This will set the right locator at Bar 2.

5 **Find and play** the key **C1** on your MIDI keyboard. You should hear the bass drum when you play it. Now **move up** to key **A1**. This is a ride cymbal, and it's what you are going to record first. **Click** the **Record button** on the Reason Transport and listen to the groove of the click. It is playing quarter notes (1-2-3-4).

6 When you are ready, **record** an **eighth-note pattern** with your ride cymbal (play 1 and 2 and 3 and 4) with your A1 key, twice as fast as the click.

7 Once you have your ride cymbal recorded, **record kick** (C1) on Beats 1 and 3 and **record snare** (C#1) on Beats 2 and 4. As the click goes 1-2-3-4, you will play kick-snare-kick-snare. Your loop is only four beats long, so you will have just two kicks and snares and eight ride cymbal hits when you are finished.

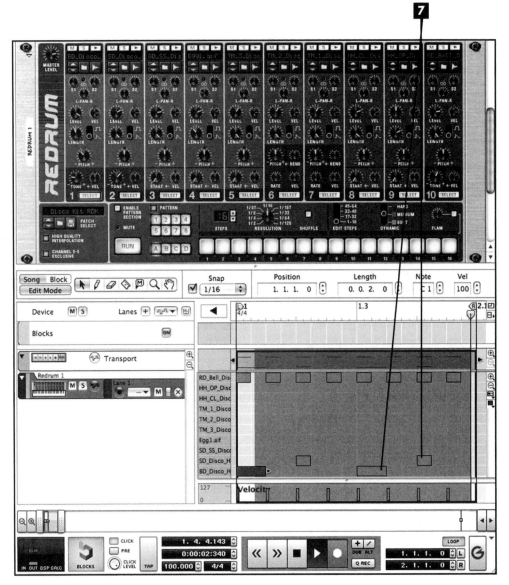

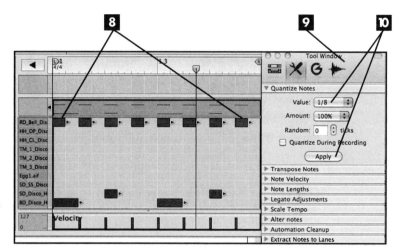

8 **Click Record** again to stop recording, but play will continue. **Double-click** in the middle of your **drum sequence** so you can edit. (Your notes will turn from gray to red.) Then **press Ctrl+A** to select all (or **choose Select All** from the Edit menu). The notes in the Sequencer will get darker, and black note-length adjustment arrows will appear to the right of each note.

9 In your Tool window (F8 shows or hides the Tool window), **click** the **Tools tab** if it's not already highlighted.

10 **Set** the **Quantize value** to 1/8 (because that's the smallest time value you played). Quantize Amount should be set to 100% by default. **Click Apply**, and you will notice that all your beats are right on the money!

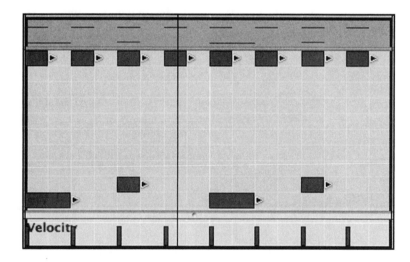

After quantizing, the start point of all the notes lines up perfectly on the grid. The timing is dead-on now.

So now you have a taste of the magic of Quantize. If you wanted the beat to sound not quite so robotic, you could have set the Quantize Amount to 80% (or something like that—you can experiment) so that your notes are moved closer to the beat, but not perfectly right-on. Now, you may be saying to yourself, "He said my beats would be right on the money, but a few of them are totally off after quantizing!" Quantize moves the notes you played to the nearest eighth note (or whatever time division you have selected). If you were closer to the wrong beat than the right beat, Quantize will move the note to dead center of the wrong beat! Not to worry—you can just click on the note and drag it to the correct beat.

Digging into the Redrum Channels

For the last few sections of this chapter, we are going to take a look at some of the controls on Redrum's 10 channel strips. Unlike the Mixer 14:2 (reMix), where each channel is identical, you will notice that Redrum's channels are slightly different from one another. For a detailed, complete rundown of all the particulars, please see your Reason manual. For now, I am just going to highlight a few of the bits I think you will want to use the most.

Redrum Effects Sends (S1 and S2)

Redrum's effects sends are especially useful when you are connecting Redrum to the reMix Mixer on one stereo channel instead of routing each individual drum to a separate channel on reMix. On reMix (as well as on the smaller MicroMix Line Mixer 6:2), each channel has its own effects sends. But when Redrum is connected to only one stereo channel of a mixer, using the effects sends on the mixer channel would apply the effects to all the drums simultaneously. Using Redrum's own effects sends allows you to send the audio signal from each individual drum to up to two separate effects at any level you want. If reMix is present at the top of the Reason Device Rack, when a new Redrum is created, Redrum's Send Out 1 and 2 outputs will be automatically routed to the first two available Chaining Aux inputs in the rear of reMix. These inputs bypass the red Auxiliary Send Level knobs on the front of reMix and send the signal directly to the effects device with no attenuation. That may have sounded more complicated than it actually is. Let's give this a spin!

1 Open the **song** you created earlier in this chapter, called Redrum_Ignite. **Drag** an **RV7000 Advanced Reverb** directly under the reMix Mixer and then **drag** a **DDL-1 Digital Delay** directly under that. The effects will be "automagically" routed with the RV7000 on Effects Return 1 and the DDL-1 on Effects Return 2 of the reMix Mixer.

2 **Flip** your **rack** around (using the Tab key on your computer keyboard), and you will see that Send Outs 1 and 2 of Redrum have been automatically routed to Chaining Aux Inputs 1 and 2 of reMix 14:2. This means that the signal from Redrum's Send 1 will be processed by the RV7000 Reverb, and the signal from Redrum's Send 2 will be processed by the DDL-1 Digital Delay. (If you are having trouble reading some of the labels because the cables are in the way, clicking L on your computer keyboard will show or hide the cables.)

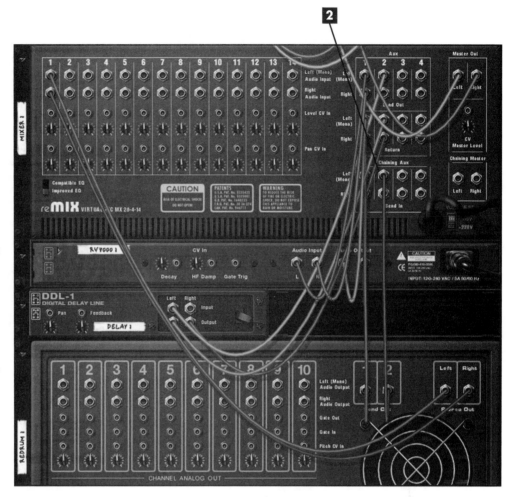

3 **Press Tab** to flip the Reason Device Rack back around so it's facing front. **Click Play** on the Reason Transport to hear that oh-so-familiar beat.

4 **Turn up** the **Send 1 knob** on Channel 2 halfway to send the snare drum through the RV7000 Reverb.

5 **Turn up** the **Send 2 knob** on Channel 8 halfway to send some hi-hat through the DDL-1 Digital Delay.

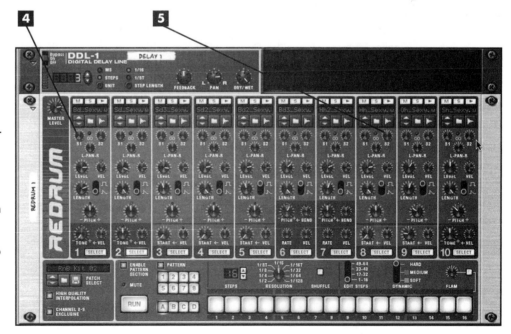

6 Turn the **Pan knob** on the DDL-1 to about 3 o'clock. Now the delayed signal is panned right.

7 Turn up the **Send 2 knob** on Channel 2 halfway to send some snare drum signal through the DDL-1 Digital Delay.

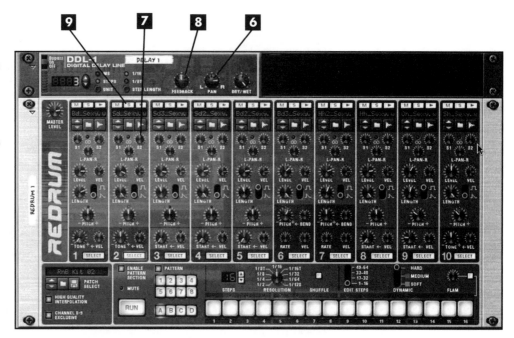

8 Turn up the **Feedback knob** on the DDL-1 to 12 o'clock for some extra snare action. Turning up the Feedback knob causes the delay to repeat more times before fading out.

9 For a cool effect, **click** the **Solo button** on the top of Channel 2. You will hear only the snare drum with its reverb and delay effects, while all the other drums will be muted.

10 Watch the progress marker in the Reason Sequencer as it travels from left to right within your loop. Just before Bar 2 of the pattern finishes, **click** the **Channel 2 solo button** again to hear all the drums come in together.

Channel 8 & 9 Exclusive

When the Channel 8 & 9 Exclusive button is activated, the sounds on Channels 8 and 9 will be exclusive of each other, meaning that when a sound is triggered on Channel 8, it will be cut off as soon as a sound is played on Channel 9, and vice versa. This is handy for adding realism to hi-hats, where a closed hi-hat is loaded into one channel and an open hi-hat is loaded into the other channel. To get a feel for this, please try the following exercise.

1 Start with an empty rack. **Create** an instance of the **Mixer 14:2** and then **create** an instance of **Redrum**. Then **open** Redrum's **Patch Browser** and **select Reason Factory Sound Bank > Redrum Drum Kits > Tight Kits > Dublab TightKit1.drp**.

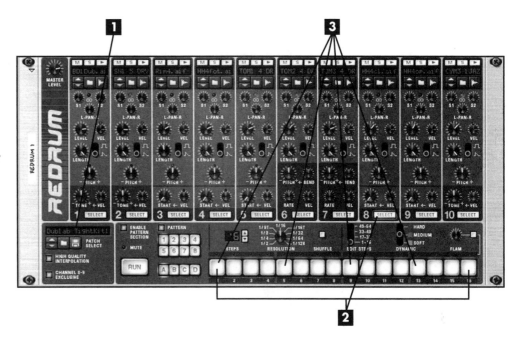

2 **Click** the **Channel 8 Select button**. This is a closed hi-hat. **Click and drag** your **mouse** across all 16 Step buttons so that they are all lit up yellow.

3 **Click** on **Step buttons 1, 5, 9, and 13** to deactivate them.

4 **Click** the **Channel 9 Select button**. This is the open hi-hat. **Click** on **Steps 1, 5, 9, and 13** so that they are lit up yellow.

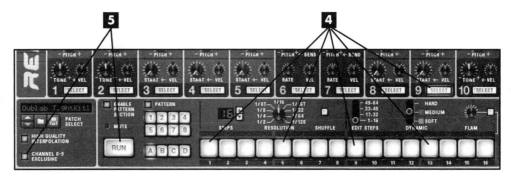

5 **Click** the **Run button**. Now **practice turning** the **Channel 8 & 9 Exclusive button** on and off. When it is on, the open hi-hat will cease to ring out as soon as the closed hi-hat is played. If the Channel 8 & 9 Exclusive button is off, the open hi-hat will continue to ring out even when the closed hi-hat is played, which would be physically impossible for a real hi-hat!

Pan, Pitch, and Level

The Pan knob included on each channel determines the selected drum's position in the stereo image. Pan settings are very important for creating a realistic-sounding acoustic kit, as well as for creating ear-catching electronic kits. The little red LED above the Pan knob (between the Send knobs) lights up to indicate when a stereo sample is being used. Its little label looks like an infinity symbol or a bipolar microphone pattern, but of course it signifies stereo in this case. When it is not lit (as in the following exercise), this means a mono sample is being used, and the Pan knob will simply move the mono sample to the left or right of the stereo image. If the Stereo Sample LED is lit to indicate that a stereo sample is being used, then the Pan knob becomes a stereo balance control, emphasizing the left or right channel of the stereo sample. In the following exercise, you will try out the Pan knob, as well as the Pitch knob (which is used for tuning the sample) and the Level knob (which makes the sample louder or quieter).

1 Start with an empty rack. **Create** an instance of the **Mixer 14:2** and then **create** an instance of **Redrum. Click** the **Trigger Sample button** on Channel 2 a few times to hear the snare drum.

2 Now turn the Channel 2 Pitch knob to the left and right. Each time you turn it to a new position, click the Trigger Sample button on Channel 2 a few times to hear the snare drum play back at a new pitch. When you are finished experimenting, turn the Pitch knob back to 12 o'clock.

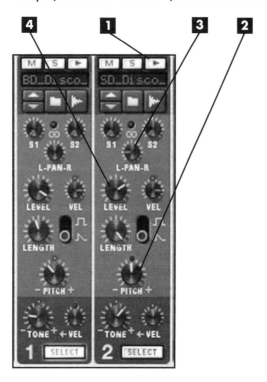

3 Turn the **Channel 2 Pan knob** to 9 o'clock. Now your snare drum sounds more or less as if it were in the same position as it would if you were sitting behind a right-handed drum kit (in front of you and to the left).

4 Turn up the **Channel 2 Level knob** all the way. Now when you trigger your snare sample, it is a bit louder.

❄ DON'T LOSE YOUR CHANNEL STRIP SETTINGS!

Loading a new individual sample into a Redrum channel (using the Browse Sample button) does not affect any of your other settings. However, when you load a new Redrum patch (using the Browse Patch button), not only will new samples (drum sounds) be loaded into each of Redrum's 10 drum channels, but new channel strip settings will be loaded as well. This is important to keep in mind. If you are working with one patch (or kit), and you have all your pan, pitch, and tone settings perfectly the way you want them, you'd better save that as a new patch, or else when you load another kit, those settings will be lost forever! You can save patches (drum kits) by clicking the diskette icon to the far right of the Patch Display window.

Sampling in Redrum

A major addition to Reason 5, without a shadow of a doubt, is the ability to actually sample from within the program. If you are unfamiliar with the term *sample*, it merely means that you are recording actual audio that will be used as a sound within certain instruments, such as Redrum!

In previous versions of Reason, if you wanted to record a kick drum from around your house and use it in Redrum or the NN-XT, it was a long procedure. You actually had to record your kick in another application (such as Pro Tools, Logic Pro, Cubase, or REAPER), and once you exported the audio from that application, you could use the Reason browser to find the actual audio file. It was not a short procedure at all.

In Reason 5, Redrum and all other devices (see the chapters on the NN-XT, NN-19, and Kong) that can use recorded audio have sample buttons on every pertinent channel, and so on.

This is amazing because it means you can record audio from your laptop mic, desktop mic, or audio interface mic and then have the audio available as a percussive part within Redrum. There's no bouncing through several programs; it can all be done in Reason.

Before you get started with actually sampling, though, you need to learn how to set up the audio input; otherwise, you'll be recording silence.

1 Go into your **Reason Preferences** or **Settings** and **go to** the **Audio page**. If you are unsure of how to do this, refer to Chapter 1 for help with setting up your audio interface.

2 On the Reason Preferences page, **verify** that you have your **audio interface** set up. This should be the case, but if you skipped Chapter 1, you may want to revisit it.

3 Press the **Active Channels input button**.

4 Check off the **audio input** to which your mic is connected.

5 If the Active Channels input button is gray because you are using a built-in audio device on a Mac, for example, **select** the **drop-down menu** at the top, where you selected your initial audio interface, and **choose Built-in Microphone+Built-in Audio or Built-in Input+Built-in Audio**.

> ❊ Audio input setups can vary dramatically depending on whether you're working on a PC or a Mac. If you are having difficulty, consult your computer's owner manual, your audio interface's owner manual, and so on.

Notice that there are two cables coming out of the Reason hardware interface, going into the Sampling Input that is new in Reason 5. You should notice green lights next to the outputs you enabled. The green lights suggest that the output is now active. By default, Reason automatically has Inputs 1 and 2 connected to the Sampling Input. However, you can connect other inputs instead by simply dragging the cables into the Sampling Input ports.

So, if you enabled Inputs 7 and 8 because your microphone or guitar is connected to them, drag the cables from Inputs 7 and 8 over to the Sampling Input. If you are on a laptop, and you selected the built-in mic or the built-in input along with the built-in output, you should be seeing signal already.

To verify that you have input, press Tab to turn the rack around, so that you see the front of the hardware interface. When you speak into your mic or strum your guitar, you should see signal coming into the Sampling Input meters.

Our ports are now set up, which means we can sample at will, so to speak. Let's try putting this new ability to good use!

1 In a new Reason session, **create** a **Mixer 14:2** and a **Redrum Drum Computer**.

2 Now press the small Sample button atop Channel 1 of the Redrum Drum Computer. A small recording interface will appear, and the recording will begin instantly, so start speaking as soon as you see it appear.

3 **Press** the **Stop button** on the Recording screen.

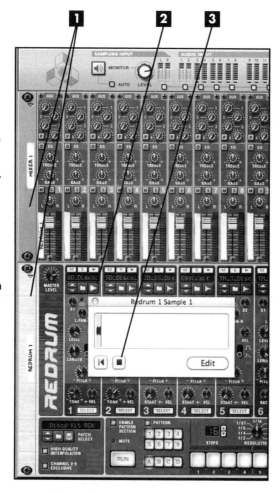

When you trigger the Channel 1 of Redrum now, you'll notice that the part you recorded is now playing back. If it's not working for you as is, remember that you can always hit the Sample button again, and a new recording will replace the old one.

Additionally, you can also edit the existing recording, but we'll save that for Chapter 7, "The Reason Samplers: NN-19 and NN-XT," where we'll get into the big-boy samplers. For now, start playing around with recording your own samples and discovering how they work with Redrum!

Now that you've spent some quality time with Dr. Rex in Chapter 2 and Redrum in this chapter, I hope you are already starting to feel pretty comfortable working with beats in Reason. Now it's time to move on to exploring the virtual synths Reason has to offer!

4 } Subtractor

Subtractor, modeled after classic analog synthesizers, was the first synthesizer ever developed for Reason. You might think that the name refers to bass (like sub-bass or subwoofer). Actually, although Subtractor does have some great bass sounds, the name comes from the fact that Subtractor uses what is known as *subtractive synthesis*. It's easy to remember that term when you keep in mind that with subtractive synthesis, you start with a basic tone and then shape that tone by filtering out (or subtracting) various frequencies. The three basic building blocks in subtractive synthesis are the oscillator (generates the basic tone), the filter (removes, or subtracts, frequencies from the basic tone generated by the oscillator), and the amplifier (amplifies the signal coming from the filter). We won't go much deeper into that subject for the moment, but you will notice oscillators, filters, and amplifiers on all of the Reason synths. For now, let's just dig in and have some fun with Subtractor.

In this chapter, you will learn how to:

* Use the various synth parameter controls on Subtractor to make your own custom sounds
* Use all the features of the RPG-8 Monophonic Arpeggiator with Subtractor
* Use the Reason Sequencer with Subtractor
* Use effects devices, such as the CF1 Chorus/Flanger, to make your Subtractor patches sound even better

Subtractor Synth Parameters

Parameter is really a pretty generic word and in this case could be replaced with the word *setting*. The Pitch Bend Range is one parameter (or setting), the Filter Frequency is another parameter, and the Master Output Level is still another parameter. The purpose of this section of the chapter is to help you get your hands on a few of the most useful Subtractor parameters so you can start getting a feel for what all those knobs, sliders, and buttons do. I'm into this sort of thing, so I think it will be fun, too!

Waveforms and Oscillators 1 and 2

Oscillators 1 and 2 are the basic tone generators for Subtractor. Each oscillator can generate any one of 32 waveforms. As you explore Subtractor's presets, you will find many skillfully programmed, rich, and elaborate sounds based on these basic waveforms. In this first exercise, however, you will hear what these waveforms sound like naked and unadulterated, prior to any filtering or modulation of any kind.

1 In a new, empty rack, **create** a **Mixer 14:2** followed by a Subtractor. Then **right-click** on the **Subtractor** and **choose Initialize Patch**. This will give you a very basic starting point.

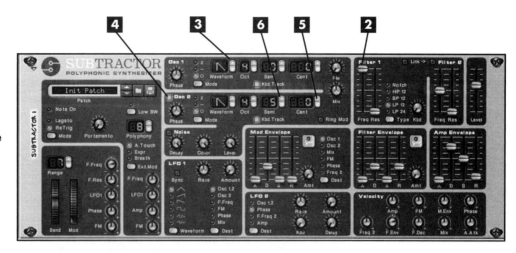

2 **Turn up Filter 1 Frequency** all the way. Now you can hear the sound of Oscillator 1 with no filtering or anything else between the oscillator and your ears!

3 As you play your MIDI keyboard, **use** the **Osc 1 Waveform up arrow** to click one by one through the 32 waveforms and listen to each sound. When you are finished, **click and hold** the **down arrow** until you are back where you started (at the sawtooth wave).

4 **Turn on Oscillator 2** by clicking the red (unlabeled) Osc 2 On/Off button.

5 While playing your MIDI keyboard, slowly **turn up** the **Oscillator 2 Cent parameter** to 10, and you will hear Oscillator 2 go just a bit out of tune with Oscillator 1. When you are finished, **turn down** the **Oscillator 2 Cent parameter** to 0. (A cent is 1/100 of a semitone, by the way.)

6 While playing your MIDI keyboard, **turn up** the **Oscillator 2 Semitone parameter** to 5. The musical interval you now have between the two oscillators is a fourth.

7 While playing your MIDI keyboard, **turn up** the **Oscillator 2 Semitone parameter** to 7 semitones. The musical interval you now have is a fifth, and I think you are ready to play the keyboard solo to "Abacab" by Genesis.

Waveforms and Low-Frequency Oscillators

When used at audible frequencies (between 20 Hz and 20,000 Hz), the type of waveform used by a synthesizer's oscillator is the first determining factor in what the synthesizer patch (or program) will sound like. However, when used at a very low, inaudible frequency (such as a few times per second) in an LFO (*low-frequency oscillator*), these waveforms can control pitch, filter frequency, or any of a number of other parameters. The following exercise will allow you to hear the shape of a few waveforms, as they will be used at very low frequencies to modulate (change) the pitch of Subtractor's oscillators (sound generators).

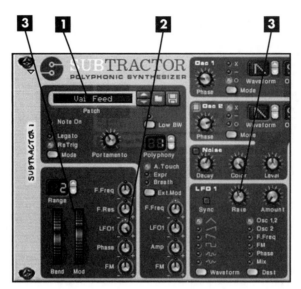

1 In a fresh rack containing Mixer 14:2 followed by Subtractor, **select** the following **Subtractor patch:** Reason Factory Sound Bank > Subtractor Patches > MonoSynths > Vai Feed.zyp.

2 Directly to the right of the Mod wheel, **turn** the **LFO 1 knob** all the way to the right. Now when you use the Mod wheel on your MIDI keyboard, you will get a lot of LFO 1 instead of just a little.

3 **Turn up** the **Mod wheel** on your MIDI keyboard (or use your mouse to move the Mod wheel on Subtractor). You will hear the pitch of the sound (the pitch of Osc 1 and 2) going up and down, just as the shape of the currently selected triangle wave under LFO 1 goes up and then down. So you can hear this more clearly, turn the **LFO 1 Rate knob** down to a value of 60.

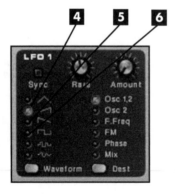

4 **Click** on the **red LED** next to the second waveform (an inverse sawtooth wave) to select it. Now you can hear the pitch of the sound ramp up over and over again, just like the shape of the waveform.

5 **Click** on the **red LED** next to the third waveform (a sawtooth wave). Now you can hear the pitch of the sound ramp down over and over again, just like the shape of the waveform.

6 **Click** on the **red LED** next to the fourth waveform (a square wave). Now you can hear the pitch switch sharply back and forth between two pitches, just like the shape of the waveform.

7 **Select** the **fifth wave-form** (random). Now you can hear the pitch change sharply in a series of random steps like the sound of a computer in some ancient sci-fi movie.

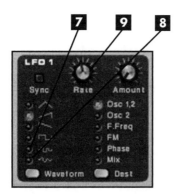

8 **Select** the **sixth** (bottom) **waveform** (soft random). Now the pitch changes more gradually (or softly) through a series of random steps.

9 **Turn** the **LFO 1 Rate knob up** and down and hear the speed of the modulation (or change) go up and down.

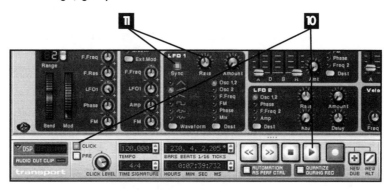

10 **Turn** on the **click** and **press Play** on the Reason Sequencer.

11 **Turn** on the **LFO 1 Sync button**. Now **play** with the **LFO 1 Rate knob** again, and you will hear that the modulation happens in time with the click. This is especially easy to hear at LFO 1 Rate settings of 2/4, 1/4, and 1/8.

In Step 11, feel free to experiment with the different waveforms as they play in time to the click. You will find that different waveforms have different characteristics when played in sync, especially at LFO 1 Rate settings of 2/4, 1/4, and 1/8. Please note that you can also use the Waveform button to click through the waveforms instead of directly clicking the LEDs to the left of the waveforms.

Portamento and Pitch Bend

Portamento is also called *glide* on some synthesizers. It controls the amount of time it takes for the pitch to rise or fall from one note you play to the next. When you switch from a low note to a high note on a piano, there is no portamento. When you switch from a low note to a high note on a trombone, there is plenty of portamento, depending on how quickly or slowly you move the slide. Portamento is good for emulating theremin sounds and for classic analog synth lead sounds. The next short, easy exercise uses a Subtractor patch that already has some portamento built in. You will also try out pitch bend at the end of the exercise.

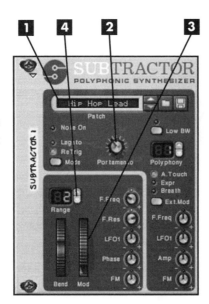

1 In a fresh rack containing Mixer 14:2 followed by Subtractor, **select** the following **Subtractor patch:** Reason Factory Sound Bank > Subtractor Patches > MonoSynths > Hip Hop Lead.zyp.

2 **Play** some **low notes and high notes** on your MIDI keyboard, and you will hear a little bit of portamento. As you play, slowly **turn up** the **Portamento knob** and hear that "glide" time increase. Then slowly **turn down** the **portamento** until the pitch changes sharply from note to note.

3 If this sound has too much treble for you, try **moving** your **Modulation wheel** forward a bit. You can use the wheel on your MIDI keyboard or the one on the Subtractor. In this patch, it is set to lower the filter frequency, which will make a more mellow sound.

4 **Turn** the **Pitch Bend Range** down to 2. You can **click** on the **arrows** or **click and drag** in the **Range window** to do this. Now **use** the **pitch bend wheel** on your MIDI keyboard (or use the one on Subtractor), and the pitch will bend up or down two microtones, which is one full step.

5 **Turn** the **Pitch Bend Range** up to 12. Now use the pitch bend wheel on your MIDI keyboard (or use the one on Subtractor), and the pitch will bend up or down 12 microtones, which is one full octave.

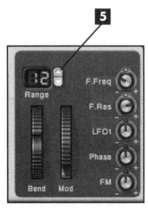

6 Finally, **turn up** the **Pitch Bend Range** to 24. Now use the pitch bend wheel on your MIDI keyboard (or use the one on Subtractor), and the pitch will bend up or down 24 microtones, which is two full octaves.

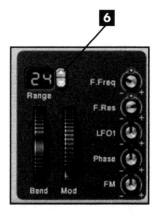

If you used your modulation wheel to mellow out the sound in Step 3, you may have noticed something if you happened to use the Reason Transport controls afterwards. When you press the Stop button on the Reason Transport, the Mod wheel setting returns to zero automatically. If this is a problem for you, you could always adjust the filter frequency directly by using the Filter 1 Frequency slider, which will not reset when you stop playback.

Polyphony

In a synthesizer, *polyphony* refers to the number of independent voices that can be played simultaneously. If only one voice (one key) can be played at a time, the synthesizer (or synthesizer patch) is *monophonic*. The classic Minimoog is an example of a famous monophonic analog synth. Nearly all the patches (or programs) in the Mono-Synths folder in Reason Factory Sound Bank > Subtractor Patches are monophonic. I'm not sure why a few of them (such as Chronic Lead) are actually *polyphonic* (as of version 4.0), but we'll skip that mystery for now. Let's play with Subtractor's Polyphony control and change a monophonic patch into a polyphonic patch.

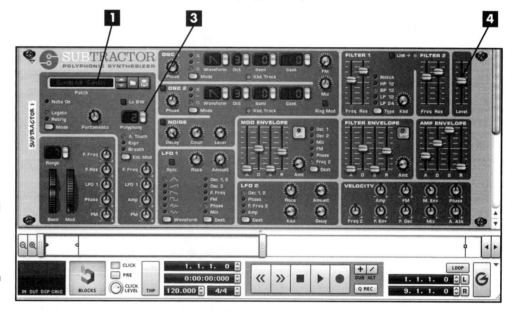

1 In a fresh rack containing Mixer 14:2 followed by Subtractor, **select** the following **Subtractor patch:** Reason Factory Sound Bank > Subtractor Patches > MonoSynths > Singing Synth.

2 **Play** around on your **MIDI keyboard**, and you will notice that you can play only one key at a time (just like with Hip Hop Lead from the previous exercise).

3 **Turn up** the **Polyphony control** to 2. Now play around and notice that every time you try to play a third simultaneous voice, the first voice you played drops off.

4 You may notice your audio *clipping* (distorting because Subtractor's output is too much for Reason's audio output). This is because the patch you are using was designed to be loud with only one voice, and adding the extra voices is just too much signal, as evidenced by the Audio Output Clipping Indicator light. **Turn down** the **(Master) Level slider** on Subtractor to about 70 to avoid any further clipping.

5 **Turn up Polyphony** to 10. Now you could make a chord with all 10 fingers if you wanted to. A whole choir of Singing Synths!

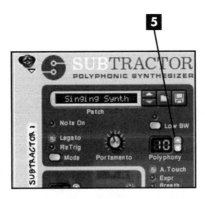

Subtractor's Polyphony control goes up to 99 voices. Some samplers or piano emulations go up to 150. Why would you need so many voices? Well, if you are playing piano and you leave the sustain pedal down, you could easily rack up more than 50 voices. (There are 88 keys, after all.) Also, if you did an entire electronic orchestral arrangement and tried to play it through one synth, you could use quite a few voices.

Of course, simply using one voice (monophonic) is great for lead playing. When Polyphony is set for 1, the most recent note you have touched will be the one you hear, even if you are holding down another note. This allows you to do some "hammer-on" or *pivot* effects. To hear what I'm talking about, set Polyphony to 1 and, while you are holding down one note, strike another key over and over again. Monophonic playing can also sound "cleaner" than higher Polyphony settings when playing fast, because you will hear only one note at a time, even if you accidentally hit two notes at the same time.

Modulation Wheel

You may have noticed that when you play with the Modulation wheel on your MIDI keyboard, stuff happens. You may not have a clear rule in your brain for which stuff happens, since it seems like different things happen depending on which patch you are using. You're not imagining that! If you look to the right of the Mod wheel, you'll see five different knobs. For our purposes, to *modulate* simply means to change. Each of those knobs to the left of the Mod wheel determines to what extent a particular parameter (such as Filter Frequency or LFO 1 Amount) will be changed (or modulated) when you move the Mod wheel. Let's take the Mod wheel for a spin! (I couldn't resist.)

1 In a fresh rack containing Mixer 14:2 followed by Subtractor, **select** the following **Subtractor patch:** Reason Factory Sound Bank > Subtractor Patches > PolySynths > Jupiter 4.zyp.

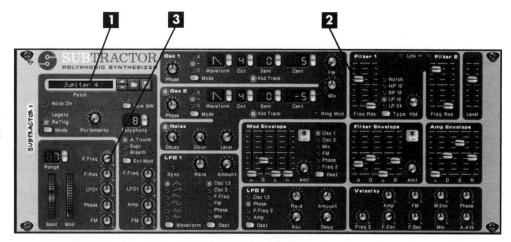

2 While playing some notes on your MIDI keyboard, slowly **turn** the **Filter 1 Freq slider** all the way up and then back down to its default value of 80.

3 **Look** at the **knob** to the right of the Mod wheel labeled F.Freq. This is the Filter Freq Mod Wheel Amount knob. As you can see, it is turned up to about 2 o'clock. Now **play** a few **notes** while you **move** the **Mod wheel** on your MIDI keyboard or on Subtractor. You can hear the filter frequency being raised when you move the Mod wheel, the same as you heard in Step 2!

4 **Turn** your **Mod wheel** all the way back down and **turn** the **Filter Freq Mod Wheel Amount knob** down to about 10 o'clock (a value of –20). Because you have set a negative value, when you turn the Mod wheel, the filter frequency will go down instead of going up.

❄ ❄ ❄

5 Set the **Filter Freq Mod Wheel Amount knob** to 12 o'clock. The little red light above it will turn off to show that filter frequency is not being affected by the Mod wheel.

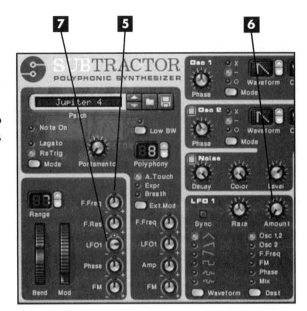

6 **Hold down** a **note** on your MIDI keyboard and slowly **turn up** the **LFO 1 Amount knob** (turn it clockwise). You will hear LFO 1 making the pitch of Oscillators 1 and 2 go up and down. When you are finished, **turn** the **LFO 1 Amount knob** all the way back down again.

7 **Turn** the **LFO 1 Mod Wheel Amount knob** up to about 3 o'clock (a value of about +38). Now **hold down** a **note** on your MIDI keyboard and ease up the Mod wheel. You will hear the pitch go up and down, the same way it sounded in Step 6.

Noise Generator

The Noise Generator does not react to pitch information, so it sounds the same no matter what key you press. It is also not controlled by the Amp Envelope. (More on the Amp Envelope later.) Instead, it has its own Decay knob, which determines how long the Noise Generator's sound will last when a note is played. Long decays can be used for wind noise or to fatten up a pad, and short decays can be used when you want the Noise Generator to provide a percussive attack. In fact, the Noise Generator can be used to create different electronic percussion patches, such as snare drums and hi-hats. The Noise Generator can also be used to add "breath" to a flute patch.

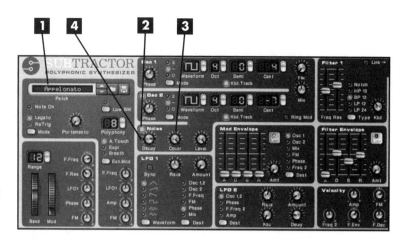

1 In a fresh rack containing Mixer 14:2 followed by Subtractor, **select** the following **Subtractor patch:** Reason Factory Sound Bank > Subtractor Patches > PolySynths > Appelonato.zyp. Play a bit on your MIDI keyboard to hear what this sounds like.

2 **Turn on Noise**, and you will hear an immediate effect.

3 While playing your MIDI keyboard, slowly **turn** the **Noise Color knob** all the way down and then back up again. Think of the Color control as a simple tone control, with brighter tone (more treble) as you turn toward the right and darker tone as you turn toward the left.

4 While playing your MIDI keyboard, slowly **turn down** the **Noise Decay knob** to 12 o'clock and then slowly **turn it back up** to 3 o'clock, listening to the effect as you go.

By the way, the reason the sound sort of goes "owe, owe, owe" when you press new keys is because of the way the Filter Envelope is set. It's the sound of the Filter Frequency falling during the Decay portion of the Filter Envelope. Come back to this thought after you read the following section, and it might make more sense!

ADSR: Four Letters You Cannot Do Without

A-D-S-R. These four letters stand for **Attack**, **Decay**, **Sustain**, and **Release**. Please say the words to yourself a few times if this concept is new to you. From here on out, you will see these four parameters again and again throughout Reason and on almost any analog or emulated analog synthesizer you ever use in the future. With these four parameters you will sculpt quite a bit of your sound. This is news you can use!

ADSR envelopes are used in Subtractor's Filter Envelope, the Modulation Envelope, and the Amp Envelope. In the exercise for this section, you will be applying ADSR to the Amp Envelope. Think of an envelope as the shape of an event over time. While Subtractor's Level control affects the overall volume (or amplification) of your sound, the Amp Envelope controls the shape of how that amplification is applied. Will the sound start sharply when you strike a key, or will it fade in slowly? Will it end abruptly when you let go of the key or will it fade out slowly? Is a short sound produced, such as a drum hit, or is a long, sustained tone produced, such as holding down a key on an organ?

Here is how ADSR relates to the Amp Envelope. You can refer to this when considering other ADSR envelopes as well.

Attack. The amount of time it takes the audio signal level to climb from 0 to its peak level.

Decay. The amount of time it takes for the audio signal to fall from its peak level to the level determined by the Sustain parameter, assuming you keep holding down the key(s).

Sustain. At the end of a note's decay, the Sustain value determines the level at which the audio signal rests as long as the note is being held. Note that Sustain is the only one of these four parameters that is not measured in time, but rather in signal level.

Release. The amount of time it takes for the level of a sound to drop to 0 from whatever level it was when you let go of a note.

If all of this seems a little confusing, don't worry. The following exercise should make this all quite clear.

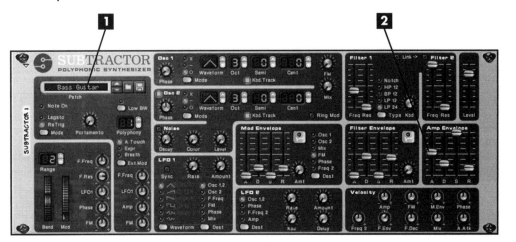

1 Start with an empty rack. **Create** an **instance of Mixer 14:2** from the Create menu at the top of the Reason window and then **create** an **instance of Subtractor**. In Subtractor's Patch Browser window, it should say Bass Guitar. Let's use this patch.

2 By default, the Attack setting on the Amp Envelope is all the way down at 0 (the fastest/shortest attack possible). So when you hit a key, you hear sound instantaneously. **Move** the **Attack slider** up to a value of about 69 (a little over halfway). **Press** a **key** on your MIDI keyboard, and you will now hear that the note fades in slowly. Feel free to experiment with different Attack values to get a feel for this.

3 **Turn down** the **Attack** to 0 and then **turn down** the **Sustain** to 0 and **play** a few **keys**. Not such a long note anymore!

4 While playing notes on your MIDI keyboard, slowly **turn up** the **Decay** to a value of about 70. If you turned it all the way up, your note would sound for as long as you held down the key.

5 Now **turn down** the **Decay** to a value of about 20. You now have a very short note.

6 With Attack still at 0 and Decay set at 20, **turn up** your **Sustain** level to about 70. **Hold down** a **key**. You will hear the sharp attack and the quick decay, but the decay will no longer fall down all the way to silence. It stops and holds at an intermediate level (the Sustain level).

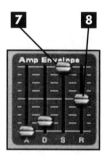

7 Now **turn up** the **Sustain** all the way. When you hold down a key, the sound stays at its maximum level until you let go. Theoretically, the Decay setting would still allow the level to fall to the value designated by the Sustain slider, but since the Sustain value is set at maximum, there is no place to fall.

8 With Attack still at 0, Decay at 20, and Sustain at maximum, **move** the **Release slider** up to a value of 64. Now **strike** a **key** and **let go**. Notice how the note continues to fade out after you release it.

9 **Move** the **Release slider** up to maximum. Now **hit** a **note**, and after you let go of the note, it will hang on for quite a long time before it finally fades out.

If that last section had you saying, "Hey, I thought this book was for beginners," then I hope you'll take the time to go over it again. ADSR is a really fundamental concept that is important to understand when producing electronic music. Anyway, if any of that last section tasted like medicine, this next section will taste like candy! You are about to have fun playing with the RPG-8 Monophonic Arpeggiator.

Subtractor, Meet the RPG-8 Monophonic Arpeggiator

According to the *American Heritage Dictionary of the English Language*, an arpeggio is "the sounding of the tones of a chord in rapid succession rather than simultaneously." RPG-8 does exactly that, automatically. You play a chord, and it plays back the notes separately in perfect time, in a variety of different user-definable patterns, at any speed you wish, using any Reason synth you wish. This feature is one I have wanted in Reason for a long, long time, and bless those Propellerheads, they finally gave it to me!

RPG-8 Octave, Mode, Insert, and Hold

Once you start playing with RPG-8, you may find it to be one of the most fun features in Reason. The following exercise will help you become familiar with some of its key features.

1 Open a new Reason **rack** and use the Create menu to **add** an **instance of Mixer 14:2**. Then use the Create menu again to **add** a **Subtractor**.

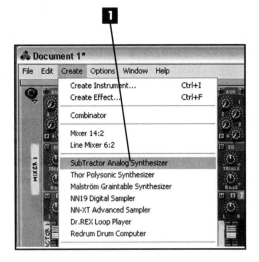

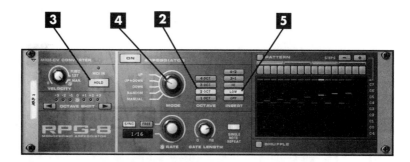

2 Now, **add** an **RPG-8** directly under Subtractor. **Play** a four-note **chord** (spanning less than one octave), and you will hear the notes in the chord separated and played in an upward repeating pattern. **Click** the **2 OCT button**, and now those notes will play in both the original octave and one octave above.

3 While still holding down the chord, **click** the **Hold button** and **let go** of the **chord**. It will keep playing.

4 You are currently using the Up mode. **Try** the **Up + Down mode**, the **Down mode**, and the **Random mode**. When you are done, **switch back** to the **Up mode**.

5 **Click** the **Low Insert button**, and you will hear the lowest note in your chord pivot with each of the remaining notes in the chord.

6 **Click** the **Hi Insert button**, and you will hear the highest note in your chord pivot with each of the remaining notes in the chord.

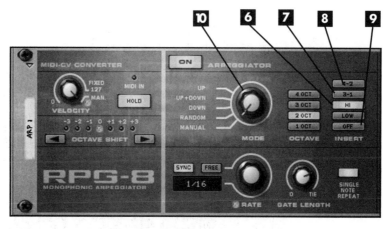

7 **Click** the **3-1 Insert button**, and you will hear an ascending triplet pattern (ascending because you are in the Up mode).

8 **Click** the **4-2 Insert button**, and you will hear an ascending four-note pattern.

9 **Turn off Insert**.

10 **Switch** the **mode** to Manual. Now **play** a **chord**, laying down the notes one finger at a time from high to low. The Arpeggiator will play the notes in that order. If you play another chord laying down the notes one finger at a time from low to high, the Arpeggiator will play them back in that order. In Manual mode, the RPG-8 plays back the notes in whatever order you played them.

RPG-8 Rate Control Videogame Trick

The next exercise uses the Rate control, which is pretty self-explanatory, but I think when used in the extreme, the sound will remind you of *Pac-Man*.

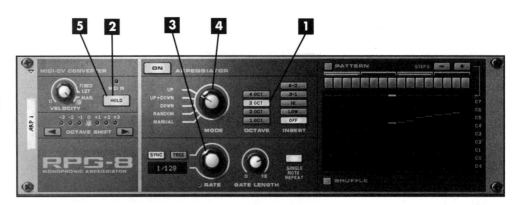

1 Open a new **song** and add **Mixer 14:2**, followed by **Subtractor** and **RPG-8**. **Click** the **3 OCT button**.

2 **Click** the **Hold button**. Then **hold down** all **five notes** from C3 to G3 on your MIDI keyboard. The first note will line up with the C3 mark on the far right of the RPG-8.

3 **Turn** the **Rate knob** all the way to the right so it reads 1/128. This sound may annoy spouses or roommates.

4 **Switch back and forth** between the following modes: **Up, Up + Down**, and **Down**. The Up + Down mode and the Down mode both sound like *Pac-Man* to me. Then try **Random**. It's pretty weird.

5 **Click** the **Hold button** to stop the madness.

RPG-8 Pattern Section

Wow, I swear, with the RPG-8 on, I can play the keyboard with my forehead and it sounds good. But wait, there's more! The RPG-8 has a Pattern section that allows you to silence certain steps in the arpeggio. To try this out, you can leave your rack as is from the preceding exercise, with Mixer 14:2 followed by Subtractor and RPG-8 in your rack.

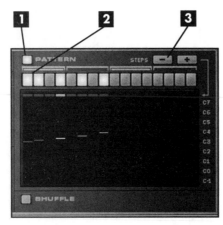

1 **Click** the **Pattern button** to turn on the RPG-8's Pattern section.

2 **Hold down** a **chord** with your left hand or **use** the **Hold button** and then **click** on a few of the **Step buttons**. You will hear silence whenever one of the deactivated steps is (not) played.

3 As you listen to this, **click** the **Remove Step button** until only eight steps are in use.

4 Drag your **mouse** across those first eight steps twice, so that all eight steps are lit.

5 **Click Play** and **turn on** the **click**.

6 With your arpeggio still playing, on the RPG-8 **click Shuffle**.

7 **Click** the **ReGroove Mixer button** and **turn** the **Global Shuffle knob** all the way to the right so you can hear the maximum shuffle amount. This works the same as it did with Redrum.

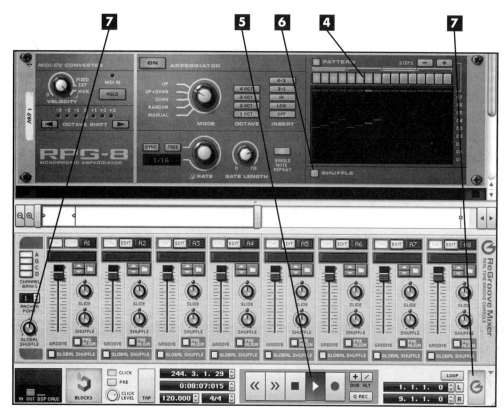

Arpeggio Notes to Track

It is possible to export the fancy fingerwork that RPG-8 creates as MIDI notes to be played by any of the Reason synths. It does take a couple of steps to do this, but it is similar to Redrum's Copy Pattern to Track function, as well as Dr.Rex's Copy REX Loop to Track function. It requires that you first record some MIDI data on the RPG-8 Sequencer track.

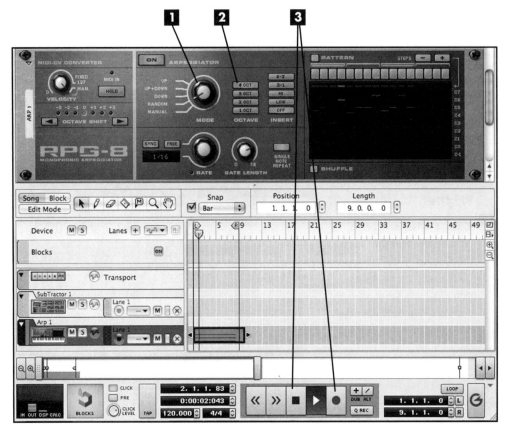

1 **Open** a new **song** and **add Mixer 14:2**, followed by **Subtractor** and **RPG-8**. **Switch** the **RPG-8** mode to Random.

2 **Click** the **4 OCT button**.

3 **Click Record** and immediately **play and hold** any **chord** on your MIDI keyboard. **Keep holding** the **chord** until the progress bar passes the right locator at Bar 9. Then **click Stop**. You should have a short recording on the Arp 1 track in the Reason Sequencer.

4 In the Tool window, **click** the **Tools tab, choose Bar** for the Quantize value, and then **click Apply**.

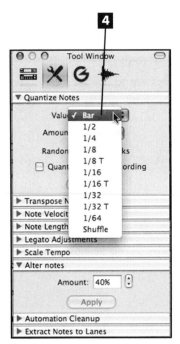

5 **Click** on the little **Subtractor icon** on the Subtractor 1 Sequencer track to select that track.

6 **Right-click** on **RPG-8** and **choose Arpeggio Notes to Track** from the context menu. You will see a mess of notes appear on the Subtractor track.

7 **Click** on the **RPG-8**. Then **press Delete**. The RPG-8 and its corresponding Sequencer track should disappear.

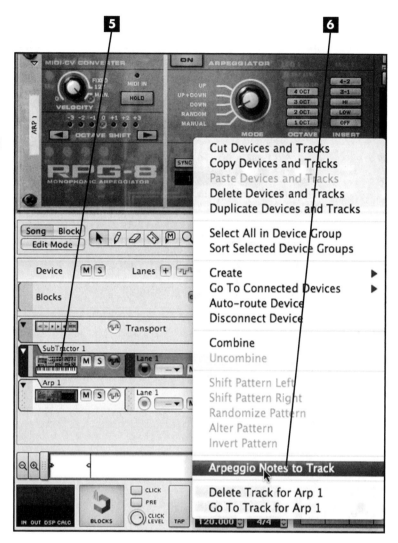

8 **Click Stop** and then **click Play**. You should hear your arpeggiated sequence, even though the RPG-8 has been deleted from the rack.

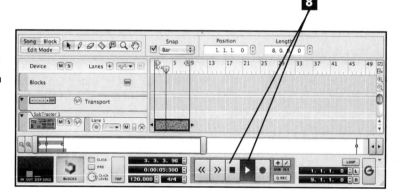

Sequencing with Subtractor

As we go forward, please remember that when I refer to *clips*, I am simply referring to the little colored rectangles that contain the notes or other information you have recorded into the Reason Sequencer. You could record one long clip that lasts three minutes (perhaps a piano solo piece), or you could record one short clip (maybe only eight notes of a bass line) and then copy and paste that clip several times throughout your Reason song. You could also cut up a long clip (using the Razor tool) into shorter clips. Perhaps the first part of a long clip is a verse, and the second part is a chorus. You can cut those into their own separate clips to help you organize your song and to facilitate copying and pasting certain defined sections into other parts of the song, perhaps onto other tracks with other instruments playing the MIDI data. Okay, it's time to practice some sequencing!

Using the Razor Tool

This exercise is a bit long but not too difficult. The idea is to get used to cutting up clips into smaller clips with the Razor tool, copying and pasting those clips, and then joining them into one clip when you are finished.

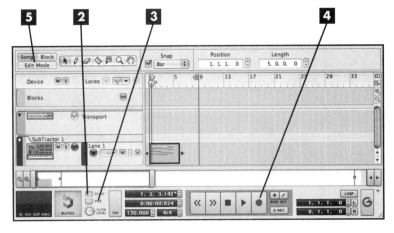

1 In a fresh rack containing Mixer 14:2 followed by Subtractor, **click** directly on the **Patch window** and **choose WarmPad.zyp**.

2 **Turn on** the **click**.

3 **Turn on Precount**. This will give you a one-bar (four clicks) count-in from the time you press Record.

4 **Click Record**, and after the four-beat count-in, **play** four whole **notes**. These could be chords or single notes. Let each note or chord hang on four beats before moving on to the next. When you are finished, you should have just passed Bar 5. **Click Stop**.

5 **Switch** to **Edit mode** by clicking the Arrange/Edit Mode button.

6 Drag the **right clip handle** to the left so the clip ends at Bar 5.

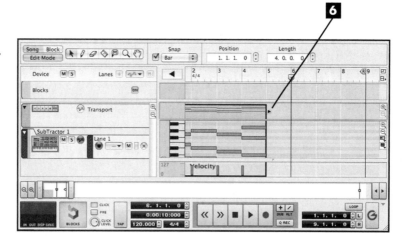

7 **Double-click** inside the **Key Edit window**. Then **press Ctrl+A** to select all.

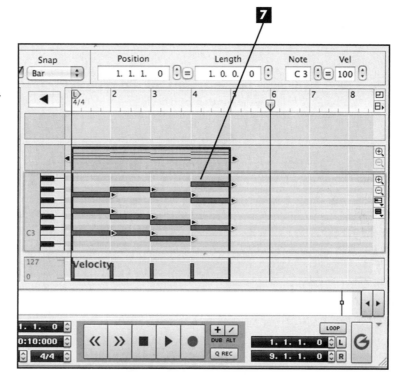

8 In the Tools tab of the Tool window, **set** the **Quantize value** to Bar and **click Apply**.

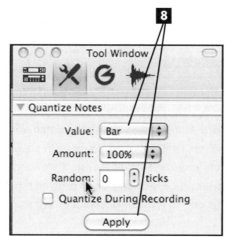

9 **Click** directly to the right of the **clip**.

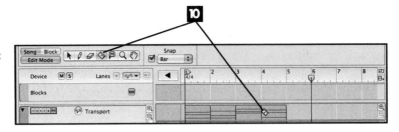

10 **Select** the **Razor tool**. Then **click** on the **clip** at each bar line. Now you have four clips.

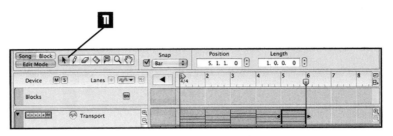

11 **Choose** your **Selection tool**. **Ctrl-click** on the **clip** at Bar 3 and **drag it** to Bar 5 and then **release** the **mouse button** followed by the **Ctrl key**. Now you have five one-bar clips.

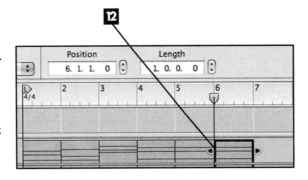

12 **Ctrl-click** on the **clip** at Bar 4 and **drag it** to Bar 6; then **release** the **mouse button** followed by the **Ctrl key**. Now you have six one-bar clips.

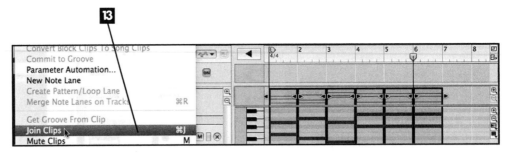

13 **Press Ctrl+A** to select all the clips. Then **choose Join Clips** from the Edit menu. (Note that you can also use Ctrl+J to join the clips.) Now you have one six-bar clip.

Of course, there are no real rules regarding when you should join your clips, when you should leave them split, or when you should cut a larger clip into smaller clips. This will depend on your own logical sense, style, and workflow and on the nature of the song you happen to be working on at a given time. I'm just trying to help you get a comfortable grip on the tools and techniques. It's up to you to decide how they best work for you!

Making a Velocity Ramp

Although you may choose to use Subtractor primarily for bass lines, lead lines, and other keyboard-oriented sounds, it also can produce some nice electronic percussion sounds. The next exercise could have easily been included in the "Using the Reason Sequencer with Redrum" section of Chapter 3, but it works just as well here.

1 In a fresh rack containing Mixer 14:2 followed by Subtractor, **select** the following **Subtractor patch:** Reason Factory Sound Bank > Subtractor Patches > Percussion > Snare Drums > Tribe Snare.

2 In the Reason Sequencer, **switch** to **Edit mode**.

3 **Alt-click** at the end of **Bar 2** to set the right locator there.

4 **Turn on** the **Loop button**.

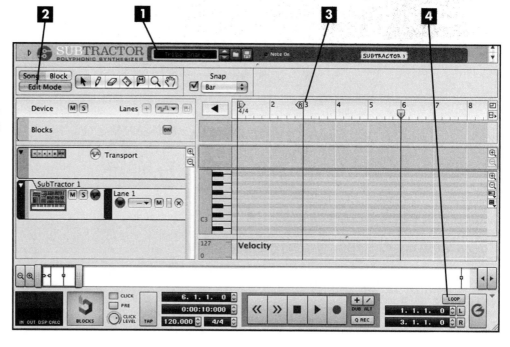

5 **Set Grid** to 1/16.

6 **Click** the **Horizontal Zoom button** until two bars take up almost the entire Sequencer window and then **drag** the **horizontal scrollbar** all the way to the left so you can see Bars 1 and 2.

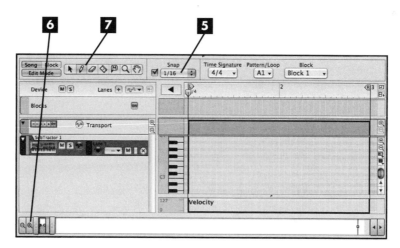

7 **Select** the **Pencil tool** and then **draw** in a **clip** by dragging your cursor from left to right across the top of the Sequencer window between the left and right locators.

8 **Pick** any **note**. The snare sound is not pitched, so it sounds the same on any note. **Click** in each **grid box** on one note between the left and right locators. That's 32 little notes. It'll take a minute or less.

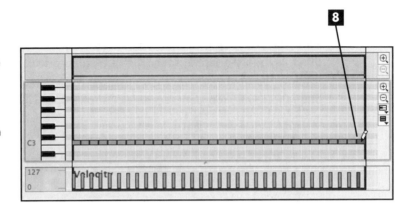

9 **Click Play**, and you will hear that all the notes are at the same volume.

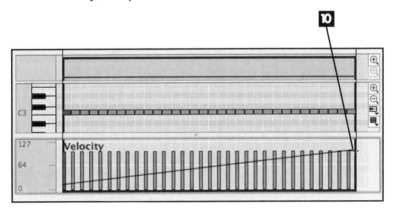

10 **Drag** up the **top handle** of the Velocity Editor so you have more room to work. Then **Ctrl-click** and **hold** (on a Mac Option-click and hold) in the bottom left of the **Velocity Editor**, and your Pencil tool will become a Line tool. (The Pencil icon will turn into crosshairs.) **Drag upwards** diagonally from left to right to draw a velocity left-to-right ramp up from 0 to 127.

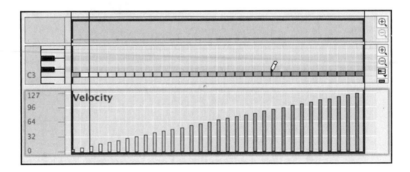

11 **Click Play** to hear the result. Notice that the higher a note's velocity is, the darker the shade of red used for the note. This is true in all the edit modes: Note, Drum, REX, and Velocity.

Quantize during Recording

Quantize during Recording is a great feature for people whose timing when playing into the Sequencer is less than perfect (which would be many or most of us!). It's especially good for any style of electronic music where a computer feel is favored over a human feel. The danger is that if you have the Quantize Amount set at 100%, you will remove 100% of the human feel in timing, so you might not want this feature on when you record your piano concerto! Let's give it a try.

1 In a fresh rack containing Mixer 14:2 followed by Subtractor, **select** the following **Subtractor patch:** Reason Factory Sound Bank > Subtractor Patches > PolySynths > Pulse Clav.zyp.

2 **Look** on the **Tools page** of the Tool window and **make sure** the **Quantize value** is set at its default value of 1/16. The Quantize Amount should be at 100%, and the Random value should be 0.

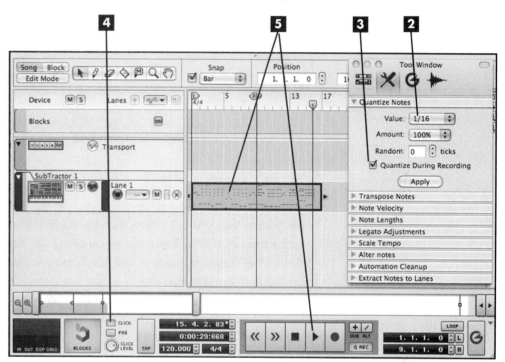

3 **Click** on the **Quantize during Recording button**, and it will light up green. Now anything you play into the Reason Sequencer will be automatically quantized to the nearest 1/16 note.

4 **Turn on** the **click** and **press Record**. Then **play whatever feels good** into the Sequencer for a minute or two and **click Stop** when you're finished.

5 **Click Play** and **double-click** on the **clip** you recorded.

6 **Zoom way in** on the **Horizontal Zoom**, and you will see that every note starts dead-on at a 1/16-note division on the grid.

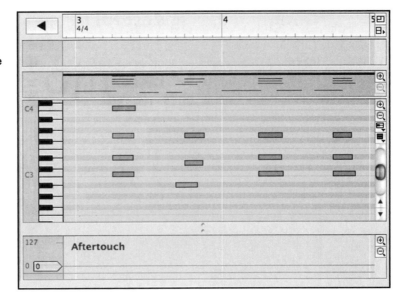

Now, if you really freaked out with reckless abandon while you recorded that last bit, some stuff may still sound off because you played the note closer to the *wrong* 1/16 note than to the *right* 1/16 note. You can move those notes to the right place in Edit mode as needed. Also, if you know you are going to record a simple 1/8-note bass part, set the Quantize value to 1/8. Or if you are playing a 1/4-note snare drum part, set the Quantize value to 1/4. You are more likely to be closer to your intended 1/4 note than to the correct 1/16 note or 1/32 note. It makes things easier. Finally, if you want to quantize as you record, but you don't want to entirely lose the human feel, set the Quantize Amount to 80% or 90% instead of to 100%.

New Dub/New Alt

New Dub and New Alt are used when recording a new take in the Reason Sequencer. When you think of New Dub, think "new overdub." If you are going to play a synthesizer melody that harmonizes with a synthesizer melody you just recorded with the same synth, use New Dub so that you can hear the older part you are harmonizing with. When you think of New Alt, think of "new alternative take." If you are playing a keyboard solo, and you want to take several passes of the same solo section and then choose the best take, use New Alt. This will mute the previous solo takes so that you won't hear them while you play the new one.

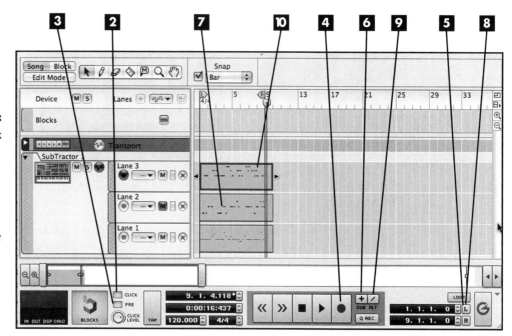

1 In a fresh rack containing Mixer 14:2 followed by Subtractor, **select** the following **Subtractor patch:** Reason Factory Sound Bank > Subtractor Patches > PolySynths > Fat Sync.zyp.

2 **Turn on** the **click**. Make sure Loop is off.

3 **Turn on Precount** so that you will get a one-bar click lead-in before recording commences after you click Record.

4 **Click Record**, and after the one-bar count-in, **record** a very basic chord **rhythm** part (or bass part if you prefer).

5 After Bar 9, **click Stop**. Then **click** the **Go to Left Locator button** to return the song position marker to Bar 1.

6 **Click** the **New Dub button**. A new lane (Lane 2) will be created above the old one, but Lane 1 will not be muted.

7 **Click Record** again and **record a melody**.

8 After Bar 9, **click Stop**. Then **click** the **Go to Left Locator button** to return the song position marker to Bar 1.

9 **Click** the **New Alt button**. A new lane (Lane 3) will be created above Lane 2, and Lane 2 will be muted. (The little button marked "M" will be red.)

10 **Record** a different **melody**. You will hear Lane 1 play back as you record, but you will not hear Lane 2.

Even when overdubbing, it's great to create these new lanes each time so that it remains easy to edit the separate performances. Also, New Alt is not only great for recording a bunch of takes and picking the best one. You can pick the best parts from several takes and edit them together into one dazzling, perfect solo using the Razor tool and cut, copy, and paste.

Subtractor, Meet Effects

Subtractor is the only Reason synth that has a mono (instead of stereo) output. For bass sounds as well as lead sounds, this may not be an issue for you. But if you want a fat pad to sound fatter, you might want it to be in stereo. This is easily done by adding effects.

1 **Create** fresh **rack** containing Mixer 14:2 followed by a Subtractor. **Click** directly on the **Patch window** and **choose WarmPad.zyp**. Now **play** a **chord** on your MIDI keyboard to hear this sound.

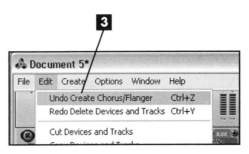

2 **Create** a **CF-101 Chorus/Flanger** directly under Subtractor. Now **play** the **chord** again. The basic feeling of the sound is the same, but now it is spread out nicely across the stereo image.

3 From the Edit menu, **choose Undo Create Chorus/Flanger**. (You can also use Ctrl+Z to undo.)

4 For a more dramatic sound, **create** a **PH-90 Phaser** directly under Subtractor. **Play** a **chord** and listen to the sound swim around between your ears.

Subtractor and Control Voltage

All of the devices in Reason have control voltage inputs and outputs on the rear of the devices. You will remember that in the waveforms exercise, LFO 1 made the sound go "wah wah wah wah" (or something like that). In slightly more scientific terms, LFO 1 modulated a parameter of the patch. You could do something similar by turning the volume or tone control up and down on a guitar or stereo system or by turning a dimmer switch up and down for a light in a room. The "virtual voltage" that LFO 1 is using to make those weird sounds can be sent to control other things as well—things outside of Subtractor! It won't make the light in your room get brighter and dimmer, but in the next exercise, it will make the sound of your Subtractor patch go back and forth from left to right in the stereo image.

1 **Open** a new empty **rack**. Instead of Mixer 14:2, **create** a **Line Mixer 6:2**. Under that, **create** a **Subtractor** and **select** the following **Subtractor patch:** Reason Factory Sound Bank > Subtractor Patches > PolySynths > Vibra.zyp.

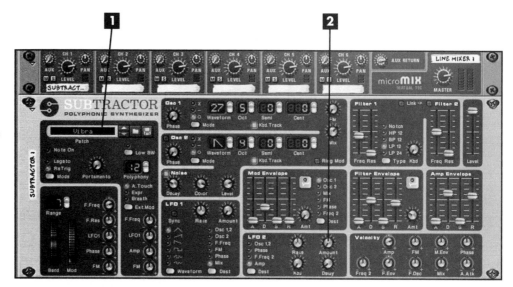

2 **Play** a few **keys** on your MIDI keyboard. You will find that this sound has some "wah wah wah wah" (it has some tremolo/vibrato), but it is still mono in the center of the stereo image. **Turn** the **LFO 2 Amount knob** all the way down, and the tremolo will stop.

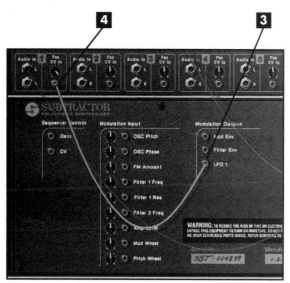

3 **Click** the **Tab key** to flip the Reason rack around. **Click and hold** on **LFO 1 Modulation Output** and **drag** a **cable** to connect to Pan CV In on Channel 1 of the Line Mixer. Of course, Pan controls left or right in the stereo image, and CV stands for *control voltage*.

4 **Turn up** the **Channel 1 Pan CV In knob** all the way to the right. **Play** your **MIDI keyboard**, and you will hear the sound moving from left to right and back as you play.

If you have any trouble hearing the stereo effect, perhaps you need to move your speakers farther apart from each other, or you might want to put on some stereo headphones.

There are all kinds of deeply crazy things you can do with control voltage in Reason, but that's another book! Seriously, the way Reason uses control voltage is one of the most fun things about the program for synth geeks like me, and it's a great link between the Reason software and the vintage synth hardware that inspired it. If you flip your Reason rack around when you are using the RPG-8 Arpeggiator or the Matrix Pattern Sequencer, you will see that they output their note, velocity, and other information to the Reason synths using control voltage connections.

All right! Now that you've gotten a good handle on Subtractor, it's time to dig into the next synth in Reason's virtual instrument line-up: Malström!

5 } Malström

The Malström Graintable synthesizer offers a whole new range of sounds, distinct from what you experienced with Subtractor in Chapter 4. Rather than producing sound by emulating analog oscillators (as is the case with Subtractor), the Malström uses Graintable synthesis, which is Propellerhead's hybrid of *granular* and *wavetable* synthesis. You will hear the difference because many of the sounds really sound like a human voice, or thunder, or some other real sound. It's not a sampler, however. The Malström Graintable designers start with a sample, chop it up, detonate it into a zillion grains, and slap it back together (as a Graintable) so that sound can be manipulated and warped in ways a simple sample might run and hide from.

In this chapter you will learn how to:

❋ Build a song in the Reason Sequencer using multiple Malströms

❋ Understand and use all the synth parameters unique to the Malström

❋ Use the Matrix Pattern Sequencer to control the Malström

❋ Use the Malström as an effects processor, playing Dr. Octo Rex through the Malström's filters and shaper section

Building a Song with the Malström

Before we start tinkering under the hood, let's just have some fun seeing what the Malström can do. In the Reason Factory Soundbank > Malstrom > Rhythmic folder, there are all kinds of sounds that play a rhythm all by themselves if you just hold down one note. This can help you build a track in a hurry. This exercise is a bit longer than average (20 steps), but it's pretty easy and really super cool.

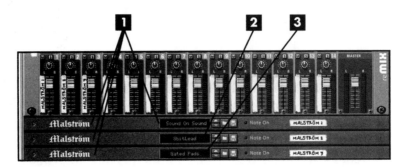

1 In an empty rack, **create** a **Mixer 14:2**, followed by **three Malströms**. In the first Malström, **load** the **patch** Reason Factory Soundbank > Malstrom > Rhythmic > Sound On Sound.xwv.

2 In the second Malström, **load** the **patch** Reason Factory Soundbank > Malstrom > Rhythmic > 8bitLead.xwv.

3 In the third Malström, **load** the **patch** Reason Factory Soundbank > Malstrom > Rhythmic > Gated Pads.

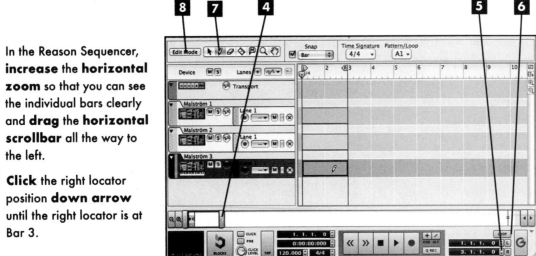

4 In the Reason Sequencer, **increase** the **horizontal zoom** so that you can see the individual bars clearly and **drag** the **horizontal scrollbar** all the way to the left.

5 **Click** the right locator position **down arrow** until the right locator is at Bar 3.

6 **Click** the **Loop On/Off button** to activate looping and **click Play**. (You won't hear anything yet.)

7 **Select** the **Pencil tool** and **draw** a two-bar **clip** into each Malström track.

8 **Click** the **Edit/Arrange Mode switch** to get into Edit mode.

9 **Make sure** the **Grid mode** is set to Bar.

10 **Click** the **keyboard icon** under Malström 1 to select the track.

11 **Choose** the **Selection tool** and **double-click** on the **clip** so you can edit it.

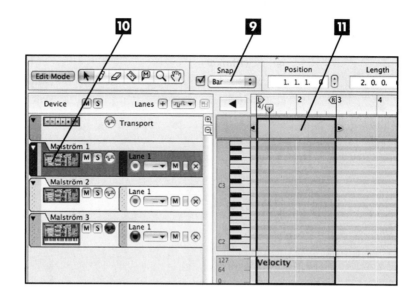

12 **Choose** the **Pencil tool** and **draw** in a **note** at D2 on Bar 1 and Bar 2. You only need to click in each grid square, and the note will fill up the whole bar. You should hear something now.

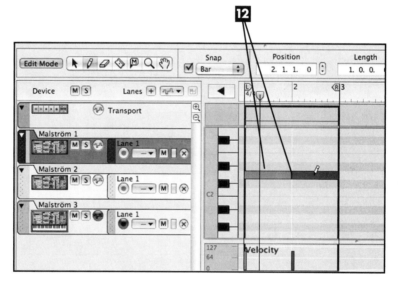

13 **Click** the **keyboard icon** under Malström 2 to select the track.

14 **Choose** the **Selection tool** and **double-click** on the **clip** so you can edit it.

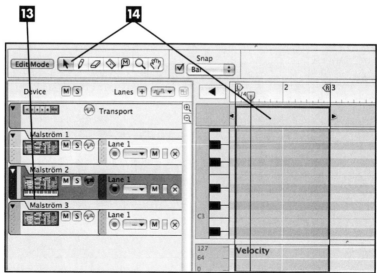

15 **Choose** the **Pencil tool** and **draw** in a **note** at F1 on Bar 1, and then **draw** in a **note** at D1 on Bar 2.

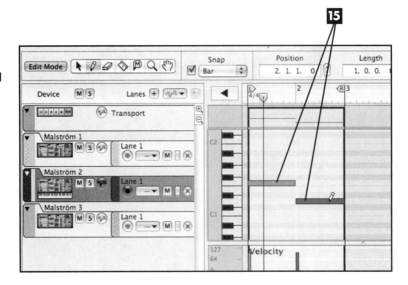

16 **Click** the **keyboard icon** under Malström 3 to select the track.

17 **Choose** the **Selection tool** and **double-click** on the **clip** so you can edit it.

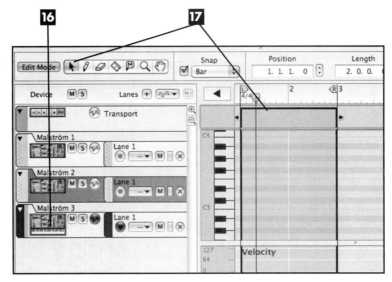

18 **Choose** the **Pencil tool**, **draw** in a **note** at C5 on Bar 1, and then **draw** in a **note** at A4 on Bar 2.

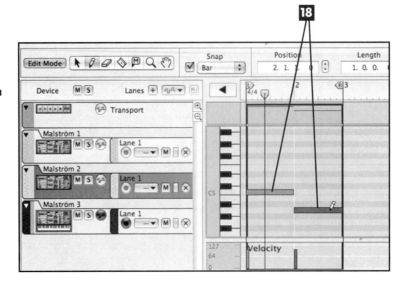

19 **Create** a **Dr. Octo Rex**
directly below the third
Malström and **load** the
patch Reason Factory
Sound Bank > Dr Rex Drum
Loops > Techno > Tec29_
Minimal_135_eLab.rx2.

20 Click the small arrow at the bottom of Dr. Octo to open up the programmer. Then **turn**
the **Loop Level knob** up all the way and **click** the **Copy Loop to Track button**.

You did a lot of work on that exercise, so save it when you're finished. We're
going to use it again in a moment, so please, really save it.

For extra fun and creativity, I suggest that while this song plays, you click in the
Patch Display window of Malström 1 and try some other rhythmic patches. You
might find that some of the other patches fit nicely also.

> ❄ **SCROLLING IN THE KEY EDITOR**
>
> If you have a mouse with a wheel on it, you may have noticed that you can use it to scroll up and
> down inside the Key Editor so you can get to the higher or lower octaves of the keyboard. If you
> do not have a wheel and you have your Sequencer window really short, you may freak out, won-
> dering how to scroll. Calm down; everything is okay. Drag the top of the Sequencer window
> upward until you see a vertical scrollbar appear on the right side of the Key Editor.

Stereo-ize That Sequence

By the way, here is a bonus trick that you can add on to the end of the previous
exercise if you want to. It'll make everything in trippy super-stereo.

1 Starting at the end of the
previous exercise (or with
the file you saved after
completing the previous
exercise), **create** a new
Malström under Dr. Octo
Rex and **right-click** and
select Initialize Patch.

2 **Click** the **Sync buttons** on both MODs A and B.

3 **Turn down** the **MOD A Rate knob** to a value of 8/4.

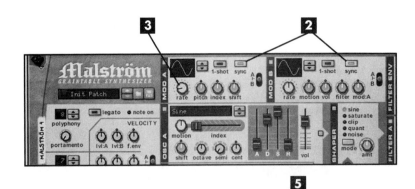

4 **Click** the **Tab key** on your computer keyboard to flip your rack around and **click Play**.

5 On the bottom Malström, **right-click** on the **MOD A Output jack, mouse over Mixer 1** in the context menu, and **select Channel 2 Pan CV**.

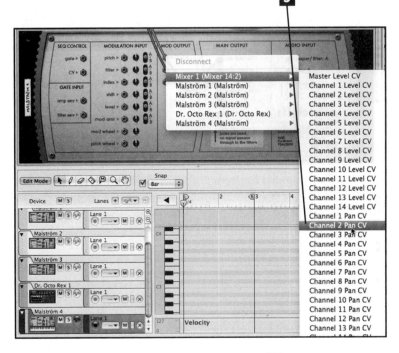

6 **Right-click** on the **MOD B Output jack, mouse over Mixer 1** in the context menu, and **select Channel 3 Pan CV**.

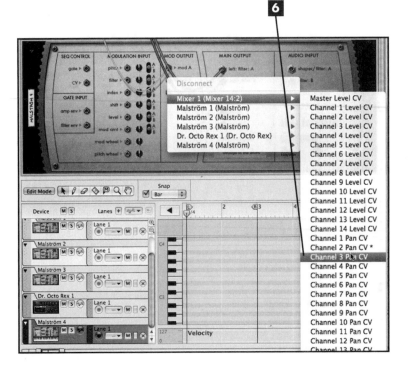

The sounds from Malströms 2 and 3 should be swimming through the stereo field now. If you have any trouble hearing this, you might want to put on some headphones. There is no sound coming out of that last Malström you created. It's just controlling the stereo pans on Channels 2 and 3 of the Mixer 14:2.

Turn That Loop into a Song

I find it can be a cool creative process to start with a short loop (maybe only two bars as we've done here) and fill it up with a lot of layers (clips) that all fit together. Then I can spread those puzzle pieces throughout an entire song, leaving some space and bringing the parts in and out. I hope you'll see what I mean after you complete the next exercise.

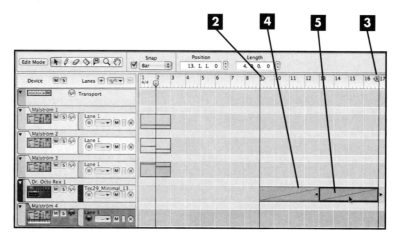

1 Reduce the **horizontal zoom** so that the hash marks between bars disappear and you can see 16 bars at a time in the Arrange window.

2 Drag the **left locator** to Bar 9.

3 Drag the **right locator** to Bar 17.

4 Drag the **Dr. Octo Rex 1 clip** over so that it starts at Bar 9 (at the left locator).

5 Ctrl-click on the **Dr. Octo Rex 1 clip** and **drag it** over so that it starts on Bar 13. Then **let go** of the **Ctrl key** first and **let go** of your **mouse button** second.

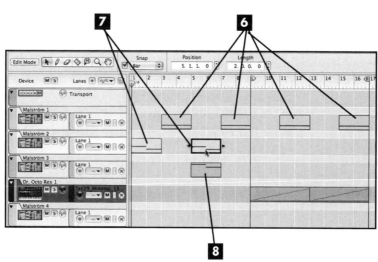

6 Drag the **Malström 1 clip** over so that it starts at Bar 3. Then **Ctrl-click** on it and **place copies** at Bar 7, Bar 11, and Bar 15.

7 Ctrl-click on the **Malström 2 clip** and **drop** the **copy** at Bar 5.

8 Drag the **Malström 3 clip** to Bar 5.

9 **Select** the **Malström 2 and Malström 3 clips** at Bar 5 by clicking and dragging a rectangle around them or by Ctrl-clicking on each one.

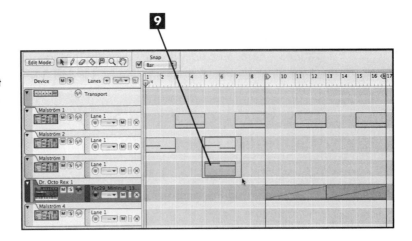

10 **Ctrl-click (and hold)** on the **Malström 2 clip**, and you will be able to drag and drop copies of both Malström 2 and Malström 3 clips simultaneously at Bar 9 and then at Bar 13.

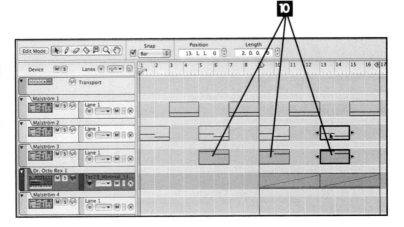

Now you can click Play and hear your little arrangement. You should still have Loop active on the Transport panel, so the song should loop between Bars 9 and 17. Of course, you can turn up the tempo a little bit if 120 bpm is too slow for you.

Exporting the Song as an Audio File

Now that you've finished your mini-song, you will need to export it as an audio file before it can be burned onto a CD or converted to MP3. This next tutorial will show you how to do that and will also give you a sneak peak at the Combinator. Why would I suddenly bring the Combinator into this exercise? Because you are going to use the MClass Mastering Suite (a Combinator preset) to give your mix a little extra oomph.

1 **Right-click** on the **Reason hardware device** (the one that says Audio Output) at the very top of the rack and **choose Create > MClass Mastering Suite Combi** from the context menu.

2 **Move** the Combinator's **On/Off/Bypass switch** into the Bypass position. This will make the audio signal pass around the Mastering Suite's electronics so that the signal is not processed.

3 **Click Show Devices** on the Combinator.

4 **Turn up** the **Input Gain knob** on the MClass Maximizer to a value of 6 dB (a little past 2 o'clock).

5 **Click Play** to hear your sequence without the Mastering Suite (which is bypassed).

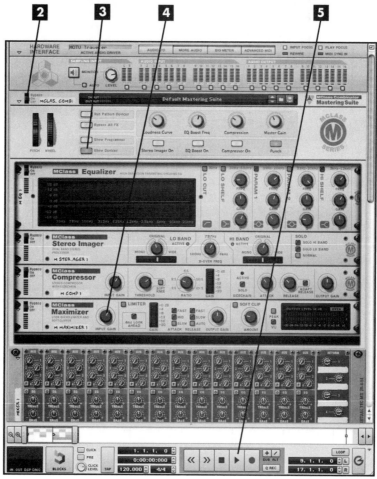

6

6 **Move** the Combinator's **On/Off/Bypass switch** into the On position. Now your mix sounds much louder but is not overloading anything.

7 **Click Stop** in the Reason Transport.

8 In the Reason Sequencer, **drag** the **horizontal scrollbar** so you can see the end marker.

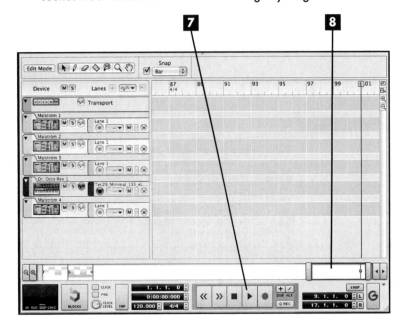

9 **Drag** the **end marker** to Bar 18.

10 **Deactivate** the **Loop On/Off button**. Then **listen** to your 30-second **song** one more time to be sure that all the echoes and sounds stop completely before the end marker so you will not cut off the end of your sound when you export.

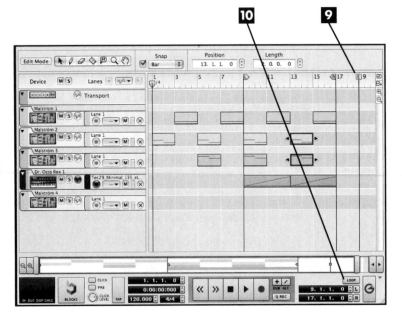

11 From the File menu, **select Export Song as Audio File**.

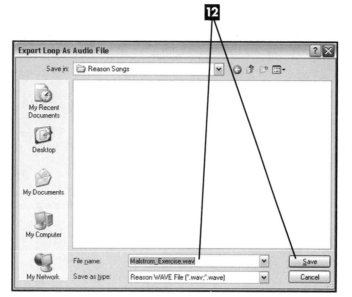

12 In the Export Song as Audio File window, **choose a filename and a location** in which to save and **click** the **Save button**.

13 **Choose** your desired **sample rate and bit depth** in the Export Audio Settings window. The default of 44,100-Hz 16-bit is perfect for CD or MP3, so you can choose that unless you are planning to master and dither in another application. You can leave the Dither box checked as well. Then **click OK**.

Now you should find a 16-bit 44.1-kHz wave file in the folder to which you saved. If you want to turn it into an MP3, one easy and free way to do that is to import it into iTunes using the iTunes MP3 encoder.

Malström Synth Parameters

I'm not going to go through every single parameter on the Malström exhaustively (you have the Reason Operation Manual PDF for further reference), but I would like to point out some of the bits that make it unique, which also happen to be some of the bits that make it such a cool and fun synth to make music with.

How the Malström Produces Its Sound

At the beginning of Chapter 4, in the first exercise (in the section "Waveforms and Oscillators 1 and 2"), you listened to each waveform that Subtractor's oscillators could produce. These oscillators work like standard analog oscillators, producing a steady tone. The only noticeable difference between the waveforms is the harmonic content (how bright or dark the sound is, and so on). The Malström is entirely different. Although a few of its Graintables are based on basic waveforms like sine and sawtooth, you will find all kinds of craziness not found in analog synthesizers.

Trying Out the Graintables

The simple exercise in this section is really a good way to start getting a handle on the personality of the Malström.

1 **Open** a new **rack** and **create a Mixer 14:2** followed by a **Malström**. Then **right-click** on the **Malström** and **choose Initialize Patch**.

2 To start from the top of the list of Graintables, **click** once in the **OSC A Graintable display window** and **click** on **Bass: AcidBass** at the top of the enormous context menu. By the way, I counted 82 Graintables in that list.

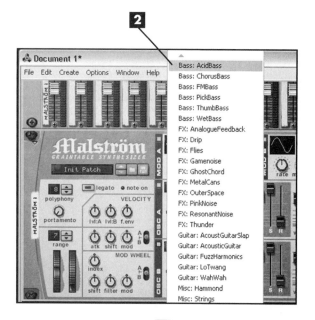

3 **Play** your MIDI **keyboard** to hear the sound. After you are finished checking out the AcidBass Graintable, **use** the **down arrow** in the OSC A Graintable selector to try each Graintable one at a time.

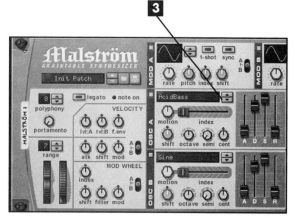

It should really only take a couple of minutes to try all the Graintables, even though there are 82 of them. Some of the weirder sounds go on for a few seconds before repeating, so you might want to hold down the key for a few seconds to hear the whole story. Several of those sounds are really interesting (and often a bit crazy), and yet you haven't even applied any filters or other tricks, and you are only using one of the two oscillators. Just the naked Graintables sound great.

Motion, Shift, and Index

These three controls have a dramatic effect on the sound and are pretty easy to understand. The Motion knob controls how fast the Graintable is played back by the oscillator, Index determines the starting point for playback of the Graintable (the Index slider represents the Graintable from left to right, with the start being at the far left and the end being at the far right), and Shift "shifts" the harmonic content of the Graintable (generally messes with the sound).

1 In a rack containing Mixer 14:2 followed by a Malström, **right-click** on the **Malström** and **choose Initialize Patch**.

2 **Click** in the **OSC A Graintable display window** and **choose Wind: Trumpet** from the bottom of the context menu. You will probably have to use the arrow at the bottom of the context menu to get all the way down there.

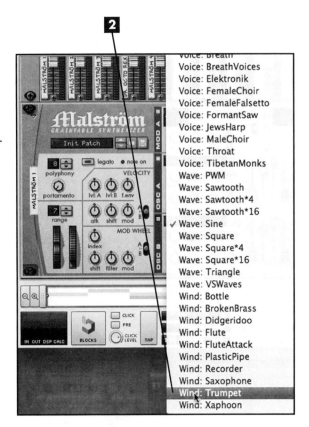

3 **Find** a **note** on your MIDI keyboard where the trumpet sounds realistic. **Move** the **Index slider** to the middle, and you will hear that trumpet line start at a different point in its phrase. Experiment with different positions, and when you are finished, **move** the **Index slider** back to the far left (start) position.

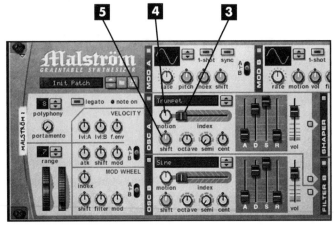

4 **Hold down** a key on your MIDI **keyboard** and slowly **turn** the **OSC A Motion knob** all the way to the left. (You will hear the trumpet speed up, but the pitch will remain the same.) Then **turn** the **knob** slowly all the way to the right. When you are finished, **return** the **Motion knob** to its middle position.

5 **Hold down** a **key** on your MIDI keyboard and slowly **turn** the **OSC A Shift knob** all the way to the left and then all the way to the right. The trumpet gets a lot weirder.

The Malström isn't really that complicated when you look at it in bite-size pieces. The stuff all makes sense. You can plainly see that each oscillator has an ADSR amplifier envelope (just like the Amp Envelope on Subtractor) as well as its own volume control. You will also recognize the tuning knobs (Octave, Semi, and Cent) just like the ones you learned about in the Subtractor and Dr.Rex chapters.

Malström Filters

The Malström has two filters (Filter A and Filter B) that are identical. Each of them has a low-pass (labeled *lp*) filter and a band-pass filter (labeled *bp*), just like on Subtractor and Dr.Rex. In addition to these familiar offerings, the Malström also includes a comb filter (with two variations) as well as ring modulation in both Filter A and Filter B.

Comb Filter

The first new type of filter I think you will enjoy getting familiar with is a comb filter. The Malström has this feature, so let's take it for a test drive.

1 In an empty rack, **create** a **Mixer 14:2** followed by a **Malström**. Then **right-click** on the **Malström** and **choose Initialize Patch**. This will give you a very basic starting point.

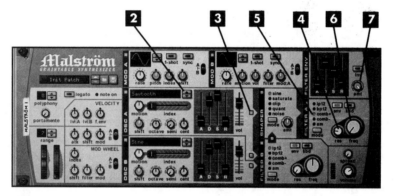

2 Right now, OSC A is the only oscillator active (indicated by the amber light above OSC A). The currently selected Graintable is Sine. **Click** the **up arrow** three times to select the Sawtooth Graintable (not Sawtooth*4 or Sawtooth*16, just plain Sawtooth). **Play** a **chord** on your MIDI keyboard to hear this raw, basic sound.

3 **Click** on the (unlabeled) **Route OSC A to Shaper button**. The signal from OSC A has to pass through the Shaper (which is turned off right now) on its way to Filter A. (See the arrows pointing the way?)

4 **Look** at **Filter A** and **play** a **chord** on your MIDI keyboard, and you will hear that the lp12 (low-pass filter) is filtering out a bunch of high frequencies. **Turn** up **Filter A Resonance** to about 9 o'clock (a value of 26).

5 **Click** on **comb+** to activate the comb filter.

6 **Turn down** the **Filter A Frequency knob** all the way to the left. Now **hold down** a **chord** on your MIDI keyboard and slowly **turn** the **Filter A Frequency knob** all the way up and all the way down a few times to hear the comb filter doing what it's good at. When you're finished, **turn down** the **Filter A Frequency knob** all the way to the left again.

7 **Turn** the **Filter Envelope Amount knob** all the way to the right. Now **play** a **chord**, and you will hear the Filter Envelope effectively turn the Filter A Frequency knob for you.

In Step 7, you're hearing the decay portion of the Filter Envelope. The very short attack instantly turns the filter frequency up to maximum, and then the very high (very slow) decay setting slowly brings the frequency back down again.

Just to be clear: Although I am using the terms *filter frequency* and *resonance* (because that is how the knobs are labeled), on Malström, when you select a comb filter, the Filter Frequency knob becomes a delay time knob, and the Resonance knob becomes a delay feedback (number of repeats) knob, just like on a flanger. A flanger is a comb filter with a delay time control, a delay feedback control, and a low-frequency oscillator (with rate and amount controls) to regularly modulate (change) the delay time. You don't really hear the delay distinctly because the delay time is so short.

Amplitude Modulation (Ring Modulation)

Although it is perhaps an odd thing to include in a filter section, the Malström has an AM selection in each of its filters. The AM stands for *amplitude modulation*. The specific application of amplitude modulation here is actually more commonly referred to as *ring modulation*. You may be familiar with the Mooger Fooger Ring Modulator pedal (or the plug-in version that looks like it). This will sound a lot like that.

1 In a rack containing Mixer 14:2 followed by a Malström, **right-click** on the **Malström** and **choose Initialize Patch** so that we can start from scratch.

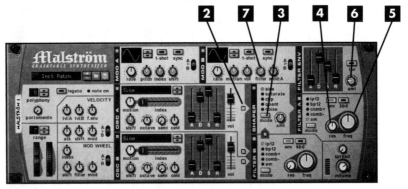

2 **Click** on the (unlabeled) **Route OSC A to Shaper button**, so that the signal from OSC A can pass on through the Shaper and into Filter A.

3 **Click** the **Filter A Mode button** until the amber LED next to AM is lit.

4 The Filter A Resonance knob becomes a "mix" knob when AM is selected. It mixes between the dry signal and the ring modulator signal. **Play** around on your MIDI **keyboard** as you **turn up** the **Filter A Resonance knob** halfway.

5 The Filter A Frequency knob controls the frequency of the inaudible carrier signal that the ring modulator uses to work its magic. **Play** around on your MIDI **keyboard** as you **turn** this **knob** back and forth. Turn it back to 12 o'clock when you're finished.

6 **Turn up** the **Filter Envelope Amount knob** to 9 o'clock (a value of 26). Now **play** a **bit** on your MIDI keyboard and hear the Filter Envelope modulate the Filter A Frequency (ring modulator frequency).

7 To get even weirder, **turn up** the **MOD B to Filter knob** to a value of 16 (about 1 o'clock). MOD B is an LFO (low-frequency oscillator), and you just routed it to control the ring modulator frequency.

Now the Filter Envelope makes the ring modulator frequency go slowly downward every time you play a note, at the same time MOD B makes the frequency rock back and forth in a sine wave pattern. Sounds like lo-fi sci-fi. By the way, Subtractor has a ring modulator, too.

Filter Envelope

You already have experience using the Filter Envelopes in Subtractor and Dr.Rex. Like Subtractor and Dr.Rex, the Malström's Filter Envelope has sliders for Attack, Decay, Sustain, and Release, as well as a Filter Envelope Amount control.

A feature that has not been covered yet in this book is Filter Envelope Invert. Dr.Rex does not have this feature. Both the Malström and Subtractor do have the feature (as do the NN-19 and Thor), and you are about to learn how to use it. Of course, one simple definition of the word *invert* is simply to "turn something upside down." And that's exactly what Filter Envelope Invert does. It turns the shape of the Filter Envelope upside down. You can hear this in the next exercise.

1 In a rack containing Mixer 14:2 followed by a Malström, **right-click** on the **Malström** and **choose Initialize Patch**.

2 **Create** an **MClass Compressor** directly under the Malström.

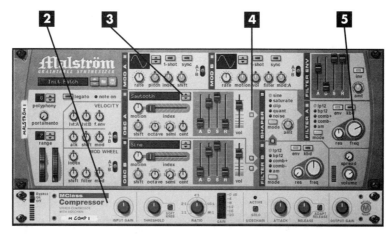

3 **Click** the **up arrow** three times on the OSC A Graintable selector to choose the Sawtooth Graintable. (Its full name with classification if you clicked in the Graintable display window is Wave: Sawtooth.)

4 **Play** a **note** on your MIDI keyboard. Then **click** the **Route OSC B to Shaper button**. Now **play** a **key**, and you will hear the lp12 low-pass filter in Filter A cutting off some high end.

5 **Turn up** the **Filter A Frequency knob** to a value of 94. **Play** a **key** on your MIDI keyboard, and you will hear that some of the highs are back because you turned up the cut-off frequency.

6 Turn up the **Filter A Resonance knob** about halfway, to a value of 62.

7 Turn up the **Filter Envelope Amount knob** about halfway, to a value of 62.

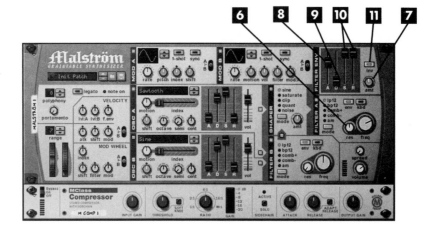

8 Turn up the **Filter Envelope Attack slider** to a value of 84.

9 Turn the **Filter Envelope Decay slider** all the way down to 0.

10 Turn the **Filter Envelope Sustain and Release sliders** all the way up to the top and **play** your MIDI **keyboard**. Do you hear the upward filter sweep as the attack rises?

11 **Click** on the **Filter Envelope Invert button** to activate it. Now **play** your MIDI **keyboard** and hear the filter start up at a high cut-off frequency and then fall down with the Attack portion of the envelope.

Once you have the preceding exercise set up, switching the Filter Envelope Invert button on and off while playing your MIDI keyboard is a great way to hear the Invert button turning the Filter Envelope upside down. Normally, pitch, filter cut-off frequency, or whatever is being modulated by an envelope will start at a low or zero level and then rise during the attack portion of the envelope. When you activate Filter Envelope Invert, exactly the opposite happens.

Velocity

You've already played with velocity, so you know that it is a MIDI value that refers to how hard a note or pad is struck. All the Reason synthesizers have velocity controls, which allow you to decide what will happen when you hit a key with more or less force. The most common use is to set the velocity controls so that when you play a key harder, the note sounds louder (like a piano) instead of having all the notes play at the same volume no matter how hard you play (like an organ). But you can choose to make that velocity information control other things as well.

1 In a rack containing Mixer 14:2 followed by a Malström, **right-click** on the **Malström** and **choose Initialize Patch.**

2 **Click** once on the **up arrow** in the OSC A Graintable selector to choose Sawtooth*4 and **play** your MIDI **keyboard** to hear what this sounds like.

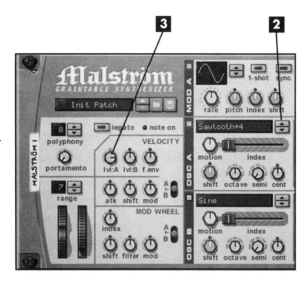

3 **Turn up** the **Velocity to Level A knob** (labeled lvl:A) to 3 o'clock. Now **play** your MIDI **keyboard**, and you will find that the harder you play, the louder the sound is. It sounds quieter than before because it used to be playing at full volume even when you played softly.

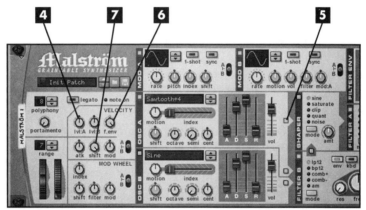

4 **Turn** the **Velocity to Level A knob** back to 12 o'clock.

5 **Click** the **Route OSC A to Shaper button** and **play** your MIDI **keyboard** to hear what this sounds like. The sound is filtered now, so there is less treble.

6 **Turn** the **Velocity to Filter Env (f.env) knob** all the way to the right. **Play** your MIDI **keyboard**, and you will hear that the harder you play, the more the Filter Envelope is turned up, which raises the cut-off frequency of Filter A, resulting in more treble in your sound. It sounds the same as if you used your mouse to turn up the Filter Envelope Amount knob.

7 **Turn** the **Velocity to Shift knob** all the way to the right. **Play** your MIDI **keyboard** and listen as the harmonic content of your sound is "shifted" the harder you play. Kind of a cool effect.

Just think of everything in terms of control voltage. Here's what I mean: The same way you connected a cable on the back of the Malström to the Stereo Pan control on the 14:2 Mixer in the "Stereo-ize That Sequence" exercise, virtual control voltage is always available to do what you want it to, even when you do not connect cables. Do you want to send control voltage from Velocity to control the Filter Envelope or the Shift amount? Would you like the Mod wheel to control the Filter Frequency? In all these cases, you are routing voltage created by one

part of the Malström to control another part of the Malström. So it is with all
the Reason instruments.

LFOs (MOD A and MOD B)

To further enjoy controlling bits of the Malström with other bits of the Malström,
there's no better place to go next than the Malström's two low-frequency oscillators: MODs A and B. Of course, the word *modulator* could be exchanged with the
phrase *automatic parameter adjuster*. This next exercise will probably remind you of
when you explored the Subtractor LFOs.

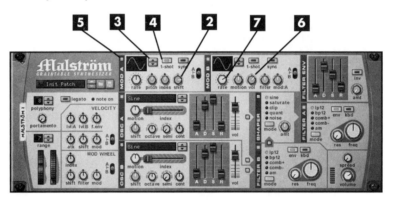

1 In a rack containing Mixer
14:2 followed by a
Malström, **right-click** on
the **Malström** and
**choose Initialize Patch.
Play** a **note or chord** on
your MIDI keyboard to
hear this plain sine wave.

2 Turn the MOD A Shift knob to 3 o'clock and **play**. Now the OSC A Shift value is
being modulated by MOD A's low-frequency sine wave. Sounds pretty, don't you think?

3 Use the **up arrow** on the MOD A waveform selector to go one by one through each
available waveform as you hold down a chord on your MIDI keyboard.

4 Click the **MOD A 1-shot button** and **play** your MIDI keyboard some more. Now
MOD A only plays its waveform once each time you strike a note, instead of cycling
over and over again.

5 Turn off MOD A by clicking the MOD A On/Off button.

6 Turn up the **MOD B to Volume knob** a bit past 2 o'clock (a value of 25). **Play**
your MIDI **keyboard** to hear the slow vibrato (tremolo).

7 Hold down a chord on your MIDI keyboard and slowly **turn up** the **MOD B Rate
knob** to a value of 90 (just past 2 o'clock). It will sound kind of like turning up the
vibrato speed on an organ.

As you probably figured out, all the blue knobs in each Modulator section are
parameters that can be modulated by the MOD A or MOD B LFO waveform.
MOD A can modulate the Pitch, Index, and Shift parameters of either or both OSC
A and B, while MOD B can modulate the Motion and Volume parameters of either
or both of the oscillators, as well as either or both of the Maström's filters, and can
even modulate MOD A for some weird effects. Finally, you should know that the
A/B "Target" switch found on each modulator (as well as in the Velocity and Mod
wheel sections) routes the modulator to either OSC A/Filter A (top position), OSC
B/Filter B (bottom position), or both (middle position).

Modulation Wheel

In the "Modulation Wheel" section of Chapter 4, you learned how to route the Modulation wheel to control LFO amount and filter frequency. You can do that with the Malström's Mod wheel as well (except that LFO is labeled "Mod" on the Malström). But since you already learned how to do that in the previous chapter, let's do something now that only the Malström can do. In the next exercise, you will use the Malström's Modulation wheel to control the Index and Shift parameters of the Malström's oscillators.

1 In a rack containing Mixer 14:2 followed by a Malström, **right-click** on the **Malström** and **choose Initialize Patch**.

2 **Click** in the **OSCA Graintable display window** and **select Perc: Anvil Hammer**.

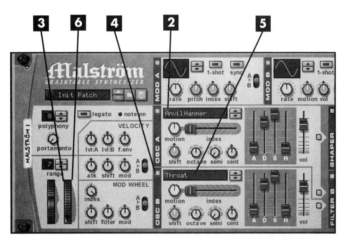

3 **Turn** the **Mod Wheel to Index knob** (labeled Index) all the way to the right. Then **hold down** some **keys** on your MIDI keyboard and **move** your **Mod wheel** up and down to hear the Graintable play forward and backward.

4 **Click** the **OSC B On/Off button** to turn on OSC B.

5 **Click** in the **OSC B Graintable display window** and **choose Voice: Throat** from the bottom of the menu. You will probably have to use the scroll arrow at the bottom of the menu to get down that low in the list.

6 **Hold down** one or more **keys** on your MIDI keyboard and **move** your **Mod wheel** (on your keyboard or the Malström) up and down. You will hear the index of both oscillators being adjusted, because the Mod Wheel Target switch is in the middle position.

7 **Move** the **Mod Wheel Target switch** into the lower, B position. **Play** your MIDI **keyboard** while moving your Mod wheel back and forth, and only the index of OSC B will be affected.

8 **Turn** the **Mod Wheel to Index knob** back to the 12 o'clock position.

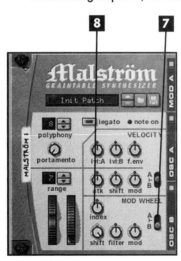

9 **Turn** the **Mod Wheel to Shift knob** all the way to the right. **Play** your MIDI **keyboard** while moving your Mod wheel forward, and you will hear the Shift parameter turned up for only OSC B, because the Mod wheel Target switch is still in the lower, B position.

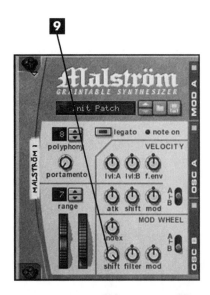

10 **Move** the **Mod Wheel Target switch** into the upper, A position. **Play** your MIDI **keyboard** while moving your Mod wheel forward, and you will hear the Shift value turned up for only OSC A.

11 **Turn** the **Mod Wheel to Shift knob** all the way to the left. Now **play** your MIDI **keyboard** while moving your Mod wheel forward. Because you have the Mod Wheel to Shift knob turned all the way down, moving your Mod wheel forward actually turns down the OSC A Shift value.

Malström, Meet the Matrix Analog Pattern Sequencer

In Chapter 4, you were introduced to the RPG-8 Arpeggiator. The RPG-8, of course, can be used with any of the Reason synths. Its use is not limited to the Subtractor. In the same way, the Matrix Analog Pattern Sequencer can be used with any of the Reason synths. The Matrix is modeled after very old sequencers that actually required plugging in a separate patch cable for each note that was to be triggered. While the Matrix is great for sequencing notes, it also can control other things, such as filters, making it useful in conjunction with almost every device in Reason.

Key Mode

You'll use Key mode to control what notes the Malström plays. By default, the Keys/Curve switch is in the Keys position. Just to the left of this switch, you will see a Pattern section that works the same way as Redrum's Pattern section, with four banks of eight patterns, a Run button, and a Pattern Enable button. Let's give it a try.

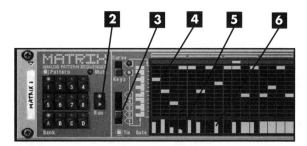

1 In an empty rack, **create** a **Mixer 14:2**, followed by a **Malström** and a **Matrix Pattern Sequencer** underneath the Malström. **Load** the following **patch** into the Malström: Reason Factory Sound Bank > Malstrom Patches > Bass > Bassic.xwv.

2 **Click Run** on the Matrix, and you will hear the default pattern.

3 **Move** the **Octave switch** down from 3 to 2. This determines which octave you will be editing but does not change the octave of the existing notes.

4 **Click** around in the left half of the upper grid section of the **Pattern window** to change some notes. By default, you are dealing with only those first 16 steps.

5 **Make** a few of the **notes** quieter or louder by dragging their velocity down or up in the lower Gate section of the Pattern window.

6 **Take out** a few of the **notes** completely by dragging their velocity all the way down.

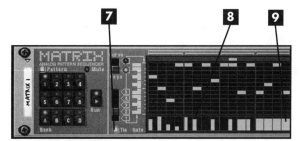

7 **Click** on the **Tie button**.

8 **Double** the **length** of a few notes by clicking on their Gate values in the lower Gate section of the Edit window.

9 If you have a few of the same note in a row, **click** and **drag** across their **Gate values** in the lower Gate section of the Edit window. Then they will all be tied together as one continuous note.

Curve Mode

Curve mode is used for controlling filters and other parameters on Reason devices. Editing in Curve mode does not change anything you did in Key mode, so you can send distinct key and curve information on the same pattern. For this exercise, you can use the same rack as the previous one, with Mixer 14:2 followed by a Malström (with the bass patch Bassic.xwv loaded) and a Matrix Pattern Sequencer underneath the Malström.

1 While still in Key mode, **draw** in some **notes** in the left portion of the Matrix grid. Use any octave you like. (I like Octave 2 for this sound.)

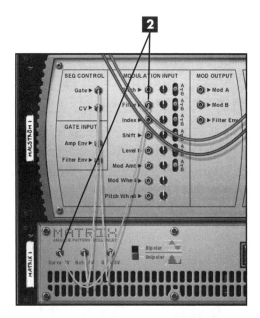

2 **Press Tab** to flip your rack around. Then **click and drag** a **cable** connecting the Matrix's Curve CV output to the Malström's Filter Modulation input.

3 **Flip** your **rack** back around facing front and **move** the **Key/Curve switch** to the Curve position.

4 **Draw** in some **curve information** in the left half of the upper portion of the grid. You will hear the Malström's filter frequency changing. (The sound will get brighter and darker.)

5 **Right-click** on the
Matrix and **click**
Randomize Pattern.
You will hear that the pitch
has been randomized, and
you will see that the Curve
has been randomized at
the same time.

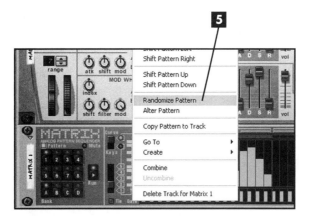

6 **Press Tab** to flip your
rack around. For a different
effect, **move** the end of
the **cable** that is in the
Malström's Filter Modulation
input so that it is plugged
into the Shift Modulation
input.

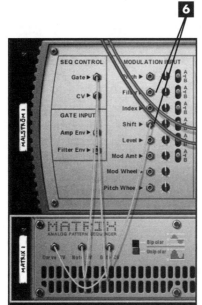

7 Finally, **move** the end of
the **cable** that is in the
Malström's Shift Modulation
input so that it is plugged
into the Pitch Modulation
input. Now you are controlling the Malström's pitch
with the Matrix's Curve output and its Note CV output
at the same time.

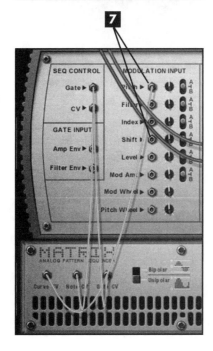

Randomize Pattern in Step 5 probably reminded you of Redrum. There are also other selections from the Matrix's context menu that work the same as in Redrum: Copy/ Paste Pattern, Shift Pattern Left/Right, and Copy Pattern to Track. There is also a Shuffle button and a Resolution knob, which also work the same as on Redrum and the RPG-9 Arpeggiator.

> ❋ **WHEN THE CABLES GET IN THE WAY**
>
> Always remember that when you are plugging and unplugging cables on the back of your Reason rack, if you have trouble reading something because a cable is in the way, you can press the L key on your computer keyboard to hide the cables. If you want to see them again, just press L again, and they will reappear.

Using the Malström as an Effects Processor

This next bit is pretty cool. The Malström actually has audio inputs. This is so you can connect the outputs of another Reason device (such as Dr.Rex or Redrum) to those inputs and use the Malström's filters and Shaper to process the sound from the other device. I hope you will enjoy trying this in the following exercise.

Playing Dr. Octo Rex through the Malström's Filters

1 In a brand-spankin'-new rack, **create** a **Mixer 14:2** followed by a **Malström** and then **Dr. Octo Rex** under that. Then **press** the **Tab key** to flip your rack around.

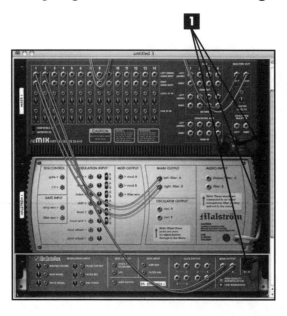

2 **Click, drag, and release** the **cable** out of Dr. Octo Rex's left Audio Output. This will actually disconnect both left and right Audio Outputs.

3 **Click and drag** a **cable connection** from Dr. Octo Rex's left Audio Output to the Malström's Shaper/Filter: A Audio Input.

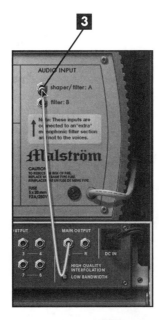

4 **Click and drag** a **cable connection** from Dr. Octo Rex's right Audio Output to the Malström's Filter: B Audio Input.

5 **Press** the **Tab key** to flip your rack around facing front. For this exercise, leave the default Rex file: Acoustic Drums | College 130 - 1.

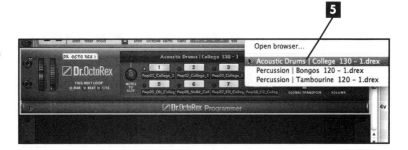

6 **Right-click** on the **Malström** and **choose Initialize Patch**.

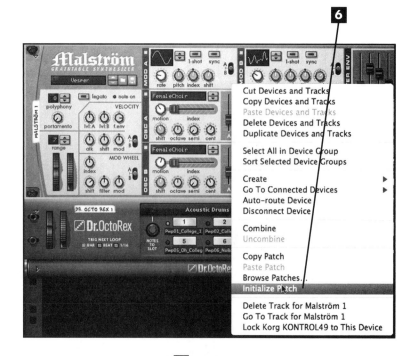

7 **Turn up** the **tempo** to 133 bpm in the Reason Transport panel.

8 **Click** the **Run button** in Dr.Rex.

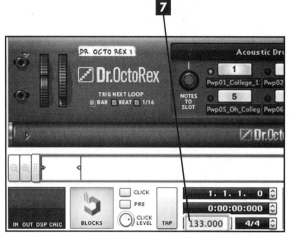

9 **Click** the **Sync button** on MOD B and **turn down** the **MOD B Rate knob** a notch to 4/4.

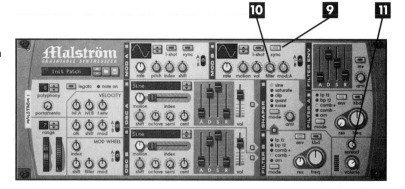

10 **Turn up** the **MOD B to Filter knob** all the way to the right.

11 **Turn** the **Spread knob** all the way to the right (to make maximum stereo separation with the output from Filter A/Shaper on the left and the output from Filter B on the right).

12 **Choose comb+** for the filter type on Filter A and **turn up** the **Filter A Resonance knob** halfway, to a value of 65.

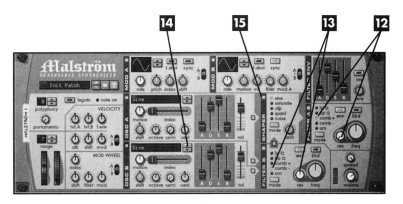

13 **Choose comb–** for the filter type on Filter B and **turn up** the **Filter B Resonance knob** halfway, to a value of 65.

14 **Use** the **up arrow** on the MOD B Waveform selector to try all the different waveforms. When you are finished, go back down to the first waveform (sine wave).

15 **Turn** on the **Shaper** and listen for a moment. Then **turn** the **Shaper Amount knob** all the way up and try each Shaper mode. The Noise mode is the freakiest!

Please feel encouraged to try different settings on the MOD B Rate knob, as well as different combinations of Shaper modes and MOD B waveforms.

Playing Dr. Octo Rex through the Shaper

Although you tried playing Dr. Octo Rex through the Shaper in Step 15 of the preceding exercise, there was so much other insanity going on that you still may not have a clear picture of the character of the Shaper. The Shaper uses a process called *waveshaping* to distort incoming signals. A good way to get a feel for what effect the Shaper has is to run a drum loop through it, with no other filtering or modulation applied to the signal.

1 In a new rack, **create** in this order: **Mixer 14:2, Malström, Dr.Rex**. Then **press Tab** to flip the rack around.

2 **Right-click** on Dr. Octo Rex's **left Audio Output** and **select Disconnect** from the context menu.

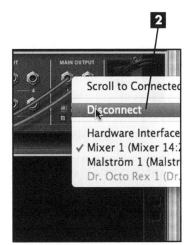

3 **Right-click** on Dr. Octo Rex's **left Audio Output** and **select Malström 1 > Shaper/Filter A Audio Input** from the context menu.

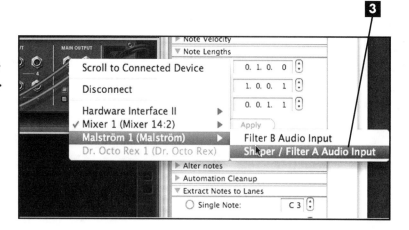

4 **Flip** the **rack** back around facing front and **use** the **default Rex file** in Dr. Octo Rex: **Acoustic Drums | College 130 – 1**.

5 **Click** the Malström's **Filter A On/Off button** to turn off the filter.

6 **Click** the **Run button** on Dr.Rex. Because neither Filter A nor the Shaper is on, you are hearing the natural, unaffected drum loop (at 30 bpm faster than the loop was originally recorded).

7 **Turn up** the **Shaper Amount knob** to 3 o'clock (a value of about 104).

8 Hang onto your hat and **click** the **Shaper On/Off button** to activate the Shaper.

9 **Click** on each **Shaper mode** to hear what it sounds like.

By now I hope you can see what a unique synth the Malström is. I find new ways to have fun with this thing every time I play with it. I invariably end up designing a new patch or becoming inspired to work on a new piece of music thanks to some interesting sound that comes out of the Malström. The logical, easily usable design with its simple yet powerful controls helps make the Malström a true classic. As you put to use what you've learned in this book and consult the Reason Operation Manual when you have questions, you will master the Malström in no time, and it will become yet another useful tool for making great-sounding music with Reason.

6 } Thor Polysonic Synthesizer

Thor is an amazing synth that comes in Reason. It's capable of very warm analog sounds; complex, deeply weird, and exciting textures and effects; lead sounds that really cut through; and tons of groove. Thor offers significant and advanced features not found on Subtractor or the Malström. It features a very cool Step Sequencer that opens up whole new areas of inspiration and rhythmic possibilities. Its oscillators and filters are modular: When you change oscillator type (analog, wavetable, phase modulation, FM pair, multioscillator, or noise) or filter type (including Formant and State Variable filter types), you are presented with a completely different user interface for that oscillator or filter. Finally, Thor's Modulation Bus Routing section allows you to easily connect almost any part of Thor to any other part of Thor.

Put Thor in a rack and click the Show Programmer button in the lower-left corner of Thor. Now you can see Thor in all its glory. Look at the size of that thing. As you can see, Thor is a big synth with quite a lot going on. You may have been a beginner at the start of this book, but now that you're becoming something of an expert on Reason 5, you are ready to learn how to use Thor's exciting and unique features. I wouldn't be giving you your money's worth if I didn't dig into this beautiful synth and show you what it has to offer.

In this chapter you will learn how to:

❋ Use Thor's Step Sequencer
❋ Make your own sounds using each of Thor's six oscillator types
❋ Use Thor's unique Formant filter
❋ Become a master of Thor's very useful Modulation Bus Routing section
❋ Use the BV512 Digital Vocoder with Thor to vocode beats instead of voice

Using Thor's Step Sequencer

One thing that makes Thor such a powerful addition to Reason is its Step Sequencer. What can you do with it? Well, there are plenty of patches in the Rhythmic and Percussion folders that use the Step Sequencer. But you can also use the Step Sequencer with any sound you like, even if the patch wasn't originally programmed that way.

All of the exercises in this section are connected to each other. When you are finished with one, don't close the window, because the next exercise will pick up where the previous one left off. You may even want to save between exercises. I promise some cool payoffs as you work through these Step Sequencer tutorials. Let's go.

Using the Step Knobs to Control Pitch

Each step in Thor's Step Sequencer has a step knob you can use to set the note value, velocity, gate length, and step duration. Which value you are editing with a step knob at any given time is determined by the position of the Edit knob. In addition to note value, velocity, and so on, you can also program a step to send modulation information to almost any other part of Thor you want, using the Curve 1 and Curve 2 positions on the Edit knob. In this first exercise, you will use the step knobs to edit pitch (note value). The Edit knob is already set to the Note position by default.

1 In a rack containing Mixer 14:2 followed by Thor, **load** the following **patch** into Thor: Reason Factory Sound Bank > Thor Patches > Lead Synths > Combing Lead.thor.

2 **Click** the **Show Programmer** button.

3 **Set Sequencer Run Mode** to Repeat.

4 **Click Run**.

5 **Turn** the **step knobs** all the way down for Steps 1, 3, 4, and 6.

6 The Octave switch is currently set for two octaves. **Switch it** to four octaves.

7 **Turn down** the **step knobs** all the way for Steps 9, 11, 12, and 14.

8 **Turn down** the **step knob** on Step 13 a hair, to a MIDI note value of A#2.

Please note that the Octave switch only affects note information. It has no effect for editing done in the Velocity, Gate Length, Step Duration, Curve 1, or Curve 2 Edit knob positions.

Using the Step Knobs to Control Gate Length

Gate Length controls the length of the note played for a given step. The step still lasts for the same duration no matter what the Gate Length value is. (By default, each step lasts for a single 1/16 note.) Gate Length determines what percentage of the step will actually have a note playing in it. The default value is 75%.

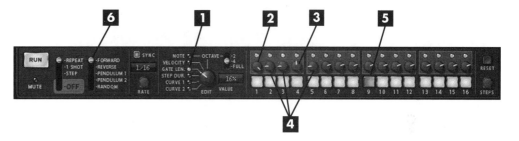

1 **Turn** the **Edit knob** to the Gate Length position. Now the control knobs will control gate length instead of note value.

2 **Turn** the **step 1 knob** all the way up.

3 **Turn down** the **step 4 knob** to 12 o'clock.

4 **Turn down** the **step knobs** on Steps 2, 3, and 5 to 9 o'clock.

5 **Click** on the **step 9 button** to turn off that step.

6 **Try** all five **Sequencer Direction switch positions:** Forward, Reverse, Pendulum 1, Pendulum 2, and Random. When you are finished, **switch it** back to Forward.

Controlling the Step Sequencer with Your MIDI Keyboard

So far, the Step Sequencer starts when you click the Run button and stops when you click the Run button again. By the end of the next exercise, not only will the Step Sequencer start when you play a note on your MIDI keyboard and stop when you let go, but it will also transpose the sequence according to which note you play on your MIDI keyboard. This exercise starts where the previous exercise left off.

1 **Click** the **Note Trigger MIDI button** to turn it off.

2 In the Step Sequencer, **click** the **Run button** to stop the sequence.

3 **Set Modulation Bus 6 Source** for MIDI Key > Gate by clicking in the first empty space in the Source column on the left side of the Modulation Bus Routing section of Thor and selecting MIDI Key > Gate from the pop-up menu and submenu.

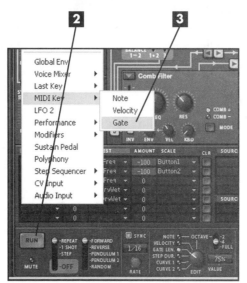

4 **Set Modulation Bus 6 Destination Amount** to 100. Do this by clicking in the Amount cell and dragging upward while you hold down your mouse button.

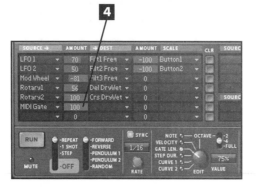

5 **Set Modulation Bus 6 Destination** to Step Sequencer > Trig. Now the Sequencer will play when you are holding down a key on your MIDI keyboard, and it will stop when you let go. The same notes are played no matter which key you play.

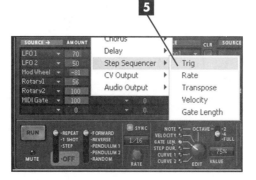

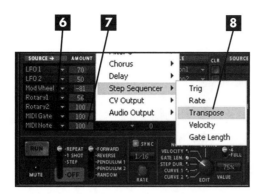

6 **Set Modulation Bus 7 Source** for MIDI Key > Note.

7 **Set Modulation Bus 7 Destination Amount** to 100.

8 **Set Modulation Bus 7 Destination** to Step Sequencer > Transpose. Now the sequence will be transposed according to what note you play on your MIDI keyboard.

Using the Step Sequencer to Gate Thor's Amplifier

In analog synths and sequencers, gate inputs and outputs transmit note on/off but do not transmit note values (such as A#1 or D2). A gate is either open or closed, on or off. Reason departs from this a bit in that Reason also transmits velocity information via its gate I/O.

Normally, when you play a note the gate is opened (note on), and when you let go of a note the gate closes (note off). In the next exercise, when you play a note, it triggers the Step Sequencer, and the Step Sequencer opens and closes the gate with each step of the sequence.

At the end of this exercise, you won't hear the notes you sequenced anymore (because note value is not transmitted via gate CV). Instead, when you play a note or chord on your MIDI keyboard, you will hear that note or chord "gated" (or triggered) to the rhythm of the Step Sequencer. This is a pretty neat trick, lending itself to some nice locked rhythmic effects. The exercise picks up at the point where the last exercise left off.

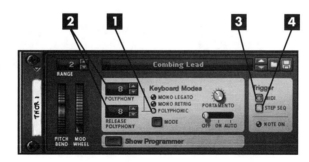

1 **Set Keyboard Mode** to Polyphonic.

2 **Turn Polyphony** and **Release Polyphony** up to 8.

3 **Turn on** the **Note Trigger MIDI button**.

4 **Turn off** the **Note Trigger Step Sequencer button**.

5 Turn the **Amp Gain knob** all the way down.

6 Set **Modulation Bus 8 Source** for Step Sequencer > Gate.

7 Set **Modulation Bus 8 Destination Amount** to 60.

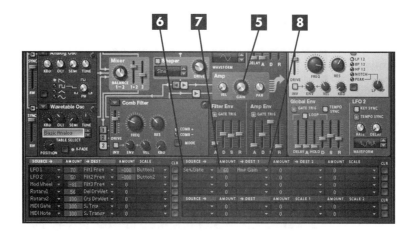

8 Set **Modulation Bus 8 Destination** to Amp > Gain. **Play** some **chords** on your MIDI keyboard, and you will hear your chords played with the rhythm from the Step Sequencer.

Using the Step Knobs to Control Curve Values

In analog hardware (and in Reason), gate information is transmitted via control voltage (CV). Curve CV (as opposed to gate CV) can transmit note value information and can be used to modulate other parameters as well.

The last two positions for the Edit knob (Curve 1 and Curve 2) are generic in nature and can be assigned in the Modulation Bus Routing section to control whatever you want. Because Thor's Edit knob already has a Note position, we will use Curve 1 to control the frequency of Filter 3. Again, we are picking up where the previous exercise left off.

1 Set **Modulation Bus 9 Source** for Step Sequencer > Curve 1.

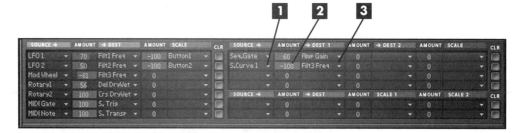

2 Turn **Modulation Bus 9 Destination Amount** all the way down to −100.

3 Set **Modulation Bus 9 Destination** to Filter 3 > Frequency.

4 Move the **Edit knob** to the Curve 1 position (or **click** directly on the **green LED** next to Curve 1).

5 Turn **down step knobs** 3, 4, 6, 8, and 10 to about 9 o'clock (a curve value of about 1:22).

6 Turn **step knob**s 5 and 11 all the way down (all the way to the left).

7 Turn **step knobs** 13, 14, 15, and 16 down to about 11 o'clock (a curve value of about 1:46). Then **hold down** some **chords** on your MIDI keyboard to hear the effect.

Here is one last trick (the cherry on top).

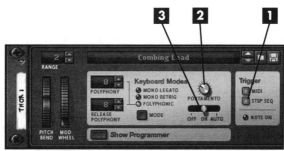

1 Turn the **Note Trigger Step Sequencer button** back on.

2 Turn **down** the **Portamento knob** to a value of 35.

3 Turn the **Portamento switch** to the on position. Then **hold** a **note** on your MIDI keyboard to hear the effect.

While you're at it, try some Modulation wheel. It's mapped to modulate the Filter 3 frequency on this patch. Okay, that's the end of the "connected" Step Sequencer exercises. The following step duration exercise starts fresh and does not reference the preceding exercises.

Using the Step Knobs to Control Step Duration

If you increase the step duration, the Step Sequencer will stay on that step longer before moving on to the next step. If the gate length is short but the step duration is long, the Step Sequencer will still stay on the step for the entire designated step duration, and you will hear silence from the time the note ends until the next step is played. However, if you set a very short step duration, the note will be short no matter what, because the gate length is a percentage of the step duration, and even 100% of "short" is still short.

You'll find a great example of step duration in action in the patch I Am Thor. This is an interesting patch to study, not only for the use of step duration, but also for the way Curve 1 and Curve 2 are used to modulate the Formant Filter X and Y sliders, which control the vowel sound.

1 In a fresh rack with Mixer 14:2 followed by Thor, **click** in **Thor's Patch Display window** and **choose I Am Thor** from the pop-up menu.

2 **Click** the **Show Programmer button**.

3 In Thor's Step Sequencer, **move** the **Edit knob** to the Step Duration position.

4 **Play** a **note** on your MIDI keyboard and watch how the lights above the steps move very quickly through the first few beats. Now **turn up step knobs** 2, 3, 4, 5, and 6 all the way to the right and **play** your MIDI **keyboard** again.

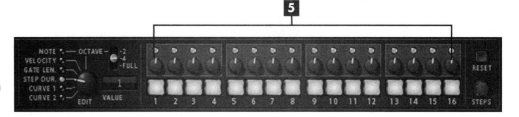

5 **Ctrl–click** on each of the 16 **step knobs** to return them to their default position of 1. **Play** your MIDI **keyboard**, and all steps will have an equal duration.

The potential drawback to messing with step duration is that you can end up with step sequences that do not line up with the rest of the track when looped. If your track is in 4/4 time, you would have to make sure your step sequence still adds up to four beats (or a multiple thereof), or else the downbeat on Thor's step sequence will not line up with the "ones" in the rest of your Reason song. This is not a problem with a one-shot, arrhythmic patch such as I Am Thor.

Building Sounds in Thor

I will not lie to you: Thor is a beast of a synth. But I mean that in a good way. You can do lots and lots with just one Thor. It's amazing how much good stuff Propellerhead built into Thor. And it all makes sense. Here it comes in bite-size pieces: making your own sounds with Thor.

Thor's Oscillators

Polysonic is probably not a word you need to learn for the Basic Synthesis 101 exam. I mean, don't most synthesizers make more than one sound, thus making them polysonic? Most likely what Propellerhead is referring to with that name is the choice of oscillator types. Each of Thor's three oscillator slots offers a choice of six completely different types of oscillators, each with its own very specific character. To give you a feel for what each oscillator type can do, I will introduce key features of each oscillator in the exercises that follow.

Each oscillator type shares one thing in common: a group of four knobs across the top of the oscillator. The Octave, Semi, and Tune knobs should be familiar to you from your experience with other Reason synths. But what's that knob labeled KBD in the upper-left corner? You will try that knob as you study the first oscillator type on your tour: Thor's analog oscillator.

Analog Oscillator

The analog oscillator will probably be the most immediately familiar to you. But it still has a couple of tricks worth mentioning. From top to bottom, you can see four familiar basic waveforms: sawtooth, square, triangle, and sine. But wait—the Reason Operation Manual does not refer to that second wave as a square wave. They call it a *pulse wave*. That's fine, because there is a Pulse Width knob, and as you can (sort of) see from the marks around the PW knob, it is only a perfect square wave when the knob is set at 12 o'clock. Otherwise, you can just think of a pulse wave as a rectangular wave, which is the way it is sometimes referred to. Let's give this a try.

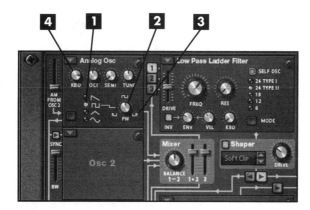

1 In a freshly initialized Thor, **select** Oscillator 1's **pulse wave**. **Play** a few **notes** to hear this.

2 **Move** the **Pulse Width knob** to 12 o'clock (a value of 64), and you will hear the classic square wave sound, with some highs rolled off thanks to the Low Pass Ladder filter it's going through.

3 **Turn up** the **Pulse Width knob** to a value of 124 and hear how thin the sound becomes. Then **play** your MIDI **keyboard** with one hand as you slowly turn the Pulse Width knob all the way to the left and then back to center. You just did pulse width modulation.

4 **Turn** the **Keyboard Tracking knob** down to about 3 o'clock. **Play** your MIDI **keyboard**, and you will find that the difference between two octaves is less than 12 semitones now.

5 **Turn** the **Keyboard Tracking knob** all the way to the left, and you will find that any key you play will play the same note.

Changing the Keyboard Tracking knob to intermediate values could be useful when dealing with non-pitched sounds (such as percussion, noise-based effects, or other sound effects). It is also useful for exotically pitched sounds, horror suspense, or general weirdness.

Wavetable Oscillator

As you know, Propellerhead combined granular synthesis and wavetable synthesis to create its own Graintable synthesis, which is the basis of the Malström's oscillators. Thor is the first Reason synth to offer a straight-up wavetable oscillator.

Imagine a WAV file of a gong crash sliced up into 100 equal slices. Each slice is a separate waveform, a tiny slice of a gong crash. String them all together, and they make a wavetable. With Reason's wavetable oscillator, the Position knob is used to choose which little waveform (slice) in the wavetable will be played when you play a note. It stays stuck looping that single waveform and will play through the entire wavetable only if you move the Position knob all the way from right to left as you play the note.

1 In a freshly initialized Thor, **click** the **arrow** in the upper-left corner of Oscillator 1 and **select Wavetable** from the menu.

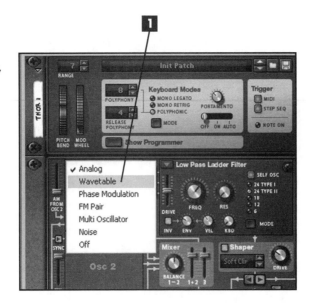

2 Use the **down arrow** to click through the 32 wavetables one at a time, trying each one on your MIDI keyboard as you go.

3 **Click** in the **Wavetable display** and **choose Sine Harmonics**. Then **play** your MIDI **keyboard**, and you will hear a basic sine wave.

4 While playing your MIDI keyboard with one hand, slowly **turn** the **Position knob** all the way to the right and then all the way back to the left (a value of zero). Now when you play your MIDI keyboard, you will hear a basic sine wave.

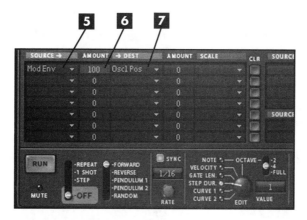

5 **Click** in the first **Modulation Bus 1 Source cell** and **select Mod Env** (modulation envelope).

6 **Click and drag** the **amount** up to a value of 100.

7 **Select Osc 1 Pos** (oscillator 1 position) for the Destination. **Play** your MIDI **keyboard**, and you will hear a smooth sweep from end to beginning of the wavetable each time you play a key.

8 On Oscillator 1, **click** the **X-fade (crossfade) button** to turn off crossfade. Now when you play your MIDI keyboard, you will hear the sharp edges of each waveform in the wavetable.

Phase Modulation Oscillator

If anyone out there remembers the Casio CZ series of keyboards (such as the CZ-1 or the CZ-101), then Thor's phase modulation oscillator may bring back memories, since it was modeled after that line of synthesizers. Thor's phase modulation oscillator can actually generate two waveforms, but instead of playing both at exactly the same time, it plays one after the other. What you hear when this happens is a second simultaneous tone that is one octave below the first tone. There is also a Phase Modulation knob that, when swept, simulates a filter sweep. This oscillator has its own unique character, providing another group of colors on Thor's palette.

1 In a freshly initialized Thor, **choose Bypass** for Filter 1, so you can hear Oscillator 1 with no filtering.

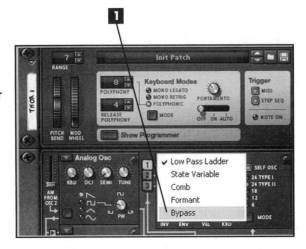

2 **Choose Phase Modulation** for Oscillator 1.

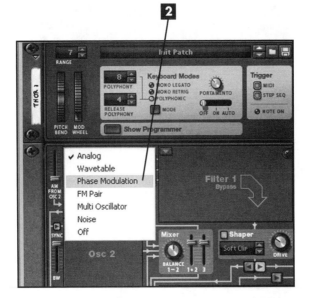

3 **Play** your MIDI **keyboard** while slowly turning the Oscillator 1 Phase Modulation knob all the way to the right, then all the way to the left, and ending back at 12 o'clock.

4 By default, the second waveform is off. **Play** your MIDI **keyboard** while using the up arrow to try each of the choices for the second waveform. When you are finished, **select** the **sawtooth wave** for the second waveform.

5 **Choose Wave number 5** for the first waveform so that your Parameter Value tooltip says OSC 1 Phase Modulation Wave 1:5 when you mouse over the waveform.

6 **Turn** the **Phase Modulation knob** all the way down to the left.

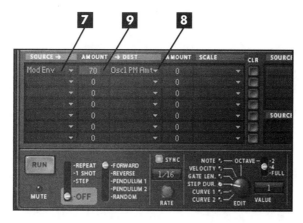

7 **Set Modulation Bus 1 Source** to Mod Envelope.

8 **Set Modulation Bus 1 Destination** to Osc 1 PM Amount.

9 **Set Modulation Bus 1 Destination Amount** to 70 and **play** your MIDI **keyboard** in the bass register.

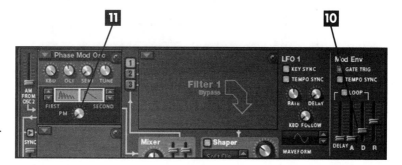

10 **Move** the **Mod Envelope Decay slider** down to 552ms (milliseconds) and **play** your MIDI **keyboard** in the bass register.

11 Continue to **play** your MIDI **keyboard** in the lower octaves while slowly turning the Oscillator 1 Pulse Modulation knob up and down through a full sweep.

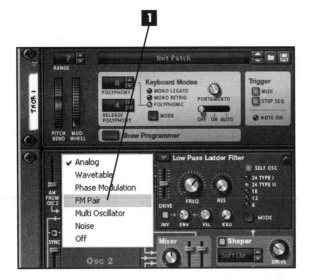

12 **Select Wave 4** for the first waveform and Wave 4 for the second waveform (they have the same number but are different waveforms) and **set Phase Modulation Amount** to 9 o'clock (a value of 20). Now you have another serviceable bass sound.

I encourage you to mix and match waveforms and Phase Modulation knob settings to hear all the different sonic characters you can come up with.

FM Pair Oscillator

Digital FM (frequency modulation) synthesis was made famous by Yamaha's hugely successful DX7 synthesizer. It can be used for all sorts of metallic or bell-like tones and can be used in combination with other oscillators to add a bit of this character, as in the following example.

1 In a freshly initialized Thor (with Programmer showing), **choose FM Pair** for Oscillator 1.

2 **Increase** the **Amp Envelope Release slider** to a value of about 3 seconds so that it is even with the Amp Envelope Sustain slider.

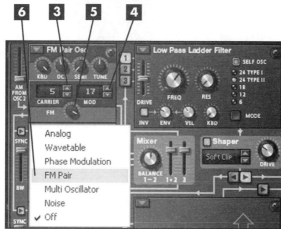

3 As you play your MIDI keyboard, **use** the **up arrow** to step through the Carrier values (one at a time) up to number 5 and leave it there.

4 As you play your MIDI keyboard, **use** the **up arrow** to step through the Modulator values up to number 17 and leave it there.

5 As you play your MIDI keyboard, slowly **turn** the **Frequency Modulation knob** all the way up to a value of 119 (almost all the way to the right). You should have a clangy, chime-like tone now.

6 **Select FM Pair** for Oscillator 2.

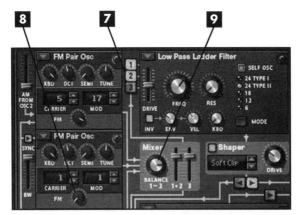

7 **Click** the **Osc 2 to Filter 1 Enable button**.

8 **Turn** the **Oscillator 2 FM Amount knob** all the way down.

9 **Turn** the **Mixer knob** to 3 o'clock and **play** your **keyboard** a bit to see where you're at with this patch.

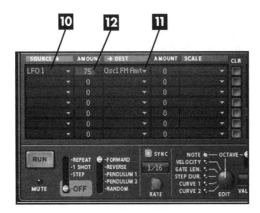

10 **Set Modulation Bus 1 Source** to LFO 1.

11 **Set Modulation Bus 1 Destination** to Osc 1 FM Amt.

12 **Set Modulation Bus 1 Destination Amount** to a value of 75 and play your MIDI keyboard to hear the effect.

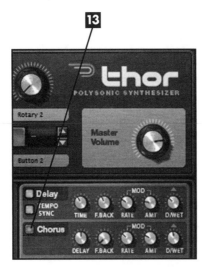

13 **Click** the **Chorus button** to activate the Chorus effect. Now you should have a pretty sound to play with. But if you want to go even further into DX7 Land, go on to the next step.

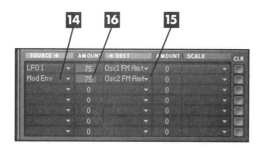

14 **Set Modulation Bus 2 Source** to Mod Envelope.

15 **Set Modulation Bus 2 Destination** to Osc 2 FM Amount.

16 **Set Modulation Bus 2 Destination Amount** to a value of 75.

17 To make this patch more expressive, **turn up** the **Amplifier Velocity knob** to 3 o'clock. Now the volume of your patch depends on how hard you play.

Wow. I feel like I'm in the 1980s. Of course, if you liked the mellower sound you had before Step 16, you can simply turn Modulation Bus 2 Destination Amount back down to zero or somewhere in between.

Multi Oscillator

Thor's multi oscillator generates its sound with multiple detuned waveforms of the same type. If you select a square wave, the multi oscillator will play multiple square waves, detuned from each other in a manner determined by the Detune Mode menu, to a degree determined by the Detune Amount knob. Of course, you are free to experiment with the five different waveforms the multi oscillator has to offer, but this exercise is focused on what makes the multi oscillator unique, which is the use of its different detune modes, so you will be sticking with the default sawtooth wave in the following easy tutorial.

1 In a freshly initialized Thor, **click** the **arrow** in the upper-left corner of Oscillator 1 and **choose Multi Oscillator**. Then **play** your **keyboard** to hear the sound of Random 1, the default detune mode.

2 Turn the **Detune Amount knob** all the way to the right. Now play some very high keys. Can you hear how this could be used to add a bell-like or metallic texture to a sound?

3 Click in the **Detune Mode display window** and **select Fifth Up** from the menu. Then **play** your **keyboard** to hear the sound.

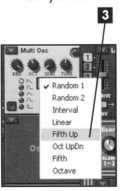

4 Click the **down arrow** once to select Oct UpDn for the detune mode and **play** your **keyboard** to hear the sound.

5 Click the **down arrow** once more to select Fifth for the detune mode, and you will hear a big mess when you play your keyboard.

6 Turn down the **Detune Amount knob** all the way to the left, and you will find that the Fifth detune mode starts with the waveforms a fifth apart (unlike the Fifth Up mode, which requires a maximum Detune Amount setting to produce a fifth interval).

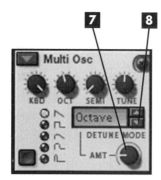

7 **Turn up** the **detune amount** to 9 o'clock, and you will hear a chorusing effect.

8 **Click** the **down arrow** to choose Octave for the detune mode. The Octave mode starts with the waveforms an octave apart (unlike the Oct UpDn detune mode, which requires a maximum Detune Amount setting to produce an octave interval).

Noise Oscillator

What's more fun to play with than straight-up noise? Thor is the first Reason synth to offer anywhere near this degree of musical sculpting of noise. The results can be subtle, eerie, atmospheric, beautiful, or all of the above. By the way, Step 9 is my favorite part. (I saved the best for last.)

1 In a freshly initialized Thor, **click** the **arrow** in the upper-left corner of Oscillator 1 and **choose Noise Oscillator**.

2 **Click** the **arrow** in the upper-left corner of Filter 1 (currently a Low Pass Ladder filter) and **choose Bypass** from the menu, so you can hear Oscillator 1 with no filtering.

3 **Move** the **Amp Envelope Decay slider** all the way to the top.

4 **Move up Amp Envelope Release** nearly halfway so it's even with the Sustain slider, and then **play** a few **notes** on your MIDI keyboard to hear pure white noise.

5 **Choose Color** for the noise type.

6 Sweep the **Modulation knob** as you play your MIDI keyboard. Turning the knob toward the left produces darker noise color settings, while turning the knob all the way to the right produces white noise.

7 **Choose Static** for the noise type and **sweep** the **Modulation knob** while playing your keyboard. Settings to the left produce lower-density static similar to turntable pops.

8 Choose S/H (Sample and Hold) for the noise type and sweep the Modulation knob all the way from left to right and back again while holding down a note on your MIDI keyboard. This adjusts the rate of the randomly generated S/H signal.

9 **Choose Band** for the noise type. **Play** your MIDI **keyboard** and **sweep** the **Modulation knob** all the way from left to right and back again.

When the noise type is set to Band, the Modulation knob controls the bandwidth, with the narrowest bandwidth at the far left. My favorite bandwidth setting is at 9 o'clock. It has sort of an ethereal, underwater sound.

AM from Oscillator 2

You are no doubt familiar with AM (amplitude modulation) from your work with Subtractor and the Malström. With Thor, AM is especially quick and easy, as you will experience in the following exercise.

1 In a freshly initialized Thor, **select** a **sine wave** for Analog Oscillator 1. (You could use another wave type, but sine will be nice for this.)

2 **Click** the **arrow** in the upper-left corner of the Oscillator 2 slot and **select Analog Oscillator**.

3 **Select** a **sine wave** for Oscillator 2. You will not hear anything change because Oscillator 2 is not routed to either filter.

4 **Turn** the **Keyboard Tracking knob** all the way down on Oscillator 2.

5 While playing your MIDI keyboard, slowly **move** the **AM from OSC 2 slider** all the way to the top.

6 For a different effect (sort of like a touch-tone phone sound), **turn up Oscillator 2 Keyboard Tracking** to 12 o'clock and **turn up** the **Oscillator 2 Octave knob** to a value of 6. Then **play** the **lower octaves** of your MIDI keyboard.

Oscillator Sync

You may have noticed some patches in the Reason synths with "sync" in the patch name. You also may have noticed that these patches have a certain sound in common. They are all using a technique called *oscillator sync*. When you use oscillator sync with Thor, Oscillator 1 is the master, and it controls the pitch you hear. When you sync Oscillator 2 or 3 to Oscillator 1, you will not hear the sync effect until you modulate (change) the frequency (pitch) of Oscillator 2 or 3. To hear this effect immediately, you will try out the patch called Big Sync.

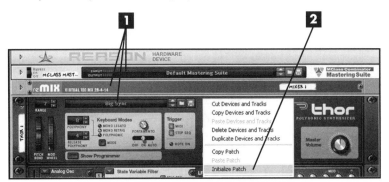

1 In an empty rack, **create** an **MClass Mastering Suite**, followed by **Mixer 14:2** and an **instance of Thor**. Then **load** the following **patch** into Thor: Reason Factory Sound Bank > Thor Patches > Lead Synths > Big Sync.

2 **Hold** a few long **notes** on your MIDI keyboard to hear the oscillator sync effect, which sounds kind of like the sweep of a comb filter. Then **right-click** on **Thor** and **choose Initialize Patch** from the context menu so you can start building your own sync patch.

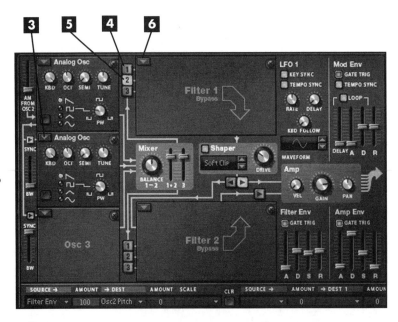

3 **Click** the **arrow** in the upper-left corner of Oscillator 2 and **choose Analog** from the pop-up menu.

4 **Click** the **Oscillator 1 to Filter 1 Enable button** to turn it off so that the audio signal from Osc 1 will not pass into the filter.

5 **Click** the **Oscillator 2 to Filter 1 Enable button** to turn it on so that the audio signal from Osc 2 will pass through the filter.

6 **Click** the **arrow** in the upper-left corner of Filter 1 and **choose Bypass** from the pop-up menu. Signal will pass through, but it will not be filtered.

7 **Click** the **Oscillator 2 Sync to Oscillator 1 button.** You will not hear much change in the sound if you play your MIDI keyboard right now.

8 **Move** the **Amp Envelope Decay slider** all the way up to the top.

9 **Set Mod 1 Source** to Filter Envelope.

10 **Set Mod 1 Destination Amount** to 100.

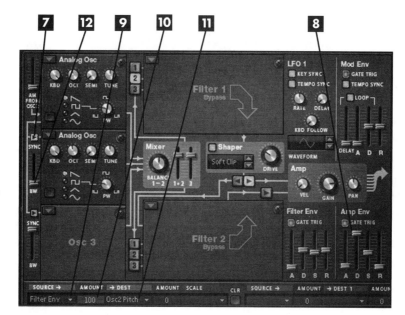

11 **Set Mod 1 Destination** to Oscillator 2 Pitch. Now when you play your MIDI keyboard, you will hear a strong oscillator sync effect.

12 **Move** the **Oscillator 2 Sync Bandwidth slider** all the way down. **Play** a **key** on your MIDI keyboard, and you will hear a slightly different effect (which will also make the higher notes quieter).

Note that the Sync Bandwidth sliders will set the bandwidth at maximum at the top and minimum at the bottom. It just says "sync" at the top and "bw" at the bottom because there wasn't room to print "sync bandwidth" in one small space.

Using Thor's Filters

Thor's filters all have a drive control (which controls the signal level going into the filter); an Envelope Invert button (which you learned about in the Filter Envelope section of Chapter 5, "Malström"); an Envelope Amount knob; a Velocity knob, which determines how much the envelope amount will be affected by how hard you play; and a Keyboard Tracking knob. Although slightly different from the filters on other Reason devices, the Low Pass Ladder filter, the State Variable filter, and the Comb filter should all feel somewhat familiar to you. The one filter type Thor offers that is radically different from anything you've seen yet in Reason is the Formant filter.

Formant Filter

The word "formant" refers to the vowel sound resulting from a filter setting. Examples of formant filters would include the rubber end of a toilet plunger used on the bell of a trombone or trumpet, the way your mouth is positioned when playing a Jew's harp or when using a talk box for guitar, or a wah-wah pedal. You will understand what I mean just as soon as you start using this thing.

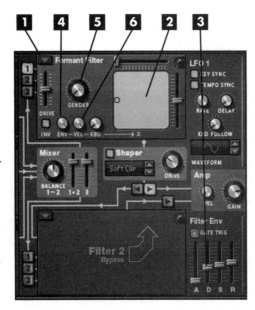

1 In a freshly initialized Thor, **click** the **arrow** in the upper-left corner of Filter 1 and **select Formant Filter** from the menu.

2 While playing your MIDI keyboard in the lower octaves, **drag** the little **"dot"** inside the gray rectangle panel up, down, and all around every which way. When you are finished, leave it in the far left of the gray rectangle, in the vertical middle.

3 **Decrease** the **Filter Envelope Decay slider** just a bit to a value of 1.9 seconds.

4 **Turn** the **Filter 1 Envelope Amount knob** all the way up to the right.

5 As you play your MIDI keyboard, slowly **turn** the **Gender knob** all the way to the right and then all the way to the left to hear its effect.

6 **Turn up** the **Velocity knob** all the way and **alternate playing** your **keyboard** very softly and very hard to hear the effect of velocity on the filter frequency.

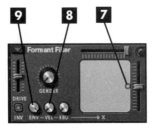

7 **Move** the **dot** all the way to the right, leaving it in the vertical middle.

8 **Turn** the **Velocity knob** all the way down (all the way to the left).

9 **Click** the **Envelope Invert button. Play** your MIDI **keyboard**, and you will hear very clearly how the filter envelope has been " flipped."

Self-Oscillation: The Original Gangsta Lead

One feature in Thor that none of the other Reason instruments has is self-oscillating filters. Thor's Low Pass Ladder filter and the State Variable filter both have this feature.

When you turn up the Resonance control on a filter, you are feeding back the output of the filter into the filter's input. This is the same as when a guitar feeds back with an amplifier (the guitar pickups and strings are part of the filter there) or when a mic feeds back with a PA system. That's why when you turn the Resonance control all the way up, the filter starts to scream. When a filter goes into self-oscillation, it feeds back on itself, even without any external input signal present. You can turn off your oscillator (sound source), and the filter will scream on its own. Specifically, it will produce a very pure sine wave.

I cannot prove this, but the word on the street is that Dr. Dre used this effect (made with an old analog synth with a self-oscillating filter) for some of the lead sounds on his highly influential solo debut album, *The Chronic*, including the hit "Let Me Ride." This lead sound became part of the musical vocabulary of rap and hip-hop. I am going to show you how to make this sound with Thor now, and if you compare it to the sound on the Dr. Dre tracks, you will find that it is about as close as it can be.

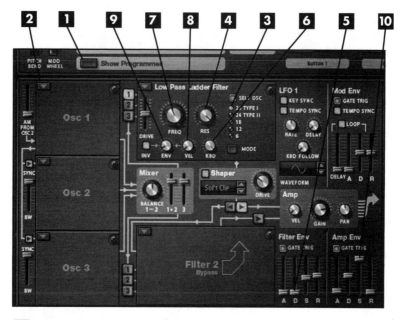

1 In an empty rack, **create** an instance of **Mixer 14:2**, followed by an instance of **Thor**. **Right-click** on **Thor** and **choose Initialize Patch**, and then **click** the **Show Programmer button**.

2 **Turn off Oscillator 1** by clicking the arrow in the upper-left corner and choosing Off from the menu. You will not hear anything when you play your keyboard now.

3 **Set** the **Filter 1 mode** to 24 Type 1.

4 **Turn up** the **Filter 1 Resonance knob** all the way. Now when you play your keyboard, you will hear a high, falling note.

5 **Move** the **Filter Envelope Decay** slider all the way down. Now the note you hear remains at a constant pitch, and every key plays the same note.

6 **Turn up** the **Filter 1 Keyboard knob** all the way. Now every key plays a different note, in semitone steps, and if you have a dog he's probably getting a bit irritated by now.

7 **Turn down** the **Filter 1 Frequency knob** to 521 Hz. Now the note is one octave lower.

8 So that velocity (how hard you play a note) does not affect the filter envelope amount (and thus affect the filter frequency), **turn down** the **Filter 1 Velocity knob** all the way to zero.

9 To fine-tune the pitch, **turn down** the **Filter Envelope Amount knob** to a value of 8.

10 **Move up** the **Amp Envelope Sustain slider** all the way.

Now you are absolutely ready to play the lead synth part from " Let Me Ride."
But what if you want to add a little pitch bend, like in "B****es Ain't S***?" If
you try your pitch bend right now, it won't do anything, because it defaults to
bending oscillator pitch, and you're not even using any oscillators. (The filter is producing the tone through self-oscillation.) No problem, thanks to Thor's Modulation
Bus Routing section. This next bit picks up at the end of the previous exercise.

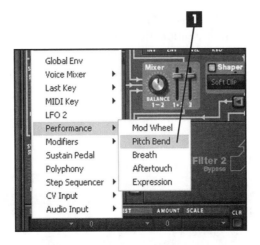

1 In the Modulation Bus
Routing section, **click** in
the **Source column** in the
first cell in the upper left
and **set Mod 1 Source** to
Performance > Pitch Bend.

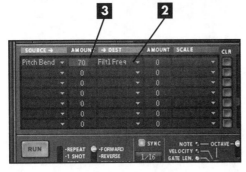

2 **Set Mod 1 Destination** to
Filter 1 > Frequency.

3 **Set Mod 1 Destination
Amount** to a value of 70.
Then try playing with the
pitch wheel on your MIDI
keyboard.

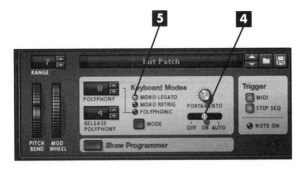

4 (Optional) **Turn
Portamento on**.

5 (Optional) **Switch** the
Keyboard mode to
Mono Legato and **play**
your MIDI **keyboard** to
hear what you've got.

There is another popular flavor of classic hip-hop lead sound that you are no
doubt familiar with, which is produced with a sawtooth wave instead of a sine
wave. You can probably think of numerous examples where this sound has been
used, but if you already have a copy of *The Chronic* handy (or YouTube.com), then
one track that uses the sound is "High Powered." There's already a Thor preset
that comes pretty close (Gangsta Lead 3).

1 **Load** the following **patch** into Thor: Reason Factory Sound Bank > Thor Patches > Gangsta Lead 3.thor. (This patch is also in Thor Patches > Lead Synths.)

2 If you want to get rid of the vibrato (I do), **click Show Programmer** and **proceed to Step 3.**

3 **Turn down Mod 1 Destination Amount** to zero.

4 If you want it to sound a little grittier and less polished, **turn off Chorus.**

5 If you really want to go dry as a bone, **turn off Delay** as well.

Thor's Shaper

Although Thor's Shaper is very similar in function to the Malström's Shaper, I will still take a moment here to introduce it to you. The Shaper provides a way to add different distortion types to a signal in Thor. It receives its signal from the output of Filter 1. I find that the more complex the signal you feed into the Shaper, the more interesting the result. I will leave much of that complexity up to your imagination and experimentation. The following example is rather simple.

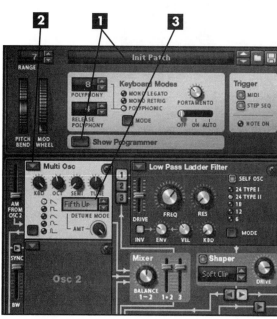

1 In a fresh rack containing Thor, **right-click** on **Thor** and **choose Initialize Patch**, and then **click** the **Show Programmer button.**

2 **Click** the **arrow** in the upper-left corner of Oscillator 1 and **choose Multi Oscillator.**

3 **Choose Fifth Up** for the Oscillator 1 Detune mode.

4 **Turn up** the **Oscillator 1 Detune Amount knob** all the way and **play** some **medium to low notes** on your MIDI keyboard to hear the sound.

5 **Click** on the **Shaper On button** to activate the Shaper.

6 **Turn** the **Shaper Drive knob** up to 3 o'clock and **play** your MIDI **keyboard** to hear the sound.

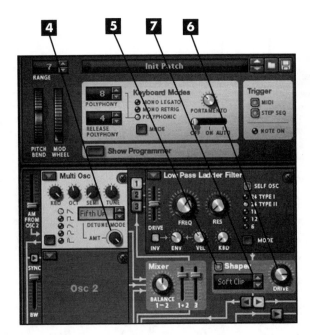

7 **Use** the **up/down arrows** to try all the different Shaper modes while you play your keyboard. Be careful. The Wrap mode is quite loud.

8 **Select Sine** for the Shaper mode.

9 While playing a low note your MIDI keyboard, smoothly **move** the **Filter 1 Drive slider** all the way down, then all the way up, and finally back to the middle to hear the effect.

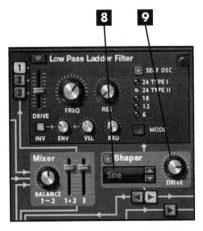

The Shaper is just one more thing you can try if you are looking to add a little extra something to your sound. You can use it to warm up your sound subtly or to not-so-subtly completely shred and obliterate your sound.

Basic Audio Signal Routing in Thor

You probably are already getting a feel for the audio signal routing in Thor, but if you ever get a bit confused, I hope the following tutorial will help set things straight in your brain. Also, just remember that Thor has little arrows all over the place showing the direction and path of the audio signal, so it's all pretty self-explanatory anyway.

1 In a fresh rack containing Thor, **right-click** on **Thor** and **choose Initialize Patch**, and then **click** the **Show Programmer button**. **Play** a few **notes** on your keyboard to hear Oscillator 1 going through Filter 1.

2 **Choose Multi Oscillator** for Oscillator 2.

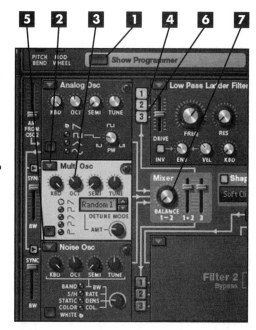

3 **Turn down** the **Oscillator 2 Octave knob** one notch to a value of 3. You will not hear anything new because Oscillator 2 is not routed anywhere yet.

4 **Click** the **Oscillator 2 to Filter 1 Enable button**. Now you will clearly hear Oscillator 2 added to the mix.

5 **Choose Noise** for Oscillator 3. You will not hear anything new because Oscillator 3 is not routed anywhere yet.

6 **Click** the **Oscillator 3 to Filter 1 Enable button**. Now you will clearly hear Oscillator 3 added to the mix.

7 **Play** your MIDI **keyboard** as you turn the Mixer Balance knob all the way to the left. You will only hear Oscillators 1 and 3.

8 **Play** your MIDI **keyboard** as you turn the Mixer Balance knob all the way to the right. You will only hear Oscillators 2 and 3.

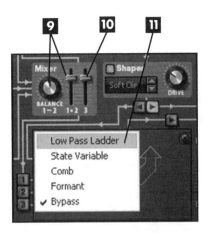

9 Turn the **Balance knob** back to the center and then **move down** the **Oscillator 1 + 2 Level slider**, and you will only hear Oscillator 3 when you play your keyboard. When you are finished, **move** the **1 + 2 slider** back up.

10 While playing your MIDI keyboard, **move** the **Oscillator 3 Level slider** all the way down and then back up again.

11 Select **Low Pass Ladder** for Filter 2.

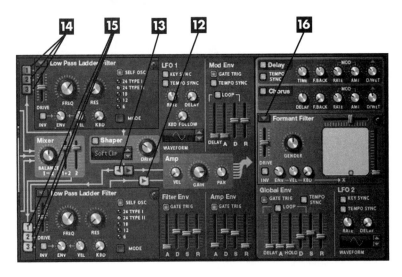

12 Click the **Filter 2 to Amplifier Enable button** to route Filter 2 to the amplifier. You will not hear anything different because nothing is routed to Filter 2 yet.

13 Click the **left routing arrow** just below the Shaper. **Play** your MIDI **keyboard**, and you will hear a mellower sound because the signal from Filter 1 is passing through Filter 2 on its way to the amp. The signal from the oscillators is being filtered twice.

14 Turn off all three of the **Oscillator to Filter 1 routing buttons**. Now you won't hear anything.

15 Turn on all three of the **Oscillator to Filter 2 routing buttons**. Now the signal from the oscillators is going straight through Filter 2 and never touching Filter 1.

16 Click the **arrow** in the upper-left corner of Filter 3 and **choose Formant Filter**. Anything coming out of the amp goes through Filter 3. **Play** your MIDI **keyboard**, and you will hear obvious proof that I am telling the truth.

The last two stops on the signal's path after Filter 3 are Chorus and Delay. Feel free to turn those on at the end of the last exercise if you want. After Delay, there is only Thor's Master Volume and then out to Thor's audio outputs. Also (going back a few steps), remember that the Shaper (not used in the preceding exercise) only processes the signal from Filter 1. It will not touch the signal from Filter 2.

Modulation Bus Routing Section

The previous section dealt with audio routing. This section deals primarily with modulation routing (although Thor's Modulation Bus Routing section can actually be used to route both modulation *and* audio). You have already been using the Modulation Bus Routing section throughout this chapter, but I want to take a moment to focus on it. The Modulation Bus Routing section allows you to modulate (control) any part of Thor with any other part of Thor in nearly any way you can think of, and it also allows you to create audio signal paths beyond those available using Thor's routing buttons.

Each row in the Modulation Bus Routing section is a separate modulation bus. For our purposes, the word "bus" simply refers to a circuit where multiple devices share the same connection. It may look complicated, but once you understand its concept, you will realize that it is actually quite simple but powerful at the same time.

Here are the terms you will see all over the Modulation Bus Routing section:

- ❋ **Source.** The modulator that will modulate the destination. For example, if LFO 1 is modulating Oscillator 1 Pitch, then LFO 1 is the source, and Oscillator 1 is the destination.
- ❋ **(Destination) Amount.** The amount by which the destination will be modulated by the source.
- ❋ **Destination.** The parameter that will be modulated.
- ❋ **(Scale) Amount.** The degree to which the destination amount will be affected by another parameter, such as Modulation Wheel or Amp Envelope.
- ❋ **Scale.** Allows you to modulate the destination amount with another parameter, such as Modulation Wheel, LFO1, and so on.

Once you try a few simple examples, you are sure to get it. As we go through the exercises, I will refer to Modulation Bus 1, Modulation Bus 2, and so on. But you will notice that the busses do not appear to be numbered. As long as you have Show Parameter Value Tool Tips selected on the General page of your Reason Preferences, then you can mouse over any Amount value and see Mod 1 or Mod 2 pop up, so you will know which bus you are on without having to count.

Modulation Busses 1 through 8

The first eight busses (rows) on the left are the simplest, so we'll start with those.

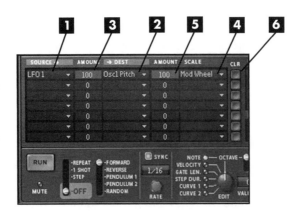

1 In a freshly initialized Thor with the Show Programmer button activated, **click** on **Modulation Bus 1 Source** and **choose LFO 1** from the pop-up menu.

2 **Click** on **Modulation Bus 1 Destination** and **choose OSC1 Pitch** from the pop-up menu.

3 **Hold down** a **note or chord** on your MIDI keyboard while you **click and drag** upward on **Modulation Bus 1 Destination Amount**, setting it to a value of 100. Sounds pretty wacky now.

4 **Set Modulation Bus 1 Scale Source** to Performance > Mod Wheel.

5 **Hold down** a **note or chord** on your MIDI keyboard while you **click and drag** upward on **Modulation Bus 1 Scale Amount**, setting it to a value of 100. Then try using the Modulation wheel (or joystick) on your MIDI keyboard to control the amount of LFO 1 to Osc 1 pitch.

6 **Click** the **Clear button** on Modulation Bus 1, and it will be as though Steps 2 through 5 never happened.

Modulation Busses 8 through 11

The second group of four modulation busses (8 through 11) allows a second destination to be modulated by the same source. You will be using LFO 2 in this exercise, which is in the brown Global section of Thor's Programmer.

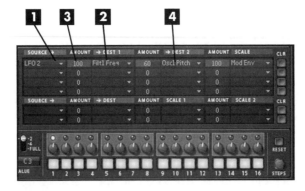

1 In a freshly initialized Thor, **choose LFO 2** for Modulation Bus 8 Source.

2 **Set Modulation Bus 8 Destination 1** to Filter 1 Frequency.

3 **Hold down** a **note or chord** on your MIDI keyboard while you **click and drag** upward on **Modulation Bus 8 Destination 1 Amount**, setting it to a value of 100.

4 **Set Modulation Bus 8 Destination 2** to Oscillator 1 Pitch.

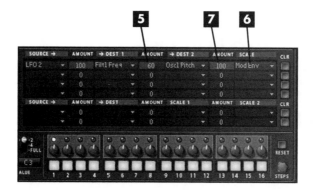

5 Hold down a note or chord on your MIDI keyboard while you click and drag upward on **Modulation Bus 8 Destination 2 Amount**, setting it to a value of 60.

6 Set the **Modulation Bus 8 Scale parameter** to Mod Env.

7 Click and drag upward on **Modulation Bus 8 Scale Amount**, setting it to a value of 100. Play a key or chord on your MIDI keyboard, and you will hear the modulation amount decrease as the modulation envelope (Mod Env) goes through the decay portion of its envelope.

8 Move up the **Mod Envelope Attack slider** so it is even with the Decay and Release sliders. Then play a note on your MIDI keyboard, and you will hear the attack portion of the modulation envelope scaling the effect of LFO 2.

9 Click the **Clear button** on Modulation Bus 8 to erase any evidence.

Modulation Busses 12 and 13

Each of the final two modulation busses has only one destination but includes an extra Scale parameter. This section provides a very simple example of how this might be used.

1 In a freshly initialized Thor, **choose LFO 1** for Modulation Bus 12 Source.

2 **Select Oscillator 1 Pitch** for Modulation Bus 12 Destination.

3 **Click and drag** upward on **Modulation Bus 12 Destination Amount**, setting it to a value of 100.

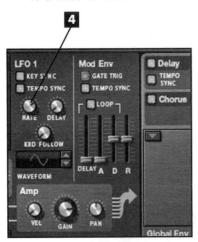

4 **Turn up** the **LFO 1 Rate knob** to a value of 10.1 Hz (just past 2 o'clock) and **play** a **note** on your MIDI keyboard. It sounds like a sound effect from a 1970s anime.

5 **Turn down** the **LFO 2 Rate knob** to a value of 0.20 Hz (almost 9 o'clock).

6 **Choose LFO 2** for Modulation Bus 12 Scale 1.

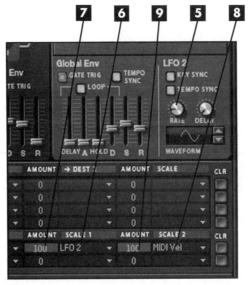

7 **Click and drag** upward on **Modulation Bus 12 Scale 1 Amount**, setting it to a value of 100. **Play and hold** a note on your MIDI **keyboard** to hear LFO 1's amount being modulated by the slow sine wave from LFO 2.

8 **Choose MIDI Key > Velocity** (MIDI Vel) for Modulation Bus 12 Scale 2.

9 **Click and drag** upward on **Modulation Bus 12 Scale 2 Amount**, setting it to a value of 100.

After you complete Step 9, playing your MIDI keyboard very gently will produce a smaller modulation effect, while playing it harder will produce a stronger effect.

Routing Trick: Backward Thor

This last trick is some pretty fancy routing. It might not get you a record deal, but you may be able to win $5 off your friend if you bet him that you can make your keyboard play backward.

1 With a freshly initialized Thor, **hit** the **Tab key** on your computer keyboard to flip your rack around and **click** the **Show Programmer button**.

2 **Click and drag** to create a **cable connection** between Thor's CV 1 Modulation Output and the CV1 Modulation Input.

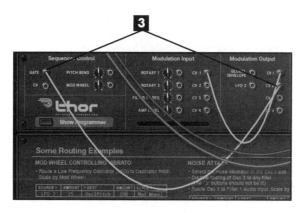

3 **Connect CV 2 Modulation Output** to the Sequencer Control Gate Input.

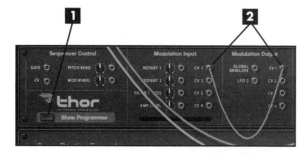

4 **Hit Tab** to flip your rack back around and **click** on the **Note Trigger MIDI button** to disable it.

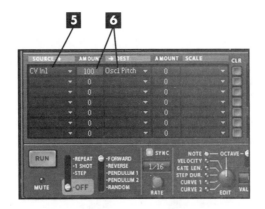

5 **Select CV Input > 1** for Modulation Bus 1 Source.

6 **Choose Oscillator 1 Pitch** for Modulation Bus 1 Destination and **set Modulation Bus 1 Destination Amount** to 100.

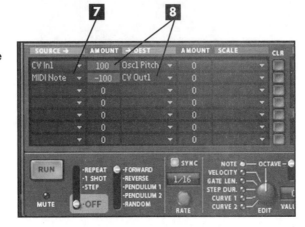

7 **Select MIDI Key > Note** for Modulation Bus 2 Source.

8 **Select CV Output > 1** for Modulation Bus 2 Destination and **click and drag** *down* on **Modulation Bus 2 Destination Amount**, setting it to a value of −100.

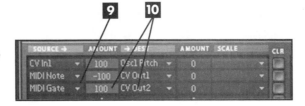

9 **Select MIDI Key > Gate** for Modulation Bus 3 Source.

10 **Select CV Output > 2** for Modulation Bus 3 Destination and **set Modulation Bus 3 Destination Amount** to a value of 100.

11 **Turn up Amp Envelope Sustain** all the way.

Now play your MIDI keyboard, and up will be down and down will be up. It will be monophonic (because CV Gate is monophonic), but you still deserve to win the $5. But remember that if you try to *save* the patch, the cable connections in the back will not be saved (unless you right-click on Thor, choose Combine, and then save the patch as a Combinator patch instead of a Thor patch). You'll learn more about saving rear-panel routing in Combinator patches in Chapter 8, "The Combinator."

I hope these exercises have taken some of the mystery out of the Modulation Bus Routing section. By the way, I truly have too much to cover in this chapter to get into it here, but the Rotary 1 and Rotary 2 knobs, as well as Button 1 and Button 2 on Thor's Controller panel (the top panel), are assignable within the Modulation Bus Routing section. They can be assigned to control whatever parameters you want. If you're curious, this is explained on the very first page of the Thor chapter in the Reason Operation Manual in the section entitled "About the Virtual Controls."

LFO 1 versus LFO 2

Thor's low-frequency oscillators are small but mighty. Their function should feel familiar to you. Before getting into the exercises, here are a few brief notes on Thor's LFO controls.

The Tempo Sync button found on LFO 1 and 2 is just like the Sync button on Subtractor's LFOs and the Malström's modulators. It simply syncs the LFO to the song tempo. The Delay knob found on LFO 1 and 2 works exactly the same way as the Delay knob on Subtractor's LFO 2. It causes the LFO to wait a second or two before it starts modulating, allowing a note to sound purely for a second before vibrato is applied, for example. The Waveform selector is similar to the Waveform selector in the Malström's modulators A and B. Of course, the Rate knob controls how fast the LFO modulates. There is no LFO Amount knob because in Thor, this will be set in the Modulation Bus Routing section.

Key Sync

The ability to turn on and off Key Sync is a feature unique to Thor. If Key Sync is off, the LFO modulation may start at any point in the LFO waveform cycle when you play a note. If Key Sync is on, each time you play a note, the LFO cycle is reset, and modulation starts from the beginning of the LFO waveform cycle. This is easy to understand if you try it out.

1 In a freshly initialized Thor, **set Modulation Bus 1 Source** to LFO 2.

2 Set **Modulation Bus 1 Destination** to Oscillator 1 Pitch.

3 Click and drag upward on **Modulation Bus 1 Destination Amount**, setting it to a value of 100.

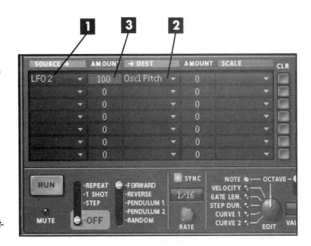

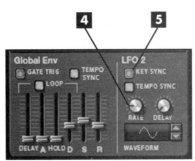

4 Turn down the **LFO 2 Rate knob** to 9 o'clock (value of 0.22 Hz). Then **play** a **note** on your MIDI keyboard and let go, over and over again, about once every second. You will hear the note start at a different point in LFO 2's slow sine wave each time.

5 Click the **LFO 2 Key Sync button** to activate it. Then **play** your MIDI **keyboard** as you did in Step 4, and this time it will start at the same pitch each time. In fact, if you look at the picture in the LFO 2 Waveform Display, you can see the shape you're hearing.

It is interesting to note that the Malström's Modulators A and B (the Malström LFOs) are always "key synced," while Subtractor's LFOs are not key synced; rather, they are always free running.

LFO 1 Keyboard Follow

Keyboard tracking is a feature you find in various forms throughout the Reason synths. In an oscillator, it determines to what extent pitch is affected by which key you play. In a filter, it determines to what extent the filter frequency is affected by which key you play. The LFO 1 Keyboard Follow knob on Thor works exactly the same way as the LFO 2 Keyboard Tracking knob on Subtractor. It determines to what extent the LFO rate is affected by which key you play. Low keys will have a slower rate, and high keys will have a faster rate.

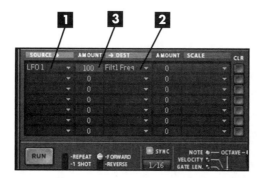

1 In a freshly initialized Thor, **set Modulation Bus 1 Source** to LFO 1.

2 **Set Modulation Bus 1 Destination** to Filter 1 Frequency.

3 **Click and drag** upward on **Modulation Bus 1 Destination Amount**, setting it to a value of 100. **Play** some **keys** on your MIDI keyboard, and you will hear that the filter frequency is modulated at the same rate no matter what key you play.

4 **Turn** the **LFO 1 Keyboard Follow knob** all the way to the right. Now when you play your MIDI keyboard, low keys will have the filter frequency modulated slowly, while high keys will have faster modulation.

Thor, Meet the BV512 Digital Vocoder

Used through the years by musical acts including Kraftwerk, Pink Floyd, Herbie Hancock, Wendy Carlos, Laurie Anderson, and Earth, Wind & Fire, the vocoder has been part of music since the 1970s. You may be surprised to find out that the technology (in its original, non-musical form) has been around since the 1930s.

Typically, a vocoder is used in the following way: A carrier signal (created by a synthesizer and controlled by a keyboard) is modulated by another signal (created by a human voice speaking or singing into a microphone). This creates the musically pitched "robot voice" with which we are all familiar. Reason's BV512 Digital Vocoder can work in the same way (provided you use a sampled voice). However, in the following examples you will be doing something a little different: You will be using Thor for the carrier signal (which is perfectly normal), but you will be modulating that signal with a beat from Dr.Rex instead of a voice.

1 In an empty rack, **create** an **MClass Mastering Suite**, followed by **Mixer 14:2** and an instance of **Thor**. Then **load** the following **patch** into Thor: Reason Factory Sound Bank > Thor Patches > Lead Synths > Combing Lead.

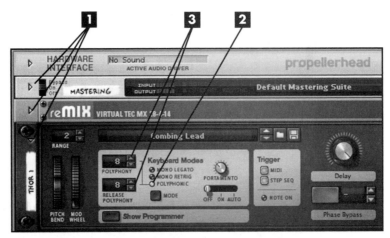

2 **Set** Thor's **Keyboard mode** to Polyphonic.

3 **Turn up Polyphony** and **Release Polyphony** to a value of (at least) 8. Then **play** a few **notes** to hear this sound.

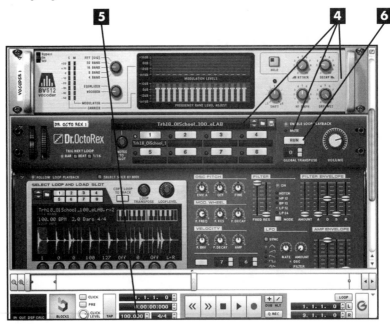

4 Underneath Thor, **create** a **BV512 Digital Vocoder** followed by an instance of **Dr.Rex**. Then **load** the following **patch** into Dr.Rex: Reason Factory Sound Bank > Dr Rex Drum Loops > Abstract HipHop > Trh18_OlSchool_100eLab.rx2.

5 In the Reason Sequencer, **turn down** the **tempo** to 100.

6 **Click** the **Run button** on Dr.Rex to hear the beat and then **click Run** again once you' ve heard the beat (so that Preview will stop).

7 **Click Tab** to flip the rack around and then **drag** the **cables** out of Dr.Rex's audio outputs. The cables should disappear.

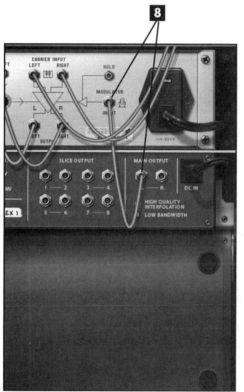

8 **Drag** a **cable** from Dr.Rex's left audio output to the BV512 Vocoder's Modulator Input.

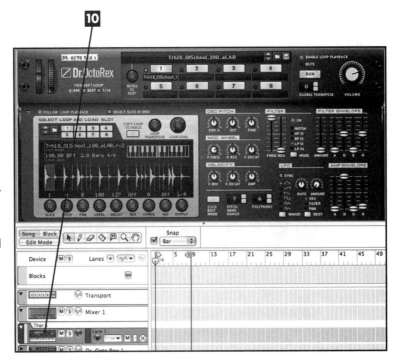

9 Click **Tab** to flip the rack back around facing front and then **click** the **Run button** on Dr.Rex to activate it. You will not hear anything yet.

10 Select the **Thor 1 track** in the Reason Sequencer by clicking on the Thor keyboard icon, and then **play** some **chords** on your MIDI keyboard. You should hear a vocoded drum beat.

Now let's set things up so you can have a sequence playing hands-free while you twiddle knobs elsewhere. The next bit picks up where the previous bit left off.

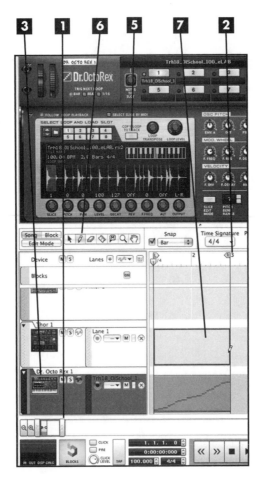

1 Drag the **Horizontal Zoom handle** to the left to increase zoom until you have a nice view of individual bars and quarter-note marks.

2 Alt–click on the **timeline** at Bar 3, and the right locator will jump there.

3 Select the **Dr.REX 1 Sequencer track** by clicking on the Dr.Rex icon.

4 Turn off **Run** on Dr.Rex.

5 Click the **Copy Loop to Track button** on Dr.Rex.

6 Select the **Pencil tool**.

7 On the Thor 1 track in the Reason Sequencer, **draw** in a 2-bar **clip** starting at Bar 1.

8 **Choose** your **Selection tool**.

9 **Double-click** on the **clip** you have just created.

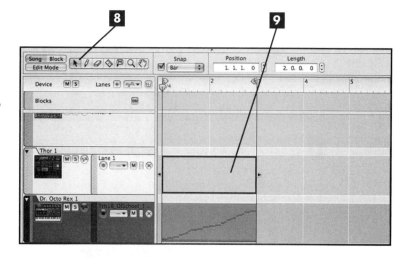

10 **Select** the **Pencil tool**.

11 **Set** the **Snap value** to Bar.

12 **Draw** in **notes** on Bar 1 and Bar 2 at D4, C4, A3, and D2.

13 **Make sure Loop** is on in the Reason Sequencer.

14 **Click** the **Play button**, and you should hear your vocoded beat.

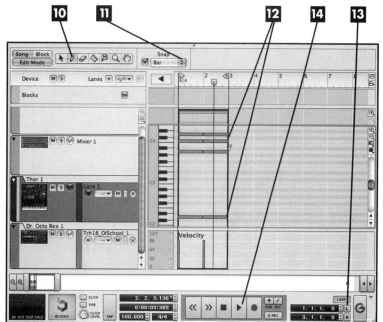

Now while you are listening to your beat:

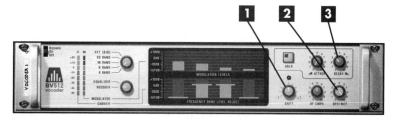

1 Slowly **turn** the BV512's **Shift knob** all the way to the right, all the way to the left, and then back to center to hear the effect.

2 Slowly **turn** the BV512's **Dry/Wet knob** all the way to the left and then back all the way to the right.

3 Slowly **turn** the BV512's **Decay knob** all the way to the right and then back to its original value of 42 (just past the 3 mark).

173

❊ ❊ ❊

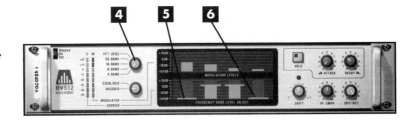

4 **Switch** the **Band Count selector knob** to the 4 Band position.

5 **Drag** the **first band** on the left all the way down in the Frequency Band Level Adjust section.

6 **Drag** the **fourth band** all the way down.

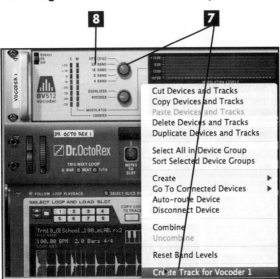

7 **Turn** all the **frequency bands** back up where they were and then **right-click** on the **BV512 Vocoder** and **select Create Track for Vocoder 1**.

8 Turn the Band Count selector knob to the 32 Band position. Then one key at a time, play the notes on your keyboard between C1 and G3. Be careful. The closer you get to G3, the more dangerously loud the sound will become. When you play up near G3, play as softly as you can.

Besides being a fun way to make cool sounds, being able to play the vocoder's individual bands on the keyboard is helpful for deciding which bands you want to boost or cut. This could be useful when using a voice recording (instead of a drum beat) as a modulator, as you may find that cutting or boosting certain bands will make the vocoded signal more intelligible or help it to fit into (or cut through) the mix better.

The last vocoder trick I want to show you may seem rather novel. Instead of using a melodic sound for the carrier signal, you will use noise. Here is a chance to try Thor's Noise Oscillator. This exercise picks up where the previous exercise left off.

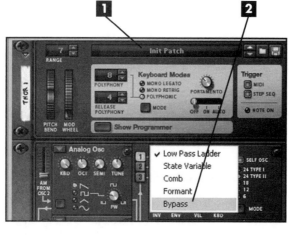

1 With your sequence playing, **right-click** on **Thor** and **choose Initialize Patch**.

2 **Click** the **arrow** in the upper-left corner of Filter 1 and **choose Bypass** from the pop-up menu.

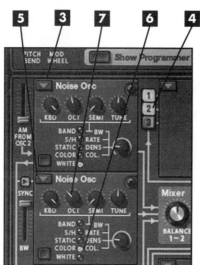

3 **Click** the **arrow** in the upper-left corner of Oscillator 1 and **choose Noise** from the pop-up menu. The noise type will be White Noise by default.

4 **Click** the **Oscillator 2 to Filter 1 Enable button** so that it lights up red.

5 **Click** the **arrow** in the upper-left corner of Oscillator 2 and **choose Noise** from the pop-up menu.

6 **Choose Color** for the Oscillator 2 Noise Type.

7 **Turn down** the **Oscillator 2 Octave knob** to a value of 3.

8 **Move** Thor's **Amp Envelope Decay slider** all the way up to the top.

9 On the BV512, **switch** the **Band Count knob** to 4 Band.

10 **Turn up Vocoder Decay** to 5 (halfway up).

11 **Turn down Vocoder Shift** all the way to −1.

12 **Turn** the **Dry/Wet knob** all the way to the Dry position to hear what you started with, and then **turn it** back to the Wet position to hear how far you've come.

Can you believe that all that sound is really just coming from Thor's noise oscillators? Sounds pretty heavy. By the way, if you turn the BV512 Decay knob all the way up, it will really sound like noise—kind of like the ocean (but with a straighter beat).

❊ BUT WHAT IF I WANT TO USE MY VOCODER FOR VOICE?

Obviously, Reason does not have an audio input, so you cannot plug in a mic and vocode your voice live through Reason. What you *can* do is record yourself in another program (for free, there's Windows Voice Recorder built into your PC or GarageBand included with your Mac). Record yourself saying "domo arigato Mr. Roboto" or "by your command" and save it as a WAV file. Browse to that WAV file from one of Reason's sample browsers (a Redrum channel or NN-19 would be simplest) and load the WAV file into the device. In the exercises you just completed, Redrum or NN-19 would take the place of Dr.Rex as the modulator, while Thor would remain the carrier. You will need MIDI info for the notes or chords Thor will play, as well as for the trigger note for Redrum or the NN-19.

Before you move on to learning about Reason's sample players, I have one last tip for you. If you enjoy making your own sounds with Thor and messing around "under the hood," then flip your rack around, make sure you have clicked Thor's Show Programmer button, and go through the routing examples printed on the back of Thor. They are really cool and useful.

The Reason Samplers:
NN-19 and NN-XT

For electronic sounds, you are most likely to use Thor, Subtractor, or Malström. For realistic acoustic instrument sounds (such as pianos, orchestral instruments, and the like), the NN-19 and NN-XT samplers are the way to go.

Technically speaking, a true sampler has the ability to sample—that is, it can record a sound and then play it back. The hardware samplers from which the Propellerhead programmers drew their inspiration had that feature. Up until now, the NN-19 and the NN-XT could not record sounds; they could only play back sounds. That is, until Reason 5 came along and added the ability to sample for several of its instruments, such as Redrum, Kong, and now the NN-XT and NN-19.

Both Reason samplers also have extensive ways to tweak the sounds once you have loaded them. For example, WAV, AIFF, Rex, or SoundFonts (.sf2) files can be loaded into either of the Reason samplers. To make things even more grandiose, Reason comes with loads of great sample patches in the Reason Factory Sound Bank and the Orkester Sound Bank.

In this chapter, you will learn how to:

❋ Record single samples into the NN-19 and NN-XT

❋ Edit samples recorded in Reason

❋ Load single samples into the NN-19 and NN-XT and assign them to specific keys

❋ Create keyboard splits so that part of the keyboard triggers one sample while another part triggers another sample

❋ Create velocity layers in the NN-XT so that playing softly triggers one sample while playing harder triggers another sample

❋ Tweak the tuning, looping, root key, and start/end points of your samples

Sampling with the NN-19 and NN-19

In Chapter 3, I showed you how to set up your sampling input within Reason 5. If you haven't done this yet, please refer back to Chapter 3. When you've completed this step, you can move on to this section and feel very confident in how this tutorial will go.

Sampling with the NN-19

Now that you're ready, let's get going! It's actually incredibly easy to sample on either sampler. Let's start with the NN-19. For this first exercise, start with an empty rack.

Create a Mixer 14:2 and an **NN-19 sampler.**

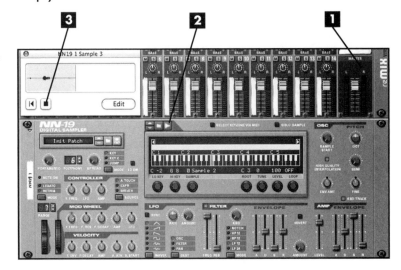

2 **Click** the **Sample button** on the NN-19. Instantly, Reason will start recording. Record into your microphone or whatever is connected to your sampling input. For more information on the setting up the sampling input, please refer to Chapter 3.

3 **Click** the **Stop button** when you have finished recording.

4 **Play** your **MIDI controller**, if you have one, or **press F4** to turn on On-screen Piano Keys. You will notice that you are now able to play back your sample across the different keys.

You can also split the keys and have different samples on different keys. Later in this chapter, we'll go over how to split keys with recorded sounds from the Reason Factory Sound Bank. It's the exact same principle, so I highly recommend going through them.

Now, let's move on to the NN-XT.

Sampling with the NN-XT

Of the two samplers of Reason, the NN-XT is by far the most complete and comprehensive. It offers everything an old hardware sampler had and more. But because it's so comprehensive, there are quite a few buttons floating around on this thing. Let me guide you to the Sampling button.

Click the small arrow at the base of the NN-XT; this will open up the sampler and reveal all of its functions. Before starting the exercise, take this opportunity to delete the NN-19 from your rack and create an NN-XT.

Now, let's sample with the NN-XT.

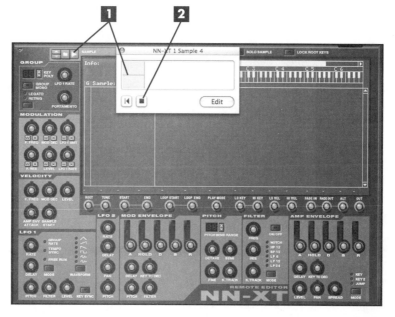

1 **Click** the **Sample button** on the NN-XT. This will immediately trigger the recording process, so have your audio source ready. (Be ready to sing, play, and so on.)

As you record, you'll see a waveform in the recorder. If nothing appears and you're screaming, you may need to refer back to Chapter 3 for information on setting up your sampling input.

2 **Click** the **Stop button**, and your recording will conclude. At this point, you can play your MIDI controller or use F4 to trigger On-screen Piano Keys. You'll be able to melodically play your recorded part.

This is pretty fun and simple so far, right? It's almost like taking a quick picture, but you're snapping off pieces of sound instead.

However, you may have run into something with the last sample you recorded that will lead to the inevitable question, " What if I want to edit what I recorded?"

You probably noticed an Edit button during the recording/sampling process. And, indeed, you can use this button to stop recording and go immediately to editing. In the next exercise, though, I'll show you another way to get there.

Editing Samples in Reason

So you've gotten the perfect sample of your dog barking! It's loud, crisp, full, and captures the spirit of canine angst amongst a world full of chaos. However, right before the dog barked, immediately after you hit the Sample button, the cat meowed!

What results is a scenario in which, when you hit the appropriate key on your MIDI controller, you hear a meow and then a bark. You'd rather set it up so you just have the bark, right?

This is a brilliant moment to learn how to cut out the cat so that the dog can shine through. Note: No disrespect is intended toward cats!

For this exercise, you can use any old sample you've recorded from the previous exercise. Odds are, your sample isn't perfect. In fact, the odds are greatest that you have a good recording, but there's some extra silence at the end. I'm going to show you how to edit that out with one of the main functions you'll use with the Editor: Crop.

Again, you'll want to have a sample already recorded before we start this exercise. If you haven't recorded a whistle, a dog bark, a burp, or whatever, go back to the previous exercise and do it now.

1 With your NN-XT loaded up with your freshly recorded sample, **make sure** the **NN-XT** is selected. (If it's selected it will have a thin blue line around it; if not, simply click the NN-XT once to put focus on it.) **Go to** the **Edit menu** and **select Edit Sample**.

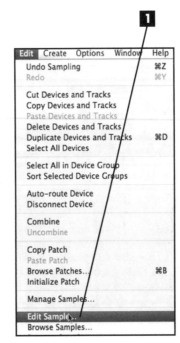

The Reason Sample Editor will appear immediately after this and present your recorded waveform to you. From this editor, you can play your sample, adjust the Loop mode, undo/redo your edits, and rename your sample. These are important functions as you move forward.

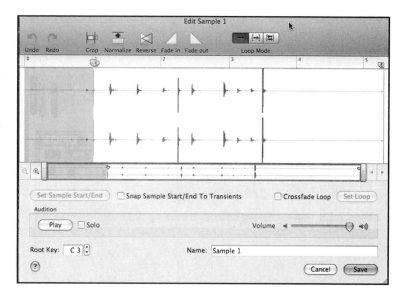

2 Let's crop the sample. **Select** the **area** of the sample that you want to keep by clicking on the waveform and dragging the blue field that will appear around the recorded area that you want.

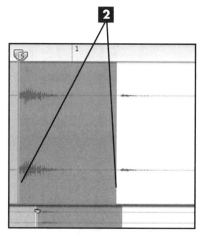

3 After you've selected the portion of the recording you want, **click** the **Play button** to verify that this is the point of the recording that you want.

4 If you're happy with the selection, **click** the **Crop button**. If you made a mistake, **click** the **Undo button**.

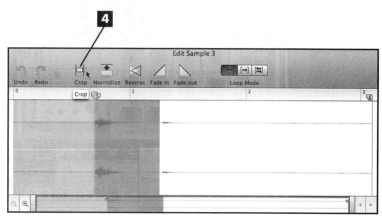

5 Now you'll notice that the waveform is much smaller and only reveals the area of the sample that you want. If this is good, **name** your **sample** and **click Save**.

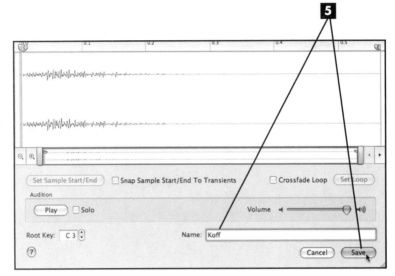

And that's really it. To manipulate the sample, simply highlight the area that you want to modify with the Crop, Reverse, or Fade command and then press the function that you want to take place. For example, if you want to fade out the end of a sample, highlight the end of the sample where you want the fade to start and end and click Fade Out.

If you want to loop your sample, select the desired Loop mode. Also, if you'd like to increase the overall volume of your sample, highlight the area of the sample that you want louder or simply click Normalize.

Now that you know how to create and edit your own samples, let's move on to loading preexisting samples into the NN-19 and NN-XT samplers.

NN-19 Brief History

The NN-19 is the older of the two Reason samplers. It has basic and familiar synth parameters, and although you may end up using the more powerful NN-XT much of the time, you may still find a place in your heart for the ol' NN-19.

Loading Samples into the NN-19

The Reason Sound Banks come with numerous patches for the NN-19 and NN-XT. These patches contain multiple samples mapped all over the keyboard, and I'm sure you will have no problem loading those preset sample patches. It is just like loading Malström or Subtractor patches. What you are going to do now is load an individual sample.

1 In a fresh rack containing an NN-19, **right-click** on the **NN-19** and **choose Initialize Patch**.

2 **Click** on the **Browse Sample button** and **select Orkester Sound Bank > Percussion > Gong GNG > GNG_F.aif**. Then **play** your **MIDI keyboard** to hear the gong automatically re-pitched for each key.

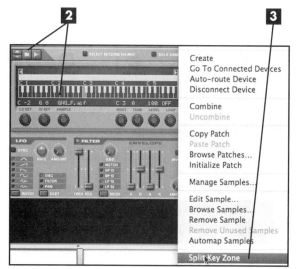

3 **Right-click** on the **NN-19** and **choose Split Key Zone**. You will not hear the gong on any keys above D♯3 anymore, and you will see the key zone handle.

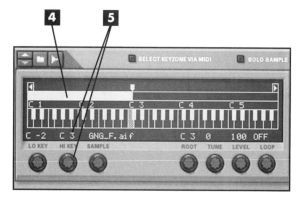

4 **Click** to select the **key zone** for the left half of the keyboard. It will turn bright blue.

5 **Turn** the **High Key knob** down to a value of C3 (which is also the root key). You will now hear the gong only when you play C3 and below.

6 **Click** to select the **key zone** for the right half of the keyboard. It will turn bright blue.

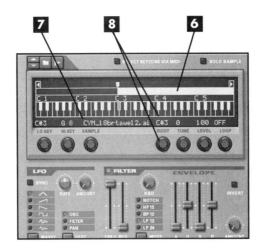

7 **Click** on the **Browse Sample button** and **select Orkester Sound Bank > Percussion > Cymbals > CYM_18brtswel2.aif.**

8 **Change** the **root key** to C#3. The cymbal sample will now play at its original speed when you play C#3 and will play faster with each key higher than that.

Now you have gongs on the left and cymbal swells on the right. By the way, think of a key zone as a container for a sample. A key zone contains only one sample. However, several key zones may be set to have the same key range (keys C0 to C6, for example).

Assigning a Single Sample to a Single Key

There are times when you want a single sample on a single key. Maybe you want to play one key and have it trigger a long sample (such as a piece of a song or beat, or even an entire song). Or you might want to trigger a vocal sample or a sound effect. Also, if you are building a drum kit, you will probably want a different sample on each key. This would be the same if you were assigning samples to drum pads (such as those found on an M-Audio Trigger Finger or on the Akai MP series controllers). All you have to do is make the key zone include only a single key.

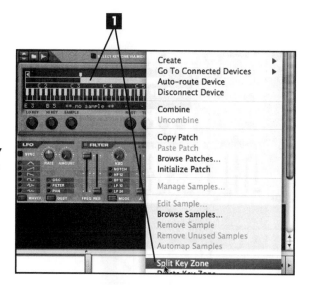

1 In a fresh NN-19 for which you have applied Initialize Patch, **right-click** on the **NN-19** and **choose Split Key Zone**. Do this four times. Then **click** in the **key zone** to the right of the key zone handle to select the key zone starting at E3.

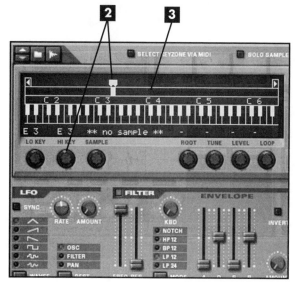

2 **Turn** the **High Key knob** down to E3. Now you have a single-note key zone.

3 **Click** in the big **key zone** to the right of the key zone handle at E3 to select it.

4 Turn the **High Key knob** down to F3. Now you have a second single-note key zone.

5 Click in the big **key zone** to the right of the key zone handle at F3 to select it.

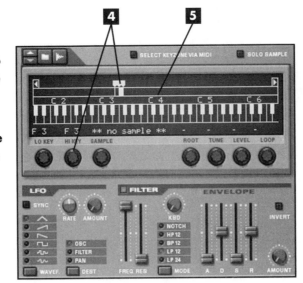

6 Turn the **High Key knob** down to F♯3. Now you have a third single-note key zone.

7 With the F♯3 key zone still selected, **click** the **Browse Sample button** and **load Orkester Sound Bank > Percussion > Castanets CST > CST_Roll.aif.**

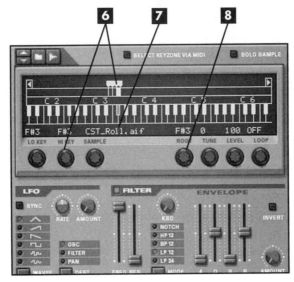

8 Turn the **root key** up to F♯3 (so it matches the low/high key of your key zone).

9 Click in the **F3 key zone** (the one in the middle) to select it and then **load** the sample **Orkester Sound Bank > Percussion > Fingercymbals FCY > FCYa_Grace.aif.**

10 Turn the **root key** up to F3 (so it matches the low/high key of your key zone).

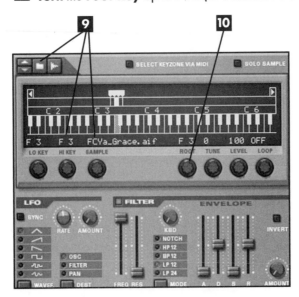

186

✻ ✻ ✻

11 **Click** in the **E3 key zone** to select it and then **load** the sample **Orkester Sound Bank > Percussion > Cymbals CYM > CYN_20swpbrsh2.aif**.

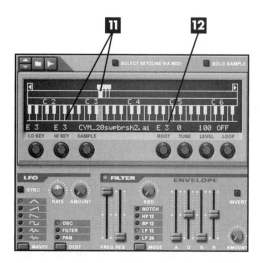

12 **Turn** the **root key** up to E3 (so it matches the low/high key of your key zone). Now you have three correctly pitched samples mapped to the individual keys of your choosing (E3, F3, and F♯3).

Note that by default, the root key (the key on which the sample plays at its original speed) of any sample you load is C3 unless the sample file actually has a root key in parentheses in the filename, such as a harp sample named HRP_F(A#5).aif. In that case, the NN-19 will correctly assign the root key as A♯5.

NN-19 Synth Parameter Exercise: Precise LFO Pitch Modulation

I assume that most people use the Reason samplers for orchestral and other "real" sounds, and they use Subtractor, Malström, and Thor for synth stuff. Those synths use mathematical algorithms to emulate synth sounds. However, the Reason Factory Sound Bank includes samples (actual recordings) of vintage synths, including Minimoog, ARP 2600 and Odyssey, Prophet V, Roland SH101, Mellotron, and Solina (Arp String Ensemble) string machine. You could argue that these short recorded samples of the original instruments contain some audio information not found in emulations.

Here is a fun thing you can do with the NN-19's LFO. Kraftwerk uses nearly the same idea on their track "Vitamin," although they are not using a sine wave as you will here.

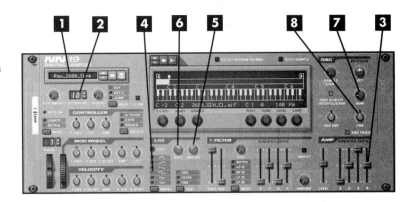

1 In a fresh NN-19 for which you have applied Initialize Patch, **load** the following **patch:** Reason Factory Sound Bank > NN19 Sampler Patches > Synth Raw Elements > Raw_2600_Sine.

2 Turn up **Polyphony** to at least 10.

3 Move the **Amp Envelope Release slider** halfway up to a value of 64. Play a few notes to hear this sound.

4 Set **LFO Waveform** to square.

5 Turn up the **LFO Amount knob** to a value of 53.

6 Turn up the **LFO Rate knob** to a value of 75. (If you want it a little faster, that's okay, but I don't think it sounds too cool much faster than 80.)

7 Turn up the **Oscillator Semitone knob** to a value of 2.

8 Turn the **Oscillator Fine Tune knob** to 12 o'clock.

❋ A NOTE ABOUT USING REX FILES WITH THE REASON SAMPLERS

Although I will not be using Rex files in any of the examples in this chapter, I want to point out that they can be loaded two ways. If you load a Rex file as a patch (using the sampler's Patch Browser), all slices in the Rex file will be automatically mapped sequentially across the keyboard (from left to right chromatically). If you use the sampler's Sample Browser to open a Rex file, you will be able to load a single Rex slice of your choosing onto a single key (or key zone).

NN-XT

For loading a single sample and having it automatically mapped across all keys, the NN-19 is the fastest way to go. However, the NN-XT offers so much more, and it is likely to be your main sampler. Not only does it offer far more synth parameters than the NN-19, several functions are easier to use. Also, unlike the NN-19, it allows you to use multilayered samples so that when you hit a key softly, it plays one sample, but when you hit it harder, it plays another sample. For example, the highest-quality piano libraries have several samples for each key, which increases realism.

You already learned how to set up single samples on each key with the NN-19, but now let's see how much easier it is to do this on the NN-XT.

1 In a fresh NN-XT for which you have applied Initialize Patch, **unfold** the **Remote Editor** by clicking the little triangle on the left side of the Remote Editor.

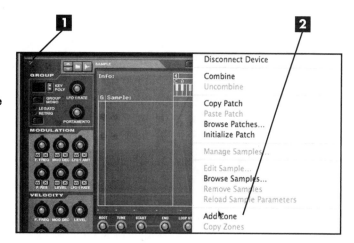

2 **Right-click** in the display window and **choose Add Zone**. Do this three times.

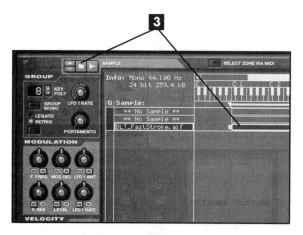

3 **Click** the third (bottom) **zone** to select it and then **click** the **Browse Sample button** and **load Orkester Sound Bank > Percussion > Belltree BLT > BLT_FastStroke.aif**.

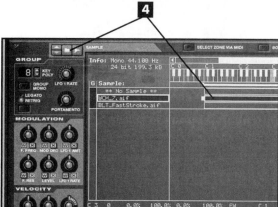

4 **Click** the **middle zone** to select it (you can click in the sample column if you want) and then **click** the **Browse Sample button** and **load Orkester Sound Bank > Percussion > Wind Chimes WCH > WCH_7.aif**.

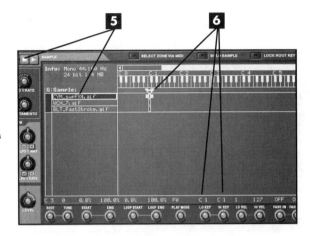

5 **Click** the **top zone** to select it and **load** in the following **sample:** Orkester Sound Bank > Percussion > Cymbals CYM > CYM_swpFX4.aif.

6 **Drag** the **right zone boundary handle** (on the tab bar) all the way to the left so that the low keys and hi keys for all three samples are C1. (You will also see this displayed above the Lo/Hi Key knobs at the bottom of the display window.)

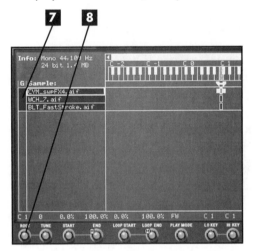

7 **Click** to the left of one of the **samples** in the Group column (labeled G) to select the whole group of all three samples.

8 **Set** the **root** to C1. This sets the root for all three samples because all three samples are selected.

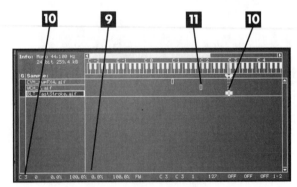

9 **Click** in a **blank area** of the display to deselect everything.

10 **Drag** the middle sample's entire **zone** to C2. Notice that the root automatically changes to C2.

11 Drag the bottom sample's zone to C3. Notice that the root automatically changes to C3.

When you are finished, you should here a weird cymbal scrape when you play C1, an upward-sweeping wind chime when you play C2, and a downward-sweeping bell tree when you play C3. All other keys will be silent. You can move the key zones for the individual samples anywhere you want, and the root will follow automatically, unless you activate the Lock Root Keys button in the upper-right corner.

Please leave this exercise as is, because you will be using it in the next exercise.

Velocity Layers

With the NN-XT, it is possible to have two or more key zones (with a separate sample in each zone) that are triggered by exactly the same range of notes. If each zone has the same velocity range, you will hear all the samples at the same time when you play a key. But if each sample has its own velocity range, you can play softly and hear one sample and play harder to hear another sample. This exercise picks up where the previous exercise left off.

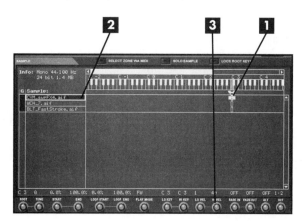

1 **Move** the **zones** for the top and middle samples to C3 so that all three samples are on C3.

2 **Click** on the top **sample** (CYM_swpFX4.aif) to select it.

3 **Turn down** the **Hi Vel** (high velocity) **knob** to 40.

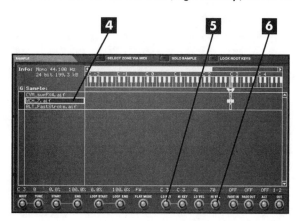

4 **Click** on the middle **sample** (WCH_7.aif) to select it.

5 **Turn** up the **Lo Vel** (low velocity) **knob** to 41.

6 **Turn down** the **Hi Vel** (high velocity) **knob** to 70.

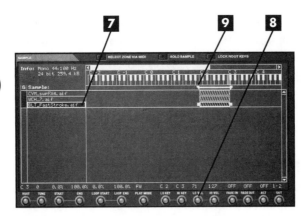

7 **Click** on the bottom **sample** (BLT_FastStroke.aif) to select it.

8 **Turn** the **Lo Vel** (low velocity) **knob** up to 71.

9 So that you can play the sounds on all notes C3 and below, on the tab bar, **drag** the left zone boundary **handle** all the way to the left (C-2).

Now if you play the C3 key (or any key below that) very softly, you will hear the cymbal scrape. If you play just a bit harder, you will hear the wind chime, and if you play very hard, you will hear the bell tree. By the way, the stripes on the key zones are there to alert you that they do not have the full velocity range of 1–127.

Velocity Crossfades

It is possible to set up velocity crossfades manually (using the Fade In and Fade Out knobs) to create smooth transitions between the samples in an overlapping zone. Here is a simple example of how to do this.

1 In a fresh NN-XT to which you have applied Initialize Patch, with the Remote Editor unfolded, **right-click** in the **display window** and **choose Add Zone**. (Do this twice to create two zones.)

2 **Select** the top **zone** (by clicking on the zone or by clicking where it says No Sample) and **load** the following **sample:** Orkester Sound Bank > Percussion > Timpani TMP > TMP_MF_(D2).aif.

3 **Select** the bottom **zone** and **load** the following **sample:** Orkester Sound Bank > Percussion > Gong GNG > GNG_MF.aif.

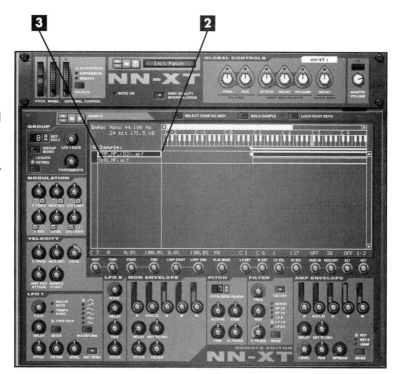

4 With the bottom zone (containing the gong sample) selected, **turn up** the **Fade In knob** to 100.

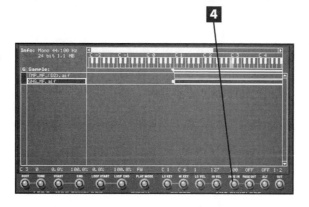

5 **Select** the top **zone** (containing the timpani sample) and **turn down** the **Fade Out knob** to 30.

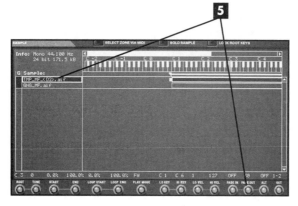

Now when you play just as softly as you can, you will hear mostly timpani and hardly any gong. As you play harder, you will hear more gong, and if you play very hard you should hear no timpani at all.

If you are interested in checking out more examples of how to use velocity crossfades (or to learn about the Create Velocity Crossfades option in the Edit menu), please see the Reason Operation Manual.

A Few More Sample Parameters

We've already covered some of the NN-XT sample parameters, including Lo/Hi Key, Lo/Hi Velocity, Play Mode, and Fade In/Out. The following exercise will introduce you to Sample Tune, Sample Start/End, and Loop Start/End.

1 **Right-click** on a freshly initialized **NN-XT** (with the Remote Editor unfolded) and **choose Add Zone**. Then **load** the following **sample:** Orkester Sound Bank > Percussion > Gong GNG > GNG_MF.aif.

2 While playing your MIDI keyboard, **turn** the **Tune knob** (used to fine-tune samples) to the left, all the way to −50, and then all the way to the right, to a value of 50. When you are finished, set it back to zero.

3 **Play** a note on your **MIDI keyboard** over and over as you slowly **turn up** the **Sample Start knob** to a value of 20%. You will hear the attack disappear, because you are starting the sample later (after the initial attack).

4 **Change** the **Play mode** to FW-LOOP.

5 **Hold down** a **key** on your MIDI keyboard and **turn down** the **Loop End** to 10%. Then, while **holding down** the **note**, slowly **turn it** down to 1%.

6 Keep **holding** the **note** and very slowly **turn down** the **Loop End** one step at a time, all the way down to 0.1%. You will hear a familiar "glitch" sound.

You will definitely want your mouse range in the General Preferences set to Very Precise for Step 6.

Backwards Piano!

Here's a fun and easy trick to wrap up this chapter.

1 **Load** a fresh **NN-XT** into a rack; it should have B Grand Piano 1.0.sxt loaded by default. **Unfold** the **Remote Editor** and then **right-click** on the **NN-XT** and **choose Select All Zones**.

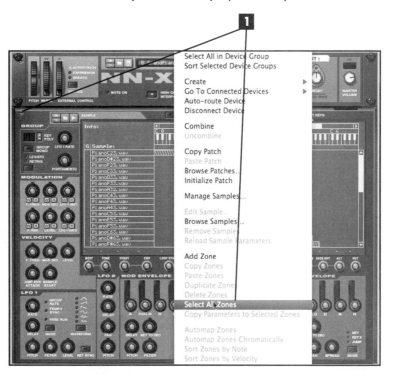

2 **Change** the **Play mode** to BW (backward).

3 In the Velocity section, **turn down** the **Level knob** to 12 o'clock.

4 In the Amp Envelope section, **turn Release** all the way up.

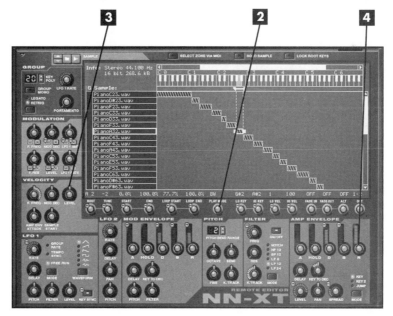

Now play your MIDI keyboard and enjoy that backwards piano sound. (Note that the samples take several seconds to fade in completely.)

If you really want to get deeply into the NN-XT, you will want to spend some time with your Reason Operation Manual. Still, many of the NN-XT's synth parameters should already look familiar to you, such as the Mod Envelope, Amp Envelope, Filter, and LFO sections. If you want to learn just about everything there is to know about creating your own sample patches with the NN-XT and NN-19, you may want to check out *Using Reason's Virtual Instruments: Skill Pack* (Course Technology PTR, 2006), which includes a CD-ROM complete with samples and contains in-depth how-tos for power users!

8 } The Combinator

First introduced in Reason version 3.0, the Combinator is a huge step forward in the power and functionality of the program. It allows you to put any number of synths and effects together, control them all with one keyboard, and save the whole thing as one patch. It saves any routing you have done with rear-panel patch cables (which could not otherwise be saved with an individual Malström or Thor patch, for example). It can be used for super-fat synth sounds built with a tower of synths or for complex effects processing (as in the MClass Mastering Suite Combi). It also allows you to create split or multilayered instruments. So you could create a Combinator patch (or Combi, for short) where when you play low notes, you hear a Subtractor bass sound; when you play high notes, you hear a Thor lead sound; or when you play *really* hard, you hear a Malström sound as well. And for the cherry on top, it is the only Reason device that is custom skinnable.

In this chapter, you will learn how to:

※ Make fat synth patches using multiple synths inside one Combinator

※ Use the MClass Master Suite Combi to make your mixes sound better (and louder)

※ Create Split Keyboard patches so one part of your keyboard plays one instrument, while another part of the keyboard plays another instrument

※ Assign the Combinator's virtual knobs and buttons to control various Reason device parameters

※ Use a single Redrum to control 10 Thors

Adding Devices to a Combinator

There are a few ways to add devices to a Combinator, as this first exercise will demonstrate. This is just an easy exercise to help you become familiar with how this works before you get on with the fun stuff in the rest of the chapter.

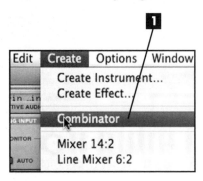

1 In a fresh rack, **choose Combinator** from the Create menu.

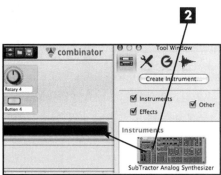

2 From the Devices pane of the Tool window, **drag** a **Subtractor** into the empty black space at the bottom of the Combinator, just under the red insertion line.

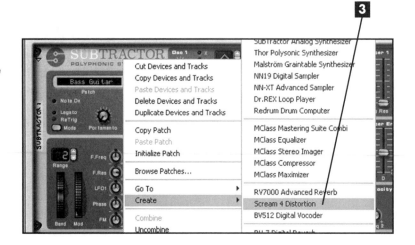

3 **Right-click** on the **Subtractor** and **choose Create > Scream 4 Distortion**.

4 **Click** on any **empty gray area** of the Combinator anywhere above the Holder to highlight the Combinator. Then **choose Subtractor** from the Create menu. This makes a Subtractor *under* the Combinator. That's not what we want.

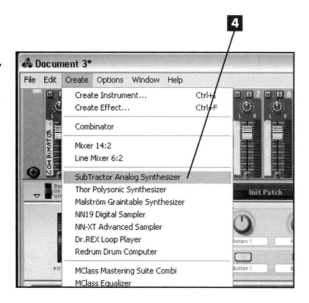

5 **Click** in the **empty slot** at bottom of the Combinator, and you will see the red insertion line appear. (Devices inside the Combinator are folded in my picture, but yours will not be folded by default.)

6 **Choose Subtractor** from the Create menu. Now it shows up in the right spot inside the Combinator. (The screenshot shows the Subtractor already in place, but you won't see yours until you create it.)

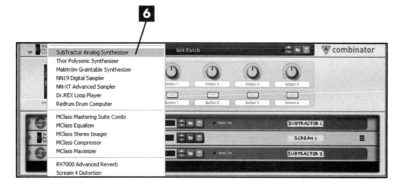

7 **Right-click** on the **Combinator** and **choose Initialize Patch**.

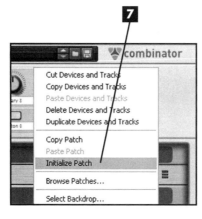

8 **Click** the **Show Devices button** to turn it off. The Holder (the area at the bottom of the Combinator that holds the devices) will disappear. There is no way to add a device to the Combinator.

9 **Click** the **Show Devices button** again. You can see the Holder again.

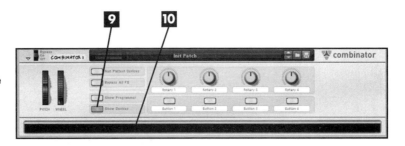

10 **Click** inside the **black space** in the Holder, and you will see the red insertion line appear. Now you are ready to add a device to the Combinator.

Obviously, you can assume they call it the *insertion line* because when it is visible, any new device that is created (or that you drag from the Tool window into the Holder) will be inserted directly below that line.

Okay, now that we have that basic bit of business out of the way, it's time to have some fun. You are about to find out how easy it is to make great sounds using the Combinator.

Fat Synth Sounds Made Easy

A really easy way to use the Combinator to make fat synth patches goes like this: Create or find a sound you like on a Reason synth. Create a Combinator containing a mixer plus two instances of the synth with your patch loaded. Pan one synth hard left and the other hard right, and then slightly change something about the sound of one of the synths. Instant fat synth patch. Let's give it a try.

1 In a fresh Reason rack containing a Mixer 14:2, use the Create menu to **create** a **Combinator** and then **create** a **Line Mixer 6:2** inside the Combinator, followed by a **Subtractor**. (This step is not pictured.)

2 **Load** the following **patch** into the Subtractor: Reason Factory Sound Bank > Subtractor Patches > PolySynths > FatThang.zyp. **Play** around on your **MIDI keyboard** to familiarize yourself with this sound.

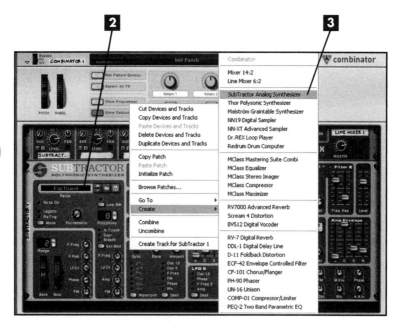

3 **Right-click** on the **Subtractor** and **choose Create > Subtractor Analog Synthesizer** from the context menu.

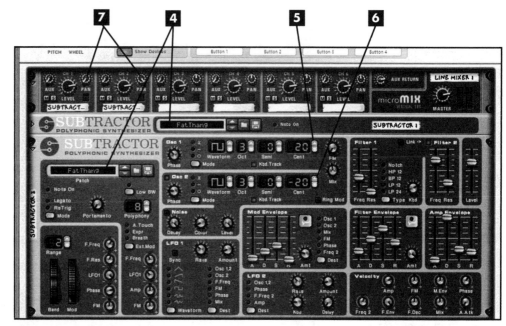

4 **Load** the same **FatThang patch** into the second Subtractor.

5 On the second Subtractor, **turn up Oscillator 1 Fine Tune** to a value of 20 cents.

6 On the second Subtractor, **turn down Oscillator 2 Fine Tune** to a value of −20 cents.

7 On the Line Mixer (micromix), **turn Channel 1 Pan** all the way to the left and **Channel 2 Pan** all the way to the right. **Play** your **keyboard**, and you will hear a nice, wide stereo image.

8 **Right-click** on the **Line Mixer** and **choose Create > RV7000 Advanced Reverb** from the context menu. It will be auto-routed to the Auxiliary Send/Return of the Line Mixer.

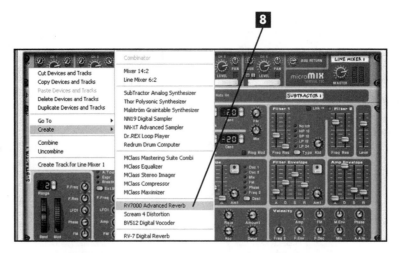

9 On the Line Mixer, **turn up** the **Auxiliary Send knobs** on Channels 1 and 2 to a value of 80.

10 If you like this patch, **click** the **Save Patch button** on the Combinator and **name it** something like Extra Fat Thang.

One additional thing you might want to add to this patch: Turn up Portamento on the second Subtractor halfway and set the Key mode to ReTrig.

Since the Line Mixer and everything are already set up nicely, let's leave this Combinator as it is and load a different patch into the Subtractors for another quick example.

1 **Load** the following **patch** into both Subtractors: Reason Factory Sound Bank > Subtractor Patches > Pads > Sweeping Strings.zyp.

2 On the second Subtractor, **turn down Filter Envelope Decay** to a value of 88.

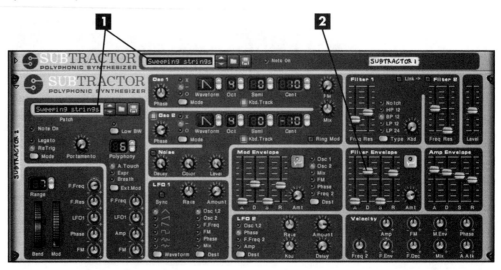

Now the filter sweep will happen just a bit faster on the second Subtractor (right channel) than it will on the first Subtractor (left channel).

To get a nice stereo spread this way, you could also use an entirely different patch on one of the two synths, or you could vary another parameter, such as the speed of an LFO or even the octave of an oscillator. I'm sure you get the idea.

❄ PRECISION VALUES WHEN MOVING KNOBS AND FADERS

If you have trouble getting precise values when dragging knobs and faders with your mouse, try holding down the Shift key on your computer keyboard while you click and drag. This will cause the knob or fader to move more slowly (increasing or decreasing values in the smallest increments possible) and will therefore allow you to select precise values. This works regardless of the Mouse Knob Range setting on the General page of the Reason Preferences. This trick also works when dragging up and down in the Amount fields in Thor's Modulation Matrix or in the Min/Max fields in the Modulation Routing section of the Combinator's Programmer window.

Combine/Uncombine

Throughout most of this chapter, you will be creating empty Combinators and then creating devices within the Combinator. However, that's not the only way to make a Combinator patch. If you find that you have a group of devices in your Reason song that are working together in a useful way, you can combine them into a Combinator patch (Combi) that can be opened later in other songs as well. This comes in especially handy when using effects devices that have no Save Patch functionality.

1 In an empty rack, **create** an **MClass Mastering Combi**, followed by a **Mixer 14:2** and **Dr. Octo Rex**. (This step is not pictured.)

2 **Load** the following **patch** into Dr. Octo Rex: Reason Factory Sound Bank > Dr Rex Drum Loops > Abstract HipHop > Trh36_Middle-Skool_090_Grif.rx2. (It's the last patch in the folder.)

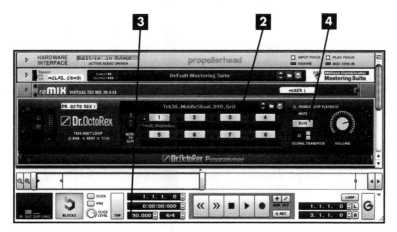

3 **Turn down** the **Tempo** to 90.

4 **Click** the **Run button** on Dr. Octo Rex.

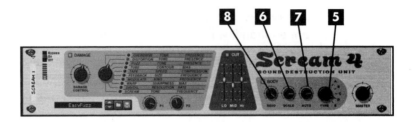

5 (These drums are going to sound very big after the next few steps.) **Create** a **Scream 4 Sound Destruction Unit** under Dr.Rex and **turn the Body Type knob** to D.

6 **Turn up** the **Scale knob** to 9 o'clock.

7 **Turn up** the **Auto knob** to 9 o'clock.

8 **Turn** the **Resonance knob** all the way up. That's what I'm talking about.

9 **Shift-click** on **Dr. Octo Rex** and **Scream 4**. Then **right-click** on either **device** and **select Combine** from the context menu.

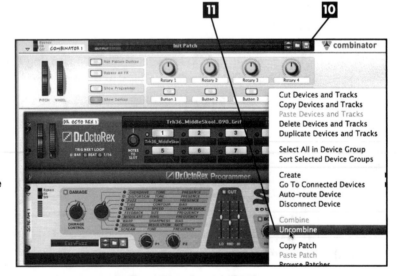

10 **Click** the Combinator's **Save Patch button** and **choose** a **name** you'll remember (such as Big Fat MiddleSkool Teacher).

11 To uncombine, **right-click** on the **Combinator** and **choose Uncombine** from the context menu.

Using the MClass Mastering Suite Combi

The MClass Mastering Suite Combi can help you add the finishing touches that can turn an okay mix into one that really jumps out and reaches the listener. Normally, you will create this Combi above the main Mixer so that the Mastering Suite Combi is the last thing the entire mix passes through on its way out of Reason. In fact, there is a song file in your Template Documents folder called Mixer and Mastering.rns that you can set as the default song on the General page of your Reason Preferences, if you like. That way, every time you open a new song, it will have an MClass Mastering Suite Combi followed by Mixer 14:2 at the top of an otherwise empty rack. (Of course, all the exercises in this book start with a completely empty rack.)

The following exercise will help you familiarize yourself with the function of the MClass Mastering Suite. Please leave everything as is at the end of this exercise with the track playing, because there will be a short second exercise that picks up where this one leaves off.

> ❋ **IMPORTANT NOTE**
>
> If you cannot find the Tutorial Song mentioned in Step 1 in the following exercise, you can download it here: www.propellerheads.se/support/files/TutorialSong.zip. It's a tiny 44-KB download. However, if you are running Reason version 4.0.1 or later, you should already have the file.

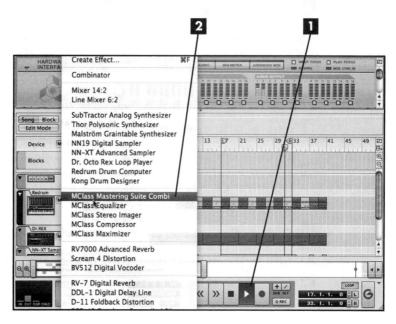

1 **Open** the **Tutorial Song** found in the Reason Program folder and **click Play** on the Reason Transport. The song will begin looping, which is perfect.

2 **Right-click** on **Reason Hardware Device** at the top of the rack and **select Create > MClass Mastering Suite Combi** from the context menu. You will hear a slight volume increase.

3 Click the **Show Devices button** on the Combinator.

4 Bypass the **MClass Maximizer** for now. Now all the devices in the Combinator are bypassed (not active) except for the MClass Equalizer.

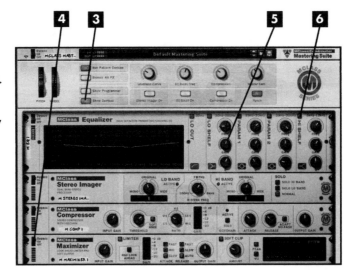

5 Turn up the **Low Shelf Gain** to a value of 2.9 dB. If your monitors or headphones are decent, you should hear an increase in bass.

6 Activate the **High Shelf,** and you will hear the cymbals ring out and "breathe" more.

7 Turn on the **MClass Stereo Imager** and **turn** the **Lo Band Width knob** all the way down to Mono.

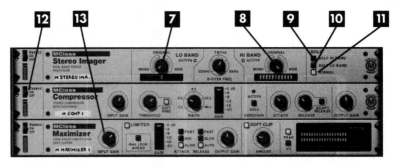

8 Turn **Hi Band Width** all the way up to Wide.

9 Click **Solo Hi Band** to hear just the Hi Band. You can play with the X-Over Freq (crossover frequency) knob and return it to 1.28 kHz when you're finished.

10 Now click **Solo Lo Band** to hear just the Lo Band (which is completely mono). You can play with the X-Over Freq (crossover frequency) knob and return it to 1.28 kHz when you're finished.

11 Click the **Normal button** on the MClass Stereo Imager.

12 Turn on the **MClass Compressor** to add a subtle bit of compression.

13 Turn on the **MClass Maximizer** and **turn Input Gain up** to a value of 4.1 dB.

14 **Bypass** the **Mastering Suite Combi** to hear the difference between what you started with and what you ended up with.

One big difference: It's much louder. And since everyone maximizes the hell out of their electronic music these days, perhaps you will want to do the same. This decreases dynamic range, but at least it ensures that your track isn't way quieter than the other guy's before it. Now, I am not claiming to have done a brilliant job mastering here. I just wanted you to hear what each device in the Mastering Suite does.

In addition to the default Mastering Suite patch, there are several presets that may sound great on your song. With the Tutorial Song still playing, please do the following:

1 **Click** the Combinator's **Browse Patch button**.

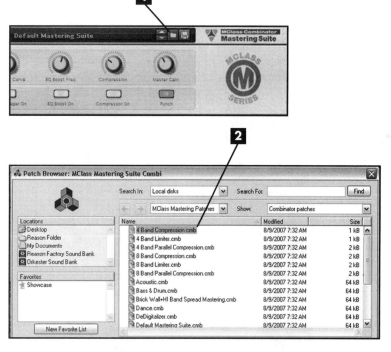

2 **Click** once on the top **patch**, called 4 Band Compression.cmb, to hear it previewed. Then use the down arrow on your computer keyboard to **select and preview** each of the patches in the MClass Mastering Patches folder.

Notice that several of these presets feature different configurations of the MClass devices. For instance, the 8 Band Compression patch contains eight MClass compressors and eight MClass Stereo Imagers. The Bass and Drum patch contains a Scream 4. Also, keep in mind that all the MClass devices can be created separately wherever you need them in your song or as part of other Combis.

Using the Programmer Panel

The Combinator's Programmer panel is where you can control the flow of MIDI messages for all the devices within the Combinator. You can use it for modulation routing (similar to Thor's Modulation Matrix), to create keyboard splits and velocity-layered sounds, and to decide what kind of MIDI information each device in the Combinator can receive. And as complex as that may sound, the good news is that the Programmer panel is set up very simply and logically.

Creating a Split Instrument with the Combinator

One easy thing you can do with a Combinator is to create keyboard splits. This is especially useful for live performances. In the following example, you will create a Combi in which the lower keys play a bass sound, while the rest of the keyboard plays a dreamy synth piano sound.

1 In a fresh rack containing an instance of Mixer 14:2, **create** a **Combinator**. (This step is not pictured.)

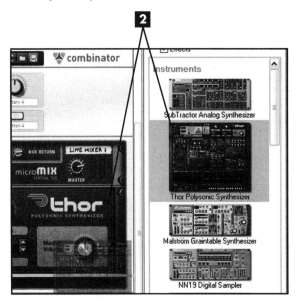

2 From the Devices pane of the Tool window, **drag** a **Line Mixer 14:2** into the Combinator, followed by **two Thors**. You will see the red insertion line appear as you drag so you know you're dropping the new device in the right place.

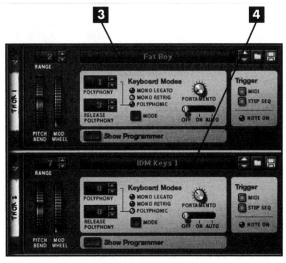

3 In the top Thor, **load** the **Fat Boy patch** (found in the default folder and also in Reason Factory Sound Bank > Thor Patches > Bass).

4 In the bottom Thor, **load** the following **patch:** Reason Factory Sound Bank > Thor Patches > Poly Synths > IDM Keys 1.

5 **Click** the Combinator's **Show Programmer button**.

6 **Drag** the **scrollbar** at the top of the Key Mapping section all the way to the right.

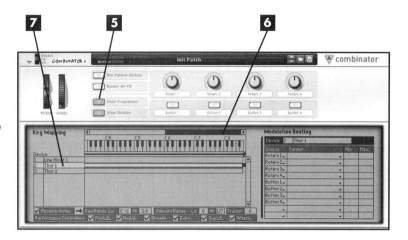

7 **Click** in the **Device area** of the Programmer, where it says Thor 1.

8 **Drag** the right edge of Thor 1's **horizontal bar** to the left until the Key Range Hi value reads E2.

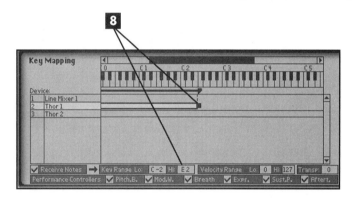

9 **Click** in the **Device area** of the Programmer where it says Thor 2.

10 **Click** in the **KeyRange Lo field** and **drag upward** until you have a value of F2.

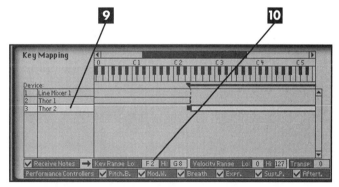

Now if you play your MIDI keyboard, notes E2 and below will trigger the Fat Boy sound in Thor 1, and notes F2 and above will trigger the IDM Keys 1 sound in Thor 2. Of course, if you wanted, you could add several synths to your Combinator—some with separate key ranges, and some with the same or overlapping key ranges.

Creating a Velocity-Layered Instrument with the Combinator

You should already be familiar with velocity layers from your experience with the NN-XT. In that context, hitting a drum sample (for example) at a lower velocity setting could trigger one drum sample, while striking the controller more sharply would trigger another drum sample. You can do this with the Combinator as well. In the next exercise, you will create a piano and strings patch where playing softly will get you piano only, while playing more forcefully will give you piano and strings at the same time.

1 In a fresh rack containing a 14:2 Mixer and a Combinator, **load** the following **devices** into the Combinator in this order: Line Mixer 6:2, RV7000 Advanced Reverb, and two instances of NN-XT. (This step is not pictured.)

2 The NN-XTs will have the B Grand Piano 1.0 patch loaded by default. In the second NN-XT, **click** in the **Patch display window** and **choose Violin Section** from the menu.

3 In the Line Mixer, **turn Channel 1 Aux** a little past 2 o'clock and **turn Channel 2 Aux** all the way up. You should have a pretty piano and strings sound.

4 The violins might be a little too loud, so **turn down** the **Channel 2 level** to a value of 85 or so.

5 **Click** the Combinator's **Show Programmer button**.

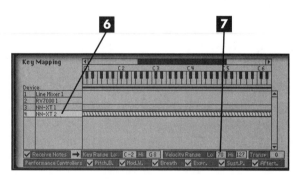

6 In the Device area of the Programmer window, **click** where it says **NN-XT 2**.

7 **Click** in the **Velocity Range Lo field** and **drag up** to a value of 70.

Now when you play very softly, you will hear piano only, and when you play more forcefully, you will hear the violins as well. Note that the horizontal bar representing the key range of NN-XT 2 now has stripes to indicate that it has a velocity range of less than 0–127. You can experiment with the Velocity Range Lo value until you find one that feels comfortable with your playing style (and with the velocity response of your MIDI keyboard). Please leave this patch up (and save it if you want), because we can use it in the next section.

MIDI Data Routing/Performance Controllers

By default, when your Combinator is selected as the active Sequencer track, all MIDI will be sent to all devices in the Combinator all the time. However, you can control this. Using your piano and strings Combinator from the previous exercise, please do the following:

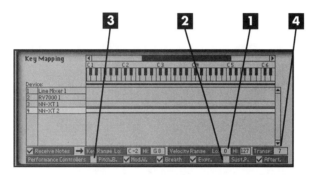

1 My fingers are getting tired of playing hard to hear the violins, so with NN-XT 2 still selected in the Device list, **drag** that **Velocity Range Lo parameter** back down to zero. (Notice that the stripes disappear.)

2 In the Performance Controllers section, **click** in the **Sust.P.** (Sustain Pedal) **check box** to deselect it. Now if you are using a sustain pedal with your MIDI keyboard, it will only sustain the piano sound, but it will cease making a mushy mess of your violins.

3 **Uncheck Pitch Bend**. Now your pitch wheel will affect only the piano but not the strings. Of course, this is a funny example, because you normally wouldn't pitch-bend piano, either.

4 **Click** in the **Transpose field** and **drag up** to a value of 7. Now **play** your **MIDI keyboard**, and the violins will be transposed up a fifth, making you sound all complex and stuff.

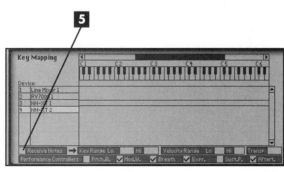

5 **Uncheck Receive Notes**. Now NN-XT 2 (Violin section) will not receive any MIDI note information, and you will hear only piano.

Step 5 may not be much fun for this patch, but it could be useful if you had a Combi containing a Redrum where you didn't want the drums to be triggered by your keyboard playing. This could also be useful in Combinators containing vocoders or other complex situations. Also, if you have a split with a bass sound and a lead sound, you might want pitch bend, Mod wheel, and sustain to affect the lead sound only, but not the bass sound.

Assigning the Virtual Controls

The Combinator's Controller panel has four virtual knobs and four virtual buttons that you can assign to control parameters of the devices inside the Combinator. By default, they are not assigned to anything. But if you want, you could make one knob (or one button) control up to 10 different parameters. You will notice that Thor has two similar virtual knobs and two virtual buttons as well. The following exercise should give you a feel for how to use these.

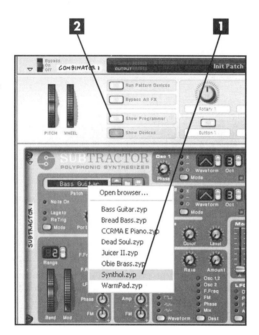

1 **Create** a **Combinator** and **create** a **Subtractor** inside of it. Then **click** inside of Subtractor's **Patch display window** and **choose Synthol.zyp** from the menu. (This patch is also in the Subtractor Patches > MonoSynths folder.)

2 **Click** the Combinator's **Show Programmer button**.

3 In the Device area of the Programmer, **click** where it says **SubTractor 1**.

4 In the Modulation Routing section, **choose LFO1 Amount** for the Rotary1 target. (You'll have to scroll down the pop-up menu to see the selection for LFO1 Amount.)

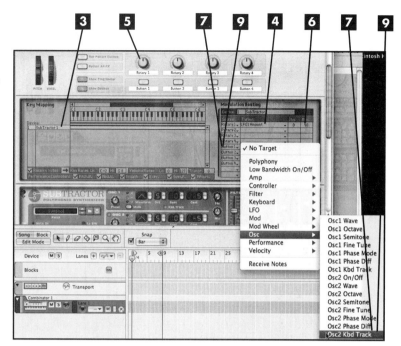

5 While playing your MIDI keyboard, **turn** the **Rotary 1 knob** back and forth and **turn it** all the way to the left when you are done.

6 If the effect is too crazy, **turn** the **Rotary1 Max value** down to 40. Now when you turn the Rotary 1 knob all the way up, the effect is tamer.

7 **Choose Osc2 Kbd Track** for the Button 1 target.

8 **Set Minimum** to 1 and **Maximum** to 0 for Button 1. Now when Button 1 is on, Oscillator 2 Keyboard Tracking will be off and vice versa.

9 In the Source column, **click** on **Button 2** and **choose Button 1** from the menu. This is how you can have the same button control two different things.

10 **Choose Ring Mod** for the second Button 1 target.

11 **Click Button 1**, and you will have a ring-modulated sound.

12 **Turn** the **Rotary 1 knob** all the way up, and people will think you are weird.

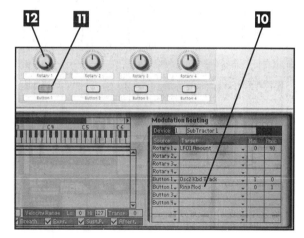

13 **Right-click** on **Button 1** and **choose Edit Keyboard Control Mapping**.

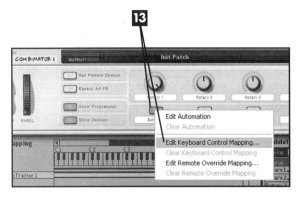

14 **Click** the **Q key** on your computer keyboard and then **click OK**. Now when you press the Q key on your computer keyboard, it will turn Button 1 on and off.

Of course, you can use that last trick on any button-style parameter in Reason. Similarly, you can right-click on any knob or button in Reason, choose Edit Remote Override Mapping, and map the knob or button to a knob or button on a MIDI controller. Your Reason Operation Manual can provide more details. It's pretty easy.

Sequencing with the Combinator

Sequencing with the Combinator is pretty much like sequencing with any other instrument in Reason, but there is one thing I'd like to point out. The Combinator track in the Reason Sequencer sends information through the entire Combinator. What if you want to automate a parameter in only one device inside of a Combinator? The following exercise shows how to do that. It also introduces you to the Create Instrument method of creating a Reason device. In the Create Instrument Patch Browser, patches are arranged by sound type instead of by device.

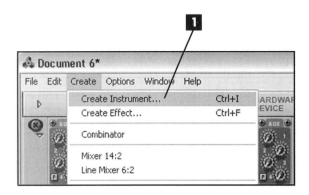

1 In a new rack containing Mixer 14:2, **select Create Instrument** from the Create menu.

2 When the browser window opens, you should already see the contents of Reason Factory Sound Bank > ALL Instrument Patches. **Select Performance Patches > Boutique > Renaissance Teebee Combi [Run].cmb** and then **click OK**.

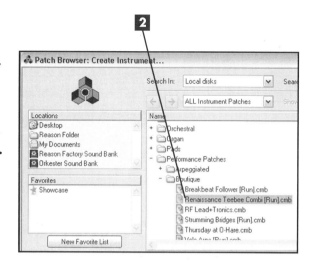

3 Click the **Run Pattern Devices button** (relabeled Run/Stop in this Combi). You should hear music.

4 Click the **Show Devices button** (relabeled Show Synth/Seq in this Combi).

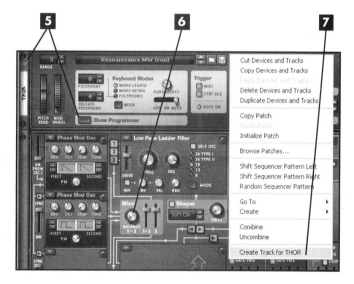

5 Unfold Thor.

6 Slowly **turn** the **Oscillator 1 and 2 Balance knob** in the Mixer section from left to right and back again to hear what this sounds like.

7 Right-click on Thor and select **Create Track for Thor** from the context menu.

8 With the Thor Sequencer track still selected, **click the Track Parameter Automation button** and **choose Osc 1 and 2 Balance** from the menu. An automation lane will appear under the note lane.

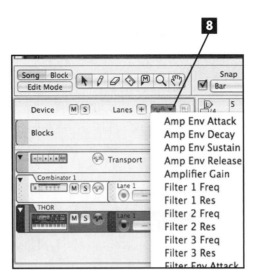

9 **Select** the **Pencil tool**.

10 **Draw** in a **clip** between Bars 1 and 9 in the Osc 1 and 2 Balance parameter automation lane.

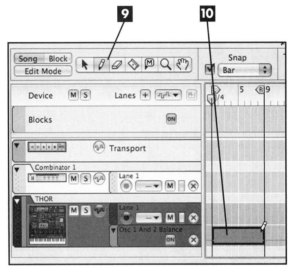

11 **Alt-double-click** on the **clip** and then **create three points** in the shape of a "V," as shown. The high points of the "V" should have a value of 127, and the low point should have a value of zero.

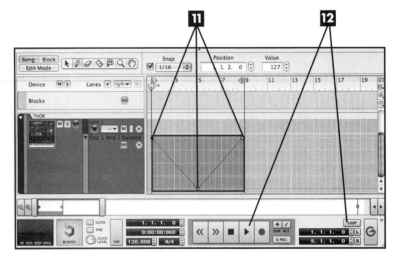

12 **Click Play** on the Reason Transport. The Transport should be in Loop mode by default, and you should hear (and see) Thor's Mixer knob moving smoothly back and forth between its minimum and maximum values.

Keep in mind that you can right-click on any Reason device and choose Create Track For from the context menu, regardless of whether the device happens to be inside a Combinator.

In the exercise you have just completed, you used Create Instrument to create your Combinator. Of course, you could have created a Malström, Subtractor, or any other instrument device using the same command. You can tell what type of device you are loading by the file extension in the patch name. In the next exercise, instead of using Create Instrument, you will use Create Effect to add effects to your sequence.

Please leave the sequence you have just created running (so that you can still hear the Renaissance Teebee Combi).

1 **Click** on the **Combinator** to make sure it's highlighted. Then **choose Create Effect** from the Create menu.

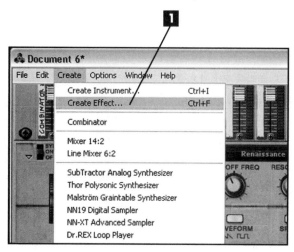

2 **Expand** the **Modulation folder** by clicking the plus symbol to the left of it (which will become a minus sign).

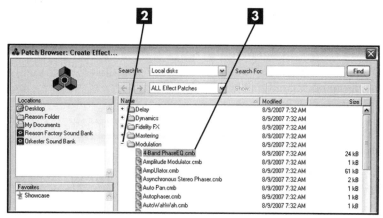

3 **Click** once on **4-Band PhaseEQ.cmb** to hear the effects patch previewed. Then **click** the **down arrow** on your computer keyboard to hear the next patch. Keep using the down arrow until you have previewed all the effects Combis in that folder.

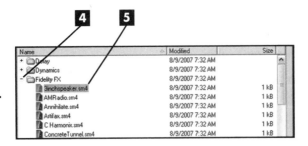

4 **Expand** the **Fidelity FX folder**. (If necessary, first **drag** the **vertical scroll-bar** up to the top so you can see this folder.)

5 **Click** once on the first patch, entitled **3inchspeaker.sm4**. (Careful—it's loud.) Then **use** the **down arrow** on your computer keyboard to preview the rest of the patches in that folder.

I realize the patches in the Fidelity FX folder are not Combis but are actually Scream 4 patches. I just thought they were pretty extreme and that you might enjoy checking them out. And at least we were processing the Renaissance Teebee Combi, so this leg of the exercise is still in the right chapter.

I should note that in Step 3 I was not able to hear anything when previewing the Tuned Thor Filters 1 & 2 patches. (I mention that in case you noticed the same thing and were wondering if your stuff was broken.) I should also note that moving the Mod wheel (relabeled Shred) and also the first rotary knob (labeled Cut Off Freq) on the Renaissance Teebee Combi can yield pretty cool results.

Custom Skins for Your Combinator

Reason allows you to change the appearance of your Combinator. The following exercise requires that you use whatever image-editing program you have at your disposal to crop or resize a JPEG image to 754×138 pixels. The image must be in JPEG format (with a .jpg or .jpeg file extension).

1 **Create** a **Combinator**. Then **right-click** on **it** and **choose Select Backdrop** from the context menu.

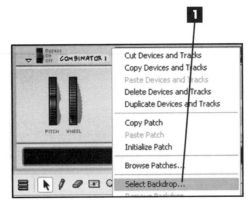

2 **Double-click** on the desired 754×138 JPEG **image** in the Image Browser window.

3 If you want to rename your Combinator, **double-click** on the piece of **tape** to the left of the display window and **type** in your **text**. (This works for any of the "console-tape style" labels in the Reason user interface.)

4 If you want to rename a rotary knob or button controller, **double-click** under **it**, **type** in the desired **text**, and **click Enter**.

5 To remove the image, **right-click** on the **Combinator** and **select Remove Backdrop** from the context menu.

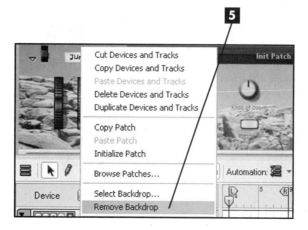

This is the quick and easy way to change the backdrop. You can try any JPEG image on your computer, but if it has the wrong dimensions, it may cover only part of the Combinator, or you may be able to see only a small portion of the image file.

If you know your way around Photoshop, you can use the Template Backdrop.psd file found in Reason\Template Documents\Combi Backdrops. It is a multilayer template. By using an image editor, such as Photoshop, you will be able to add custom text as well. If you plan to include custom text for the knob and button labels in your image file, you will have to double-click on the existing label and delete the contents.

Backdrop image information is saved when you save your Combinator patch. It is also saved with the song in which the Combinator is used. For more information on creating your own custom Combinator look, please see the Read Me file located in Reason\Template Documents\Combi Backdrops.

Advanced Combi in Which Redrum Controls 10 Thors

In the following exercise, you will create a Combi in which Redrum controls 10 Thors. Because there are so many steps, I have broken up the exercise into two parts. In the first part, you will set up the devices in the Combinator. In the second part, you will load patches into all the Thors.

Setting Up Your Thor Drum Combi

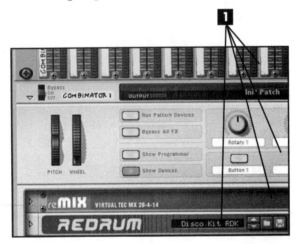

1 In a fresh rack containing a Mixer 14:2, **create** a **Combinator**. Inside the Combinator, **create** a **Mixer 14:2**, followed by a **Redrum**.

2 **Click** the **Tab key** to flip your rack around, **drag** the **cables** out of Mixer Channel 1 Left and Right inputs, and **plug them** into Mixer Channel 11 Left and Right inputs.

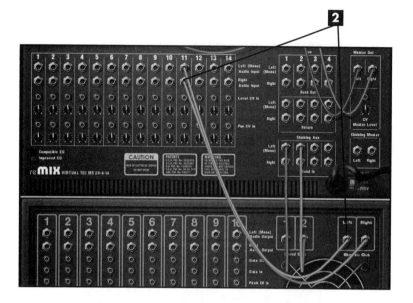

3 **Click** the **Tab key** to flip your rack around facing front and then **mute Channel 11**. Then **create 10 Thors** under Redrum. After creating each Thor, **fold it**.

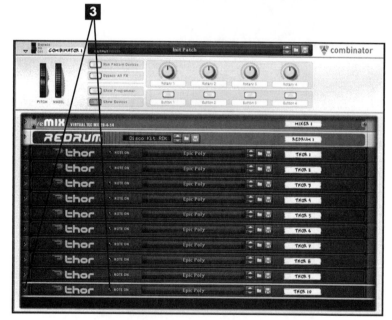

4 **Flip** your **rack** around, **unfold Thor 1**, and **connect Redrum Channel 1 Gate Out** to Thor 1 Sequencer Control Gate In.

5 **Connect** all remaining **Redrum Gate outs** to the remaining Thor Gate ins (Redrum Channel 2 Gate Out to Thor 2 Gate In, Redrum Channel 3 Gate Out to Thor 3 Gate In, and so on). Unfold as needed. Folding Mixer 14:2 helps.

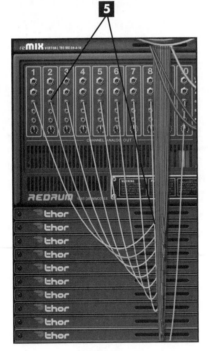

6 **Flip** your **rack** around facing front. **Click** the Combinator's **Show Programmer button**.

7 **Click** on **Thor 1** (in the Device area of the Programmer) and **uncheck Receive Notes**. Then do the same for each of the remaining Thors in the Device list.

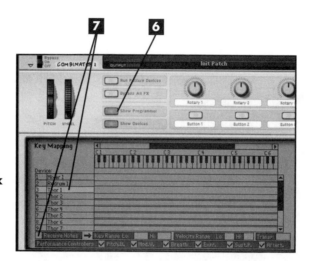

8 On the Mixer 14:2 inside the Combinator, **mute Channel 11** (the one Redrum is plugged into).

Remember that in Reason, Gate CV carries note on/note off information, as well as velocity information.

Selecting Sounds for Your Thor Drum Combi

Tastes vary widely, so you may find that my choices bear little relation to the music you want to make; however, you can certainly make your own modifications later. Of course, this picks up where the previous bit left off.

1 Load the **following** into Thor 1: Reason Factory Sound Bank > Thor Patches > Percussion > BassDrums > 808 BD.

2 Load the **following** into Thor 2: Reason Factory Sound Bank > Thor Patches > Percussion > SnareDrums > ER Snare Construction.

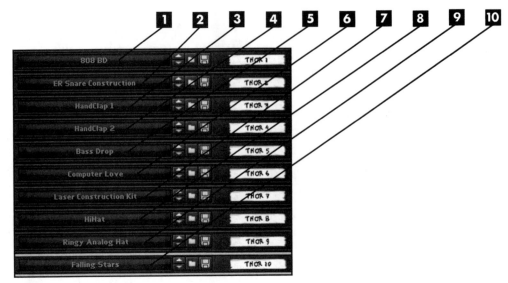

3 Load the **following** into Thor 3: Reason Factory Sound Bank > Thor Patches > Percussion > Claps > HandClap 1.

4 Load the **following** into Thor 4: Reason Factory Sound Bank > Thor Patches > Percussion > Claps > HandClap 2.

5 Load the **following** into Thor 5: Reason Factory Sound Bank > Thor Patches > Percussion > Misc Percussion > Bass Drop.

6 Load the **following** into Thor 6: Reason Factory Sound Bank > Thor Patches > Fx > Computer Love.

7 Load the **following** into Thor 7: Reason Factory Sound Bank > Thor Patches > Fx > Laser Construction Kit.

8 Load the **following** into Thor 8: Reason Factory Sound Bank > Thor Patches > Percussion > HiHats > HiHat.

9 Load the **following** into Thor 9: Reason Factory Sound Bank > Thor Patches > Percussion > HiHats > Ringy Analog Hat.

10 Load the **following** into Thor 10: Reason Factory Sound Bank > Thor Patches > Fx > Falling Stars.

Now that you've got your sounds all set up, you can save this Combinator patch. (I'm going to call mine Throbinator. It throbs, and the name reminds me of Thor.)

Here are some tips for using this Combi:

❋ You may want to build your beats with Mixer Channel 11 soloed (so that you can hear a regular kit as your make your beat) and then turn Channel 11 Solo off (so that Channel 11 is muted, and you can hear all your Thors instead).

❋ Another great starting point for making beats with this Combi is to leave Mixer Channel 11 muted so you can hear the Thors. Then right-click on Redrum and choose Randomize Pattern.

❋ You may want to alternate left and right panning of Remix Channels 2 through 10 so that you have a nice stereo kit. Once you're happy with the sound, you can save the Combi again.

❋ If the 808 BD or the Bass Drop is not tuned to your liking, you can unfold the appropriate Thor, Show Programmer, and adjust the Octave and Semi knobs on the analog oscillators. The Tune knobs on Redrum will have no effect.

❋ If you don't like the sound in a particular Thor, you can use the arrows next to the Patch display window to scroll up and down between patches in the same folder as the currently selected patch.

❋ Remember that your pitch bender and modulation wheel will control all Thors simultaneously.

Something for Adventurers: Spider CV Merger and Splitter

This is definitely the most advanced exercise in this book, but if you're into it, it's just a matter of following the steps. Could be fun. This exercise uses the Throbinator you just constructed. Before beginning the exercise, please use Redrum's Pattern Sequencer to create a beat. If you need help, please refer to Chapter 3 or check your Reason Operation Manual. If you're in a hurry, you can use Randomize Pattern to create instant chaos. Once you have a beat, do the following:

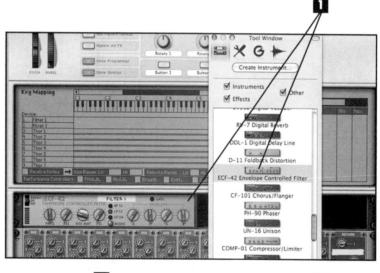

1 Drag an **ECF-42 Envelope Controlled filter** into the Holder directly above the Mixer 14:2.

2 **Flip** your **rack** around and **disconnect** the **cables** going into the Left and Right inputs of the Envelope Controlled filter.

3 **Disconnect** the **cables** going out of the Mixer Master outs and into the Combinator's From Devices jacks.

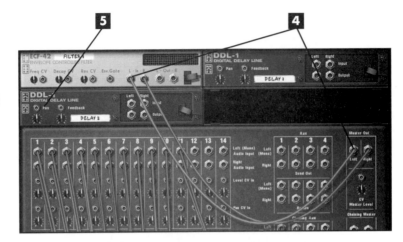

4 Connect the **Left and Right Master outs** of the Mixer 14:2 to the L /R In of the Envelope Controlled filter.

5 Create two **DDL-1 Digital Delay Line devices** after the Envelope Controlled filter and **disconnect** all **cables** from the Digital Delays.

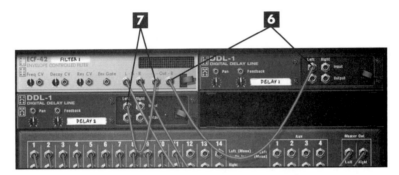

6 Connect the **Right output** of the Envelope Controlled filter to the **Left input of the** first Digital Delay, but **disconnect** the **cable** that automatically **appears to connect** the right channel.

7 Connect the **Left output** of the Envelope Controlled filter to the **Left input of the sec-**ond Digital Delay.

8 Connect the **Left output** of the first Digital Delay to the Combinator's Right from Devices input.

9 Connect the **Left output** of the second Digital Delay to the Combinator's Left from Devices input.

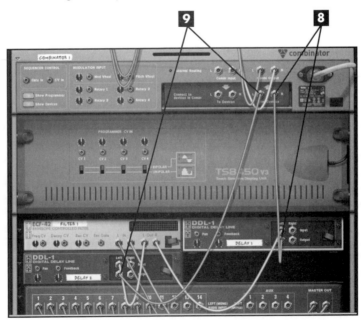

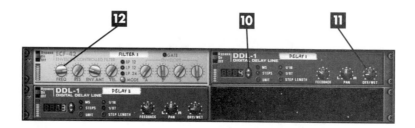

10 Flip your **rack** around and **change** the **delay time** on the first Digital Delay to 4 Steps.

11 Turn down the **Dry/Wet knob** on both delays to 9 o'clock.

12 Play your **beat** while turning the Frequency knob on the Envelope Controlled filter back and forth. (You can play with Resonance, too, if you want. You've been good.)

You may now be wondering where the Spider is. It's coming next. If you have been puzzling over the Envelope Controlled filter and wondering how you get the envelope to control it, the answer is that we haven't hooked up that part yet. We will in the next section of this crazy exercise. Picking up where we left off:

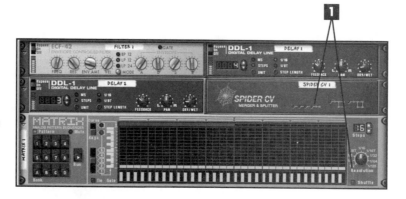

1 Create a **Spider CV Merger & Splitter** after the second Digital Delay and then **create** a **Matrix Analog Pattern Sequencer** under that.

2 Flip your **rack** around and **disconnect** Redrum **Channel 1 Gate Out** from Thor 1 Gate In.

3 Disconnect the **cables** coming out of the Matrix. Then **connect Redrum Channel 1 Gate Out** to Spider CV Split A input. (Click the L key to hide or show cables if the spaghetti is in the way.)

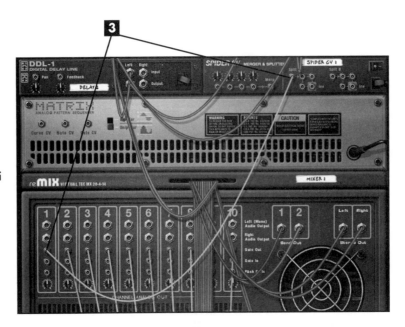

4 Connect **Spider CV Split A Out 1** to Thor 1 Gate In.

5 Connect **Spider CV Split A Out 2** to the Envelope Gate input of the Envelope Controlled filter. Now Redrum's Channel 1 Gate Out is controlling Thor 1 (as before) plus the Envelope Controlled filter.

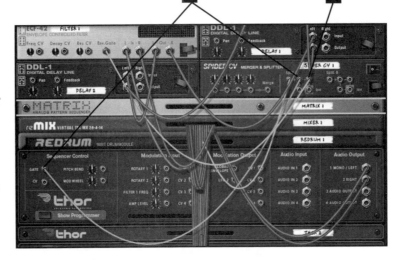

6 Switch the **Matrix** to Bipolar Curve mode.

7 Connect the Matrix's **Curve CV output** to the Envelope Controlled filter's Freq CV input.

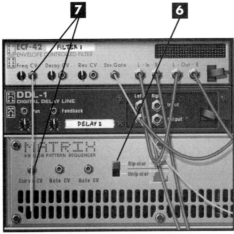

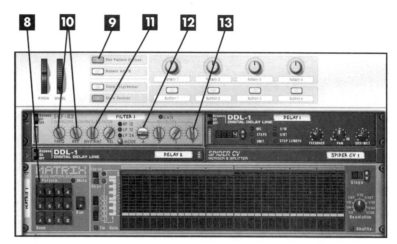

8 Flip your **rack** around and **turn off** the **Pattern Enable button** on the Matrix. We're not using the Matrix yet.

9 Click Run Pattern Devices on the Combinator to start your beat (if it's not already playing).

10 Turn up the **Freq and Res knobs** to 11 o'clock on the Envelope Controlled filter.

11 Turn the **Envelope Amount knob** slowly all the way up and all the way down. Then set it at 12 o'clock.

12 Slowly **turn** up the **Envelope Attack knob** to 12 o'clock and then down to 9 o'clock.

13 Slowly **turn** the **Envelope Release knob** all the way to the right, then all the way to the left, and then back to 12 o'clock.

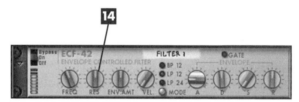

14 Slowly **turn up Resonance** all the way to the right and then back down to 12 o'clock. (It's fun to play with the filter frequency when Resonance is turned up, too. Be careful of your ears/speakers.)

Did I throw that Matrix in there just for looks? In the final leg of this mammoth exercise, you will use the Matrix to modulate the cutoff frequency of the Envelope Controlled filter, and you will also do a little bit of routing in the Combinator's Programmer.

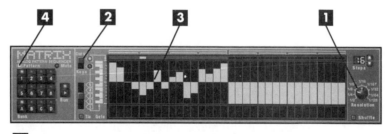

1 On the Matrix, **turn down** the **Resolution knob** to 1/8.

2 Set the Matrix's **Edit mode** to Curve.

3 Using your mouse, **draw** a **random pattern** in the first eight steps.

4 Click the Matrix's **Pattern Enable button** so it lights up red, and you should hear the Envelope Controlled filter's frequency being modulated by the Matrix.

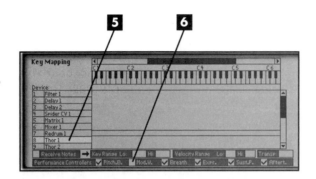

5 In the Combinator's Programmer, **select Thor 1** from the Device list.

6 **Turn off Mod.W.** for Thor 1. Then **do** the **same** for the remaining nine Thors.

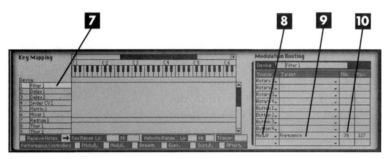

7 **Select Filter 1** from the Device list.

8 In the Modulation Routing section, **choose Mod Wheel** for the first empty Source slot.

9 For Target, **select Frequency**.

10 **Select** a **value** of 38 for Minimum by clicking and dragging up in the Minimum box. Now you can control the Envelope Controlled filter frequency with the modulation wheel on your MIDI keyboard.

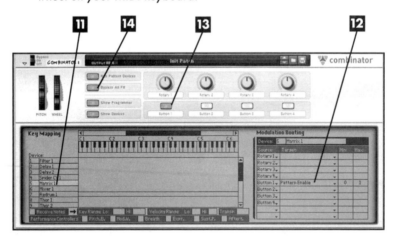

11 **Select Matrix 1** from the Device list.

12 For the Button 1 Target, **choose Pattern Enable**.

13 **Click Button 1** on the Combinator's Controller panel to turn the Matrix on and off.

14 Just so you will have touched every part of the Combinator in this exercise, **click** the **Bypass All FX button** on the Combinator, and the Digital Delays will be bypassed.

Whew. Did you make it through all that? If you did, I hope you enjoyed it, and I hope it gave you some ideas. By the way, there is also a Spider Audio Merger and Splitter that works the same way as the Spider CV, but it is used for merging and splitting audio signals instead of control voltage signals. Whenever you need one thing to go out to several things or several things to merge into one thing, the Spiders are there for you.

One last word about the advanced exercise: I hope you will take that idea with you regarding processing the left channel with a Digital Delay set to three steps and processing the right channel with a Digital Delay set to four steps (or two steps). This can be a very effective combination for processing rhythms in a variety of electronic music. You may even want to design a little Combi based on that idea.

External Routing Indicators

Here's the last little bit of the Combinator I want to tell you about before moving on to the next chapter. The Combinator includes external routing indicators (on both the front and the rear of the Combinator) to warn you if you have connected any of the devices inside the Combinator directly to a device outside the Combinator. The following exercise shows how to do something that you normally want to avoid.

1 In a fresh rack containing a Mixer 14:2, **create** a **Combinator** with a Subtractor inside it. (This step is not pictured.)

2 **Press** the **Tab key** to flip your rack around and then **drag** a **cable** connecting Subtractor's LFO 1 Modulation output to the Mixer's Channel 1 Pan CV in. The External Routing light will turn on.

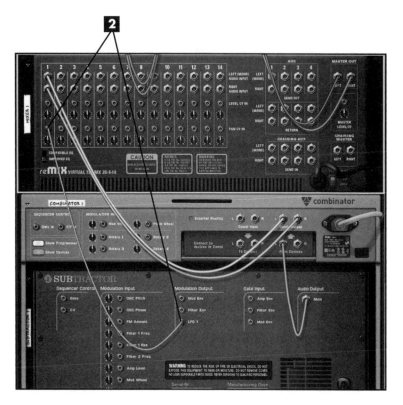

Press the **Tab key** to flip your rack back around, and you will see that external routing is indicated in the Combinator's display window as well.

Although using the Subtractor's LFO to auto-pan Channel 1 of the Mixer is a neat idea (and I wouldn't try to stop you), the reason it is generally good practice to avoid external routing is because those connections will not be saved with the Combinator patch. External routing is saved with the Reason song file, however. If you choose to route externally in this manner, be aware that when you open that Combi in another song, you will be missing any external connections.

The Combinator is truly one of the most powerful tools in Reason. I hope that after making it through this chapter, you are comfortable and confident with using the Combinator in your Reason songs.

Now it's time to move on to the next chapter and learn about the ReGroove Mixer.

9 } The ReGroove Mixer

The ReGroove Mixer is an innovation that gives you unprecedented hands-on control over the rhythmic content of your Reason songs. It offers powerful real-time control of several rhythmic aspects of the individual tracks in your sequence, and it also controls the relationship between those tracks (using the Slide control).

In this chapter, you will learn how to:

* Apply preset groove patches to a drum pattern
* Make your own groove patch
* Permanently apply your ReGroove Mixer settings to a MIDI track
* Apply Random Timing to a programmed beat to add a "human feel"
* Use the Slide control to move individual drum parts ahead of or behind the beat

Applying a Preset Groove Patch

The exercises in this chapter will be a bit long, simply because we have to set up a beat before we can apply the ReGroove Mixer to it. The first part of this next exercise will be setting up the beat, and the second half will be actually using the ReGroove Mixer. In this exercise, you will use the RPG-8 Arpeggiator to help you construct your beat.

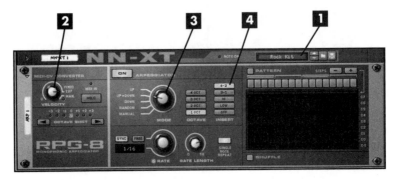

1 In a fresh rack containing a Mixer 14:2, **create** an **NN-XT** and **load** the following **patch:** Reason Factory Sound Bank > NN-XT Sampler Patches > Drums and Percussion > Drums and Kits > Rock Kit.sxt.

2 Under the NN-XT, **create** an RPG-8 **Monophonic Arpeggiator** and **turn** the **Velocity knob** to Fixed 127. Now all notes from the Arpeggiator will be at max volume, regardless of how hard you play.

3 **Turn** the **Mode knob** to Up + Down.

4 **Turn** the **Insert mode** to 4–2.

5 In the Reason Sequencer, **turn down** Tempo to 95.

6 **Click** on the **Arp 1 device icon** to select the track and then **hold down** the **C1 and D1 keys** on your MIDI keyboard, just to hear the RPG-8 Arpeggiator in action. You can try other key combinations as well.

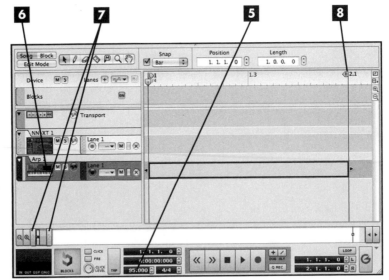

7 **Press** the **Zoom In Button** to the left until Bar 1 takes up almost the entire window.

8 **Alt-click** on **Bar 2** to place the right locator there.

9 **Select** your **Pencil tool** and **draw** in a one-bar **clip** on the Arp 1 track.

10 **Click** the **Switch to Edit Mode button**.

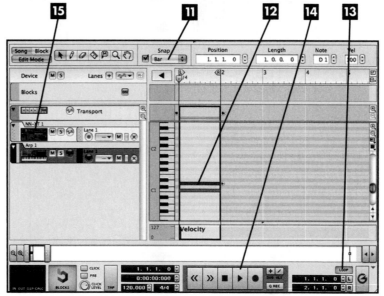

11 **Make sure Bar** is selected for the Grid mode.

12 **Draw** in **notes** at C1 and D1. You need only click once in the C1 and D1 grid squares, and the entire note will be drawn automatically, since you set the Grid mode to Bar already.

13 **Make sure Loop** is on.

14 **Click Play**, and you will hear a very robotic beat with a fixed velocity and perfect timing.

15 **Select** the **NN-XT track** by clicking its device icon.

16 **Right-click** on the **RPG-8** and **select Arpeggio Notes to Track**. You will hear the sound of double-triggering.

17 **Mute** the **Arp 1 Track** in the Reason Sequencer. The double-triggering will go away.

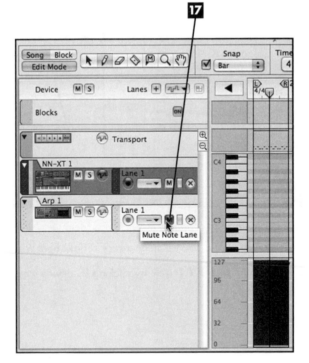

Now your beat is set up, and you can start using the ReGroove Mixer. You might want to save first, since you went to all the trouble of making this little beat.

1 Select Groove Channel **A1** from the Select Groove menu on the NN-XT 1 track.

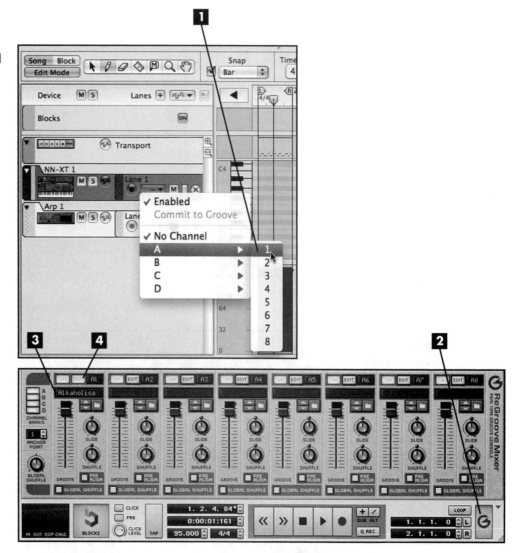

2 Show the ReGroove Mixer.

3 Click the Channel A1 Browse Groove Patch button and load the following patch: Reason Factory Sound Bank > ReGroove Patches > Drummer > Vintage Soul-RnB > Alkaholics.grov.

4 Click the Channel A1 **Edit Channel button**. This will open the Tool window to the Groove tab, with Groove Channel A1 already selected for editing.

5 If a shuffle was not what you had in mind, **move down** the **Timing Impact slider** to about 31%.

6 To dial back the variation in velocity, **move down** the **Velocity Impact slider** to 70%.

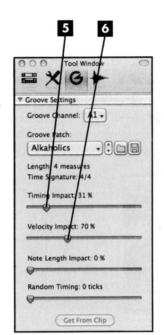

7 Slowly **move** the Channel A1 **Groove Amount slider** all the way down until you have that stiff robo-drummer back behind the kit.

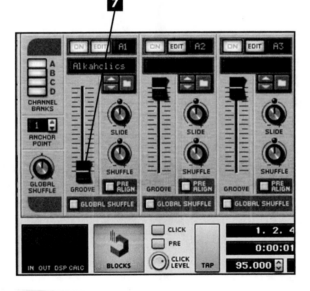

The next exercise picks up where this one left off, so you might want to save again.

Get Groove from Clip (Making Your Own Groove Patch)

You are not limited to the groove patches in the Reason Factory Sound Bank. You can create your own groove patch from any MIDI clip in Reason. So if you play a keyboard bass part with a certain groove into the Reason Sequencer, or maybe you play a cymbal part on a drum pad controller that has a groove you want to use, you can easily turn the MIDI clip in the Reason Sequencer into a groove patch.

This exercise picks up where the previous exercise left off.

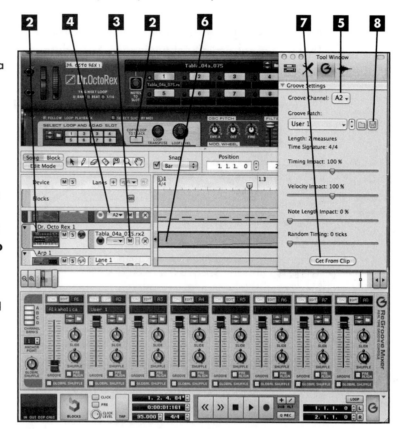

1 Under the RPG-1, **create** a **Dr. Octo Rex** and **load** the following **patch:** Reason Factory Sound Bank > Dr Rex Percussion Loops > Tabla 075 bpm > Tabla_04a_075.rx2.

2 **Make sure** the **Dr. Octo REX 1 track** is selected in the Reason Sequencer and then **click** the **Copy Loop to Track button** on Dr. Octo Rex.

3 **Mute** the **Dr. Octo REX 1 track** in the Reason Sequencer.

4 **Select Groove A2** for the NN-XT 1 track.

5 On the Groove tab of the Tool window, **select Groove Channel A2**.

6 Using your Selection tool, **click** once on the **clip** on the Dr. Octo REX 1 track to select it.

7 **Click** the **Get Groove from Clip button** at the bottom of the Tool window.

8 **Click** the **Save button** in the Groove Settings window if you want to save your groove patch in a user folder of your choosing (optional).

Now when you play your track, you will hear the shuffle timing you got from your Dr.Rex clip applied to your NN-XT 1 track. You won't hear the cool velocity performance in the tabla REX loop, however, since that was in the audio recording of the tabla player— not in the MIDI data of the REX loop. Of course, if you used Get Groove from Clip on a clip you had actually played into the Reason Sequencer, you'd have all the velocity, timing, and note-length information from your performance in your new groove patch.

Note that instead of using the Get Groove from Clip button in the Tool window, you can also right-click on any Sequencer clip and select Get Groove from Clip from the pop-up menu. Whenever a clip is selected in the Reason Sequencer, you can also choose Get Groove from Clip from the Edit menu. In either case, the groove will be applied to whatever is the currently selected groove channel on the Groove tab of the Tool window.

Let's save once more, because the next exercise picks up where this one left off.

Commit to Groove

So far, everything we've done with the ReGroove Mixer has been nondestructive. That is, it is not actually changing the MIDI data in our Sequencer tracks. Commit to Groove allows you to apply the groove to the MIDI track, so that the track will sound "groovy" even if you do not have a groove channel enabled on the track. This exercise picks up where the previous exercise left off.

1 Right-click on the **Dr. Octo REX 1 track** and choose **Delete Track and Device**.

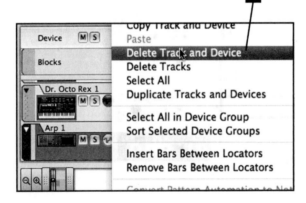

2 Right-click on the **Arp 1 track** and choose **Delete Track and Device**.

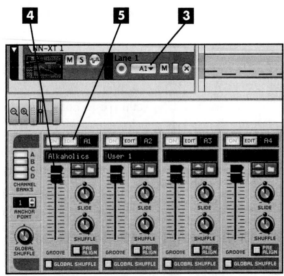

3 Assign Groove Channel **A1** for the NN-XT 1 Sequencer track.

4 Move the Channel A1 **Groove Amount slider** all the way up.

5 Click the Channel A1 **Edit Channel button**.

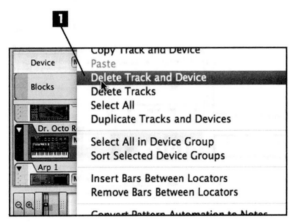

6 In the Tool window, **turn up Timing Impact** to 100%.

7 **Double-click** on the **NN-XT 1 clip**.

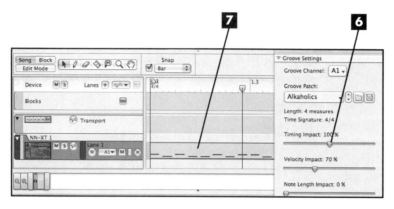

8 **Drag** the **Horizontal Zoom slider** to the left so that Bar 1 takes up almost the whole window.

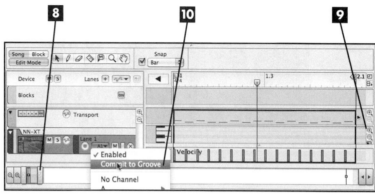

9 **Use** the **vertical scrollbar** so you can see the notes on C1 and D1. (If you don't see a vertical scrollbar, you need to drag the top of the Sequencer window up by its handle to make it taller.)

10 From the Select Groove drop-down on the NN-XT 1 sequencer track, **select Commit to Groove**. You will see the notes move in the clip, and the velocities will become varied.

Notice that no groove channel is enabled anymore on the NN-XT 1 track. If you look in the Select Groove menu, you will see that after you selected Commit to Groove, No Channel was automatically selected.

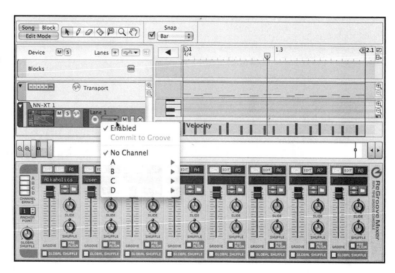

Of course, the reason why No Channel is automatically selected when you use Commit to Groove is so that you don't have the groove applied twice (once to the actual MIDI data in the clip and once again through the ReGroove Mixer). Please save your song so we can head into the last leg of this multipart exercise.

Random Timing

You can use random timing to add a subtle amount of human-feel to a cymbal part or to drastically mess up a beat. This exercise picks up where the previous one left off.

1 While playing the beat you've made, **select Groove Channel A3** on the NN-XT 1 track.

2 **Click** the Channel A3 **Edit button** so you can adjust Channel A3's groove settings in the Tool window.

3 Slowly **move** the **Random Timing slider** all the way to the right and **listen** as your **drummer** becomes ever more avant-garde!

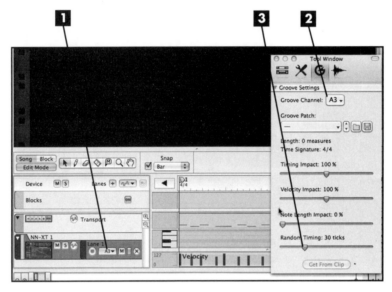

We are finished with this setup (at long last!). The next exercise will start with a fresh rack.

Redrum, ReGroove, and the Slide Control

In the past, when using the Copy Pattern to Track feature in Redrum, you have copied the entire pattern (kick, snare, cymbals, and all) to a single note lane in the Reason Sequencer. However, to get the most out of the ReGroove Mixer, it's nice to have each drum on a separate note lane so that you can apply shuffle, groove patches, and slide separately instead of to the entire drum kit. The next exercise shows you how to do this.

Also included in this exercise is the use of the Slide control, which allows you to move an individual track slightly behind or slightly ahead of the beat. This allows you to build some tension by playing slightly on top of (or in front of) the beat or to lay back slightly behind the beat.

1 In a fresh rack containing a Mixer 14:2, **create** an instance of **Redrum**. It will have Disco Kit RDK loaded by default. **Click** Redrum's **Channel 8 Select button** so you can program a hi-hat part.

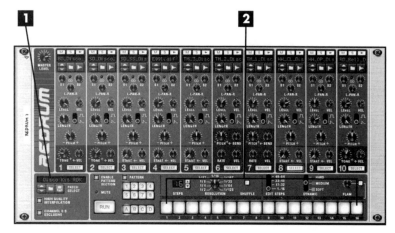

2 **Click and drag** from left to right across **all 16 Step buttons** so that they are all lit orange.

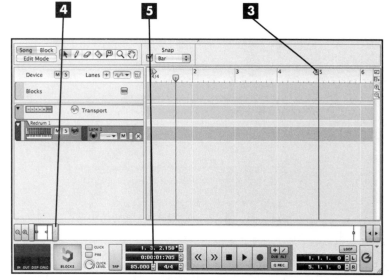

3 In the Reason Sequencer, **drag** the **right locator** to Bar 5.

4 **Increase** the **horizontal zoom** until the first four bars fill up most of the Sequencer window.

5 **Turn down** the **Tempo** to 85.

6 Right-click on Redrum and choose Copy Pattern to Track.

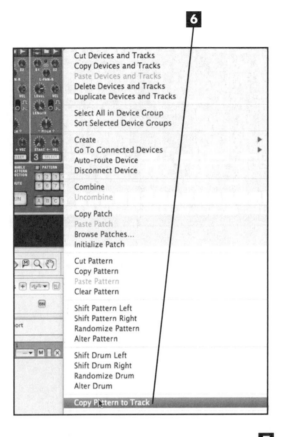

7 Right-click on Redrum and choose Clear Pattern.

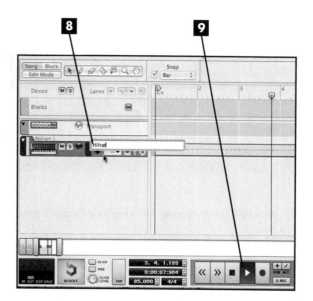

8 **Double-click** on the **Redrum 1 note lane** (where it says "Lane 1") and **rename it** "Hihat." Then **press Enter** on your computer keyboard.

9 **Click Play** in the Reason Transport.

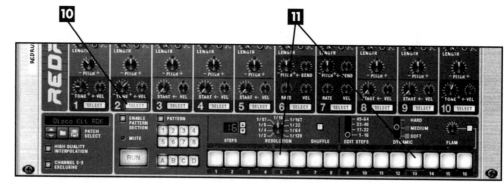

10 On Redrum, **click** the Channel 2 **Select button** so you can program a snare part.

11 **Click Step buttons 5 and 13**.

12 **Right-click** on **Redrum** and **choose Copy Pattern to Track** (not pictured).

13 **Right-click** on **Redrum** and **choose Clear Pattern** (not pictured).

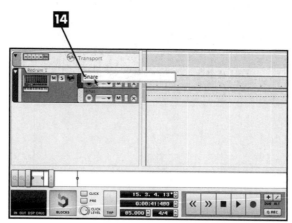

14 In the Reason Sequencer, **double-click** on the Redrum 1 **Lane 2 label** and **rename it** "Snare."

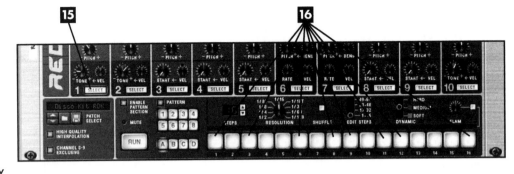

15 On Redrum, **click** the Channel 1 **Select button** so you can program a kick drum part.

16 **Activate Step buttons 1, 3, 6, 8, 9, 11, 12, and 16**. Now you've got a fairly busy kick drum part.

17 **Right-click** on **Redrum** and **choose Copy Pattern to Track** (not pictured).

18 **Right-click** on **Redrum** and **choose Clear Pattern** (not pictured).

19 In the Reason Sequencer, **double-click** on the Redrum 1 **Lane 3 label** and **rename it** "kick."

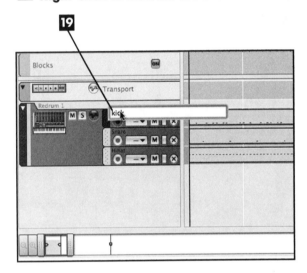

Okay, now you have a simple drum part set up with separate note lanes for each drum. You might want to save the song before going forward. You are now ready to start setting things up for the ReGroove Mixer. Of course, you will be picking up where you left off.

1 **Select ReGroove Channel A1** from the Select Groove drop-down menu in the "kick" note lane.

2 **Select ReGroove Channel A2** from the Select Groove drop-down menu in the "snare" note lane.

3 **Select ReGroove Channel A3** from the Select Groove drop-down menu in the "hi-hat" note lane.

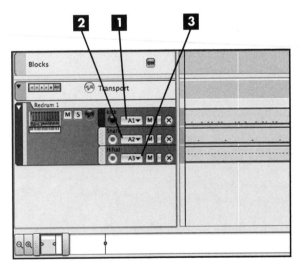

4 Click the **ReGroove Mixer button** in the Reason Transport to show the ReGroove Mixer.

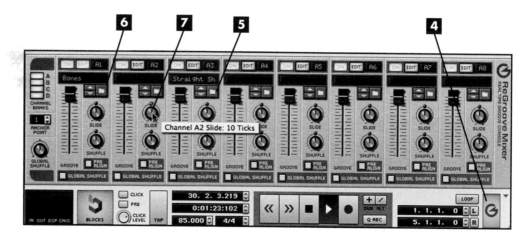

5 Click the Channel A3 **Browse Groove Patch button** and **load Factory Sound Bank > ReGroove Patches > Percussion > Shaker > Straight Shaker.grov**. You will hear a difference in velocity emphasis and timing in the hi-hat track.

6 Click the **Browse Groove Patch button** on ReGroove Channel A1 and **choose Factory Sound Bank > ReGroove Patches > Programmed > HipHop > Bones.grov**.

7 On ReGroove Channel A2 (controlling the snare drum), **move** the **Slide knob** to a value of 10 ticks. This will make the snare hit just a bit late. (Hold down the Shift key as you drag the knob to get precise values.)

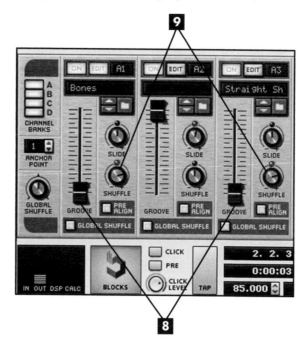

8 To go back to robot feel, **move** the **Groove Amount sliders** all the way down on ReGroove Channels A1 and A3 (kick and hi-hat).

9 **Turn up** the **Shuffle Amount knobs** to a value of 64 on ReGroove Channels A1 and A3.

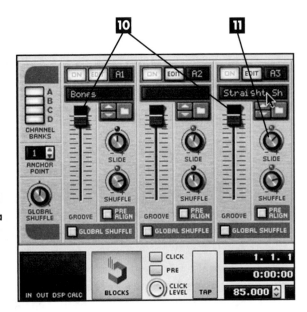

10 To re-humanize the feel, **move** the **Groove Amount sliders** all the way back up on ReGroove Channels A1 and A3.

11 Slowly **turn** the Channel A3 **Slide Amount knob** all the way to the right and then slowly dial it back to a value of 40, which will leave the hi-hats just a bit behind the rest of the beat.

Hmm...sounds like the drummer could use some Red Bull or something!

We're finished with that setup now. The next (and final!) exercise will start with a fresh rack.

Pre-Align

Pre-Align is a feature that nondestructively aligns (quantizes) the notes in a track to a 1/16-note grid so that when a groove patch is applied, it doesn't produce unpredictable results due to an imperfect live performance on the MIDI keyboard or drum pad.

1 In a fresh rack containing Mixer 14:2, **create** an **NN-XT** and **load** the following **patch:** Reason Factory Sound Bank > NN-XT Sampler Patches > Drums and Percussion > Drums and Kits > Dry Kit.

2 Turn on Click.

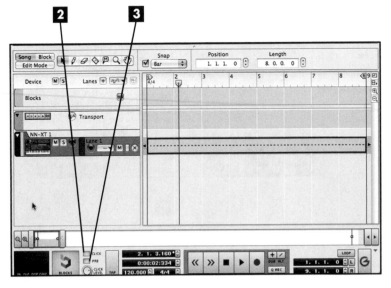

3 **Turn on Precount** so that you will have a one-bar count-in when you press Record in the next step.

4 **Press** the **F#1 key** on your MIDI keyboard. You should hear a closed hi-hat. **Click** the **Record button** and **record** an 1/8-note **pattern** for eight bars (filling the space between the L/R locators).

5 **Click Stop**.

6 **Click Play**.

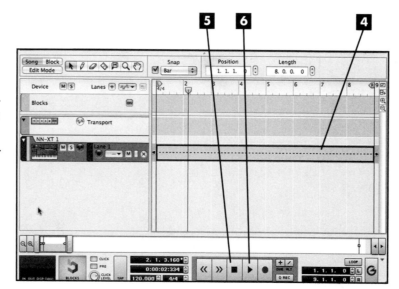

7 **Click** the **button** to show the ReGroove Mixer.

8 **Select Groove Channel A1** for the NN-XT 1 track.

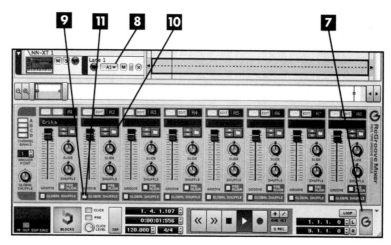

9 **Click** the Channel A1 **Pre-Align button**. You should hear your hi-hat hits quantized right on the 1/8 notes, even though the MIDI notes don't actually move on the grid (if you were to look at them).

10 **Click** the Channel A1 **Browse Groove Patch button** and **choose Reason Factory Sound Bank > ReGroove Patches > Drummer > Hiphop > Erika**.

11 **Turn off Pre-Align**, and if your performance was less than perfect, you may hear some pretty weird stuff! **Turn Pre-Align back on**, and you should be good.

All right, in the next chapter, we're going to get into the king of drums! It is known simply as *Kong*, and you're going to be blown away by all of its capabilities!

10 } Kong

And now it's time to talk about the big, new bad boy in Reason 5—Kong.

Whereas Thor has raw and sometimes ethereal majesty, Kong is all brute power. Why? Because Kong is all about percussion! Whereas Thor is the alpha and the omega of synthesizers, Kong is the king of drums.

Modeled on the MPC series of drum machines made famous by Akai, Kong allows you to create and perform by pressing pads (either onscreen or through your controller) that are set up to trigger drum sounds or loops.

But Reason already has drums, so what gives? Kong allows for advanced drum patch creation that can go far beyond Redrum, and like everything else in Reason, it is quite complementary to all that exists within the closed Reason environment already. And while it's great for post-production, it also adds new possibilities for live performance with its ability to allow you to trigger loops on the fly—something that has been mostly missing up until now.

Before we go further, though, let me explain a big difference between Redrum and Kong. Kong is a drum module, designer, and performance tool that is part synthesizer, part sampler, and part loop player. It has no sequencer. Redrum, on the other hand, is a drum machine in the classic sense—it has a built-in sequencer as well as the ability to trigger drum samples. Starting to see the difference?

Bottom line: Kong is exactly what the doctor ordered for sprucing up drums in your songs and adding a new tool to your live performance.

And now that you're excited, let's start playing with it.

In this chapter, you will learn how to:

* Browse for new patches in Kong
* Work with the Quick Editors
* Use pad settings and groups
* Work with external FX with Kong

Anatomy of Kong

Let's start by getting to know Kong on the surface. As you can see, Kong looks very simple. There are the classic drum pads that we all expect from a drum module in this day and age, and only a small number of buttons. Although it may seem simple, believe me when I say that we have a lot to cover. Let's jump into the thick of it by learning how to browse for a Kong patch.

Browsing for New Patches

To begin this exercise, create a new, blank Reason rack. Create a Mixer Remix 14-2 and a Kong Drum Designer. If you are unclear about how to create devices in Reason, refer to earlier chapters of the book for instructions on how to do this. When you're ready, put focus on Kong!

Now, let's learn how to load a patch, which couldn't be easier.

1 Click the **Browse Patch button**.

2 When the Reason Browser appears, **click** on the **Reason Factory Sound Bank**.

3 Double-click on the **Kong Patches folder**.

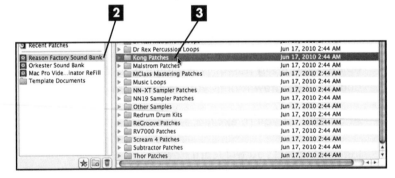

4 Double-click on the **Kong Kits folder** and then on the **Vintage Kits folder**.

5 Inside the Vintage Kits folder, **choose Classic Disco.kong**.

Congratulations, you've loaded your first Kong patch! The world of disco lays waiting at your feet. Look out, Bee Gees!

But this only opens the door; now let's take a look inside and see how the pads work!

Getting to Know the Pads

Before we go any further, try pressing some pads and get a feel for what they sound like. If you have a MIDI controller, try pressing some buttons there, too.

On a MIDI keyboard, it's important to note that the Kong key mapping is very easy-going. You can start triggering from key C-1 on up. Also, the mapping repeats again at C-3. This makes it easy for people who are using Trigger Fingers and so on.

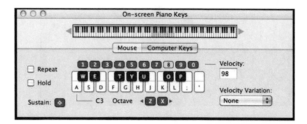

Remember, you can also use the new On-screen Piano Keys by pressing the F4 button on your keyboard. This allows you to press keys on the screen, or, by pressing the Computer Keys button, you can use your QWERTY keyboard as a music keyboard.

One thing you may notice when you tap a pad with your mouse is that a blue field will appear one pad at a time each time your cursor taps the pad.

You'll also notice that the Drum Control Panel in the lower-left corner of Kong will change. This Drum Control Panel allows you to modify specific things about that pad, or drum. For example, if you tap on a pad right now—let's say, Pad 9—the Drum Control Panel will list Drum 9. Try it!

Browsing for New Drums

While we're playing around with the drum pads, you might as well learn how to change the drum sound of a pad altogether. Reason actually comes with tons of individual drums, as well as drum pads. Let's see how to do it!

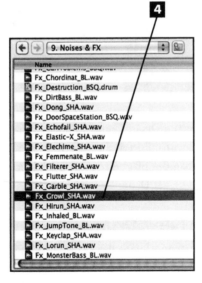

1 Select **Pad 9** and **click** the **Browse Patch button**.

2 Select the **Reason Factory Sound Bank**.

3 Select the **Kong folder** and then **select** the **Kong Sounds & Samples folder**.

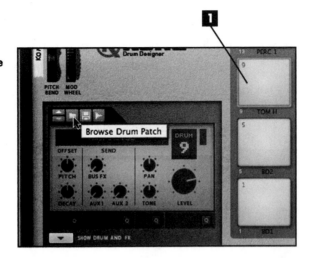

4 Double-click the **Noise and FX folder** and **select FX_Growl_SHA.wav**.

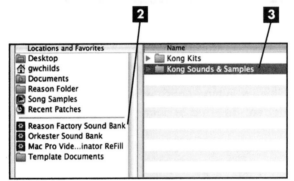

Okay, now you know how to change the drum pads of individual pads within a Kong patch, but before we get deeper, let's discuss a little more about the Drum Control Panel.

Understanding the Drum Control Panel

The Drum Control Panel is just a place where you can modify the properties of individual drums in your Kong patch—like earlier, where when we pressed a pad, the control panel listed a different drum within its window. Also within this window, you can modify the volume of a specific drum, adjust its pitch, change what speaker it's panned to, and modify how much FX it will get from the auxiliary inputs and the internal FX bus, discussed more later in this chapter.

While you're still on Pad 9, try adjusting its volume. After you've adjusted it, click Pad 11 and notice how the volume jumps back to another setting. The Drum Control Panel will change to show the setting of each pad as it is selected.

The Quick Editors

Although the Drum Control Panel is great, you may decide you want to see the volume, pan, or other settings for all the pads at once. This is where the Quick Editors come into play.

You will see these little Q buttons all over Kong. When you click one of these buttons, you bring up a Quick Editor that pertains to the function that it's closest to. For example, if you were to click the Q button near the Level knob in the Drum Control Panel, you would bring up a Quick Editor that controls the level for all of the pads within the current Kong patch. Let's try it now.

1 **Click** the **Q button** near the Volume knob within the Drum Control Panel.

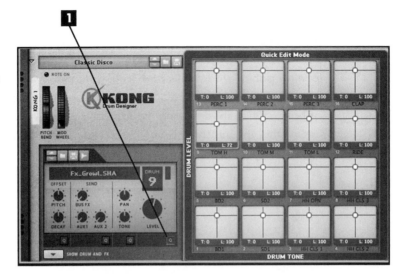

When you do this, you bring up the Quick Edit mode for Drum Level. This Editor allows you to adjust the level of each pad by moving the little white circles up and down and adjust the tone by moving the white circles left and right. Try moving one or two around.

As you move each white circle, you'll notice that the Drum Control Panel parameters will change as well. For example, if you move a white circle around on Drum Pad 3 while Drum Pad 3 is selected, you'll notice that the Level and Tone knobs will move, too.

There are Quick Edit modes for many facets of Kong, including:

※ Decay

※ Offset

※ FX

※ Pad group

※ Drum assignments

※ And more...

If you don't understand what some of these parameters I'm naming are, don't worry; we'll cover those in depth as we move through this chapter. Now, let's talk a bit about the pad settings.

Pad Settings

To effectively demonstrate pad settings, let's record something with Kong using the current drum patch.

1 Set your **left loop loca-tor** at Measure 5 and then set your **right loop locator** at Measure 7.

2 Enable **Loop Record, Quantize during Record**, and the **click**, or **metronome**.

3 Record any old **pattern**. Note that if you don't have a MIDI controller, you can record by simply tapping Kong's pads along to the metronome or using the Show On-Screen Piano Keys function by pressing the F4 button.

4 **Stop recording.**

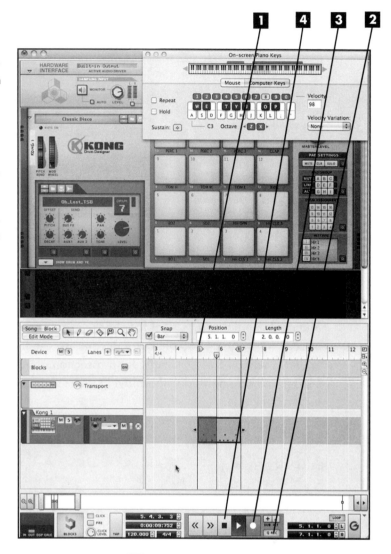

5 Now, **press** the **Play button** to hear back your recorded loop.

6 While the loop is playing, **click** on one of the **drum pads** you used to make your loop. This will cause the blue field to appear around the pad.

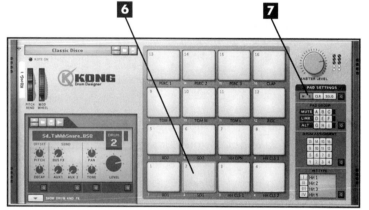

7 **Press** the **Mute button**. Notice that everything but that pad can be heard now. The pad will also turn red to indicate that it is muted.

8 Next, **press** the **Solo button**. Notice how the pad turns green, and you can only hear this drum pad. This means you have soloed this pad. Every other pad is now muted, and this one is enabled. To undo this, **press** the **Solo button** again.

9 **Press** the **CLR button**. This will clear the current muted state from where you pressed the Mute button in Step 7. It will also take care of any other pads that may have been muted as we've been playing around.

Muting and soloing are great for checking out certain parts individually to inspect quality, mix, EQ, and so on. But you can also use these functions for live performance, as seen in Step 9. Simply loop a section of your Sequencer and then start muting and soloing during the playing process to give the feel of parts dropping out or coming in.

> ❋ **NOTE**
>
> Reason has many settings, functions, and so on that seem to be very straightforward in their usage. However, by experimenting, you may find that functions such as pad settings can be used in other ways than how Propellerhead intended. Never be afraid to experiment and think outside the box!

Pad Groups

You may run into situations where you want to either increase the realism of how your drum patch works or set it up so you can trigger multiple pads at once. This is where pad groupings come into play. Let's start with the Mute groups.

Mute Groups

Sometimes you may want Kong to behave in a very electronic way, and sometimes you may want some realism out of it. One way to simulate realism is through mute groups. Let's start off with an example.

When you strike a hi-hat that is closed, meaning that the two cymbals that make up the hi-hat are pressed together, it produces a markedly different sound from when the two cymbals are apart. When they are open, the cymbal strike is sustained, long, and crisp. When the cymbals are closed, the sound is muted, clipped, and so on.

Mute groups let you duplicate this behavior. Let's do a little experiment to see how the mute groups work.

1 **Open** a new **Kong patch** following the instructions from earlier in this chapter. **Select Reason Factory Sound Bank > Kong Patches > Kong Kits > House Kits > Deep House.kong.**

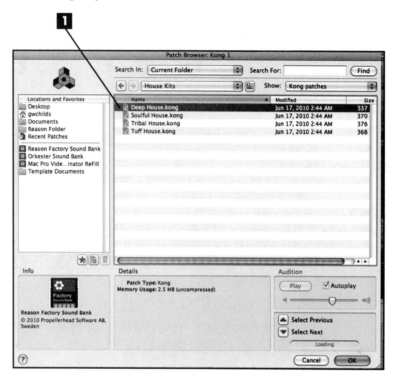

2 **Click Pad 7**, labeled HH CLS 2, so that the blue area appears around the pad.

3 **Click Mute Group A.**

4 **Click Pad 12**, labeled Crash, so that the blue area appears around the pad.

5 **Click Mute Group A.**

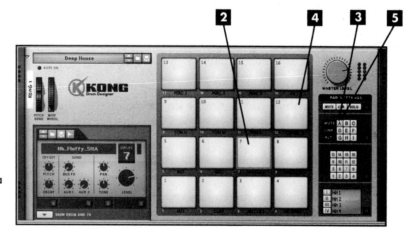

6 Now, **press Pad 12** and notice the long decay of the crash. While the decay is taking place, **click Pad 7**. Notice how Pad 7 mutes the crash when you press it. This happens because you've set up a mute group. One pad will mute the other.

Not only are mute groups great for simulating realism, but they are also great for using a drum to stop a loop and so on. Bottom line: Use your imagination!

So, we now have a better understanding of mute groups. Let's talk a bit about link groups.

Link Groups

Feel as if you don't have enough fingers for all those pads? Well, good news! Link groups allow you to trigger more than one pad at once. Let's see how they work!

1 **Click Pad 1**, labeled BD1, so that the blue field appears around it.

2 **Click** the **Link Group D button**.

3 **Click Pad 5**, labeled BD2, so that the blue field appears around it.

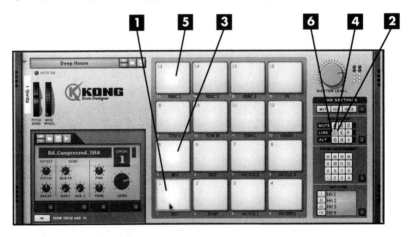

4 **Click** the **Link Group D button** again.

5 **Click Pad 13** so that the blue field appears around the pad.

6 **Click** the **Link Group D button** again.

When you click Pad 1, 5, or 13, do you notice how they all light up and sound off together now? You've grouped these pads! Until you ungroup them by simply selecting one with your mouse and clicking the Link Group D button again, they will continue to play in unison!

This can be great for triggering multiple drums at once during a live performance or recording or for simply stacking a couple of kick drums to get that big, big sound.

Now, let's add a little randomization into the mix.

Alt Groups

Randomization can be really nice at times. It affords your computer the chance to throw in some ideas of its own, so to speak. This isn't bad, as creativity can be taxing sometimes!

With alt groups, you clump a few (or more) pads together, but when you hit any one or more pads out of this group, which pad will actually play will be random. This could be great for hi-hats, bongos, toms, and so on. Let's try this out to get a feel for it!

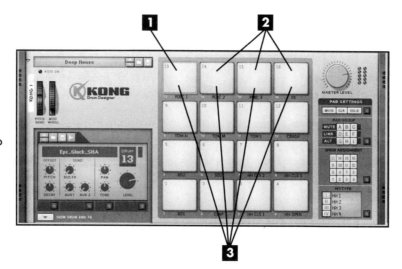

1 **Click Pad 13**, labeled Perc 1, and **assign it** to Alt Group G.

2 **Repeat Step 1** for Pads 14–16; **assign them** all to Alt Group G.

3 **Play** any of the **pads** out of this top row (Pads 13–16).

Notice that when you hit any of these pads now, other pads tend light up in place of the one that you are pressing. For instructional purposes, try pressing Pad 13 over and over again. Notice how a different pad plays and lights up each time?

By pressing one pad rhythmically and repetitiously, you can record percussion, a drum loop, and more with little to no effort!

There's definitely more to be learned about pad assignments. But before we go further into that, let's reveal a deeper secret that Kong keeps: drum modules.

The Different Drum Modules

Up to this point, we've seen how to modify pads, change levels, and so on. But we really haven't encountered what is actually responsible for the sounds coming from Kong. In this section, I'd like to take you inside the Kong machine so that you get an idea of how to modify and create your own Kong patches.

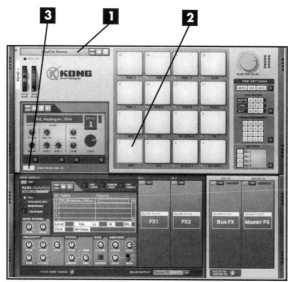

1 **Load** the **Soulful House.kong preset** found in Reason Factory Sound Bank > Kong Patches > Kong Kits > House Kits. This is a great way to get to know Kong from the inside out.

2 **Click Pad 1** so the blue field appears around it.

3 **Click** the **Show Drum and FX button** in the lower-left corner of Kong.

What appears below Kong is its internal area for drum and FX modules. Here you can choose what kind of drum module you want to use to generate sounds and what kind of FX you want your drum modules to go through. Each pad can have up to one drum module and two FX modules. Additionally, there's a Bus and Master FX module area that we'll get to later in this chapter.

What's currently shown in this drum channel is the NN-Nano, a little-brother sampler to the NN-XT also available in Reason. As with the NN-XT, you can sample directly into this drum module by clicking the Sample button shown in the upper-left corner of the module.

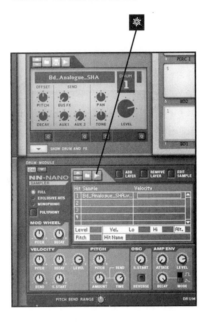

Additionally, if you click the Sample button on Kong itself, Kong will start sampling and then, when finished, will automatically create an NN-Nano for whatever pad was selected when the sampling started and will place the sample immediately on the newly created NN-Nano for that drum channel.

Now, let's take a look at some of the other drum modules and how to access them.

Press the small arrow next to the On button of the NN-Nano. This will bring up a list of the assorted modules available for Kong. I'll start explaining them now.

NN-Nano Sampler

I already went into some explanation of this module earlier, but before I move on to the others, let me expand on this one a bit. As mentioned earlier, the NN-Nano is the smaller, Kong version of the NN-XT. As with the NN-XT you can map multiple samples to the NN-Nano. Why?

The NN-Nano lets you assign up to four slots per NN-Nano unit and then take each slot even further by assigning additional layers to each one using the Layer buttons at the top of the module. You can use these samples in different ways, but the most common usage is for either stacking samples or velocity mapping.

NN-Nano also provides you with quick and easy sample mangling and manipulation on the fly. For example, there are Reverse button, pitch adjustment, and velocity refinements.

You can even access the Sample Editor directly from the NN-Nano by clicking the Edit Sample button in the upper-right corner of the NN-Nano.

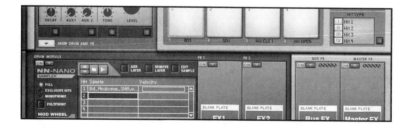

Also, you can assign each sample slot in the NN-Nano to different hit types in the Hit Type section of Kong.

Nurse REX Drum Loop Player

The Nurse REX drum loop player is the devoted little sister to—who else?—Dr. Octo Rex. And Rex files are rich in this family's history.

Nurse REX allows you to assign drum loops or segments of drum loops to specific Kong drum pads. This is a very welcome addition to Reason, because now you can bring up a loop with the press of a button and have it be in the actual tempo of your song, because the loop is a Rex file! For more information on Rex files, refer to Chapter 2.

By modifying the hit type of the pad assigned to the Nurse REX, you can also modify whether Nurse REX will play in these modes:

❋ **Loop Trig.** When a pad triggers Nurse REX, she plays the loaded loop one time. Click again, and the loop repeats.

❋ **Chunk Trig.** This hit type allows you to assign multiple pads to one Nurse REX and then assign portions of the loop to the assigned pads. Let's try it now.

1 Right-click on **Kong**. **Select Initialize**.

2 Click the **Show Drum and FX button** in the bottom-left corner of Kong to expose the Drum Module area of Kong.

3 Click Pad 1.

4 Select Nurse REX as your drum module and then use the Browse button to load the Acs01_Straight-Ahead_130.rx2 loop from the root of the Dr. Rex Drum Loops folder within the Reason Factory Sound Bank.

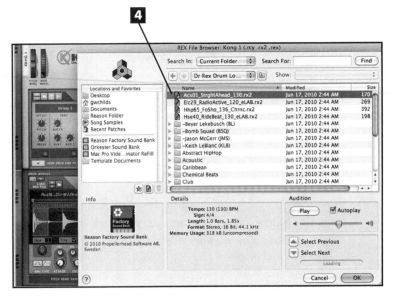

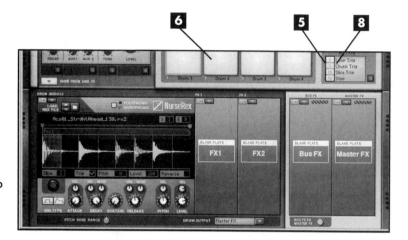

5 **Click** the **Hit Type II button**, also labeled as "Chunk."

6 **Click Pad 2**.

7 **Press** the **Drum Assign Button number 1**. Doing this will cause Pad 2 to also trigger the Nurse REX assigned to Pad 1.

8 **Click Hit Type II** again for Pad 2, setting it to Chunk as well.

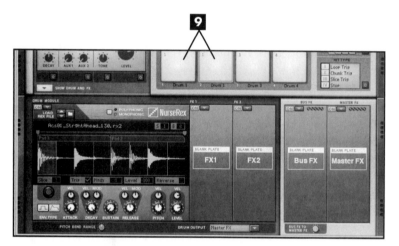

9 Now, **play Pad 1 and 2.** Notice how they both play a portion of the loop.

Having different parts of one loop assigned over multiple pads can be quite handy. One pad can be the main drum beat, while you can set up the second pad to be the fill. Just press the main loop continuously and then work in the fill pad when you need to. This can make your drums seem very live and fluid with very little effort.

❀ **Slice Trig.** With this hit type, you can play either single or multiple slices from a Rex loop on a single pad. (For more information on Rex loops and slices, refer to Chapter 2.) If you assign more than one slice to a pad, it will simply alternate between slices each time the pad is pressed.

❀ **Stop Trig.** With this hit type, use the Pad Assignment section like we did with the Chunk Trig exercise to assign two pads to one Nurse REX. Set one pad to Loop or Chunk and the other pad to Stop Trig. This will allow you to trigger a loop with one pad and immediately stop the loop with the other pad. It's great for creating instant silence or variations on an assigned loop.

Now, let me finish up the section on drum modules (with descriptions), as we have a lot of ground to cover!

※ **Physical Bass Drum, Snare Drum, and Tom Tom.** These modules do exactly what their description says they do: simulate authentic drum kit pieces. Through physical modeling, you have access to the same parameters you would tweak on a real kit. For example, you can tune your snare drum, tom, and kick drum with the Tune knobs on each module. Each module sounds wonderful and really does give that live-drummer feel. When you couple a module with FX, covered later in this chapter, you can have a very real-sounding kit. Or, you can simply mix and match and come up with something new!

※ **Synth Bass Drum, Synth Snare Drum, Synth Hihat, Synth Tom Tom.** The synth-based percussion modules within Kong closely resemble the drum synths found within classic Roland drum machines, such as the TR-808, TR-909, and so on. These tones are meant to sound synthetic, of course, and can assist in giving either that very retro sound or just more of an electronic, dance type of sound to your Kong patches.

Kong FX

Okay, so we have a good idea of what's generating the sounds within Kong, but what do we use to thicken them up, create some atmosphere, and make the sounds stand out?

Kong comes complete with its own line of effects, as luck would have it, and in this section I'd like to show you how to instantiate them.

FX 1 and 2

First, we'll talk about the FX 1 and 2 slots. There are two of these slots for each drum pad, or each drum channel (16 total). These act as inserts and only affect the drum module that each sits next to. If you switch to a different pad, those slots will be empty again because no inserts have been assigned to the pad yet.

At this moment, you should still have Kong available with a Nurse REX assigned to Pad 1. We'll pick up from where we left off.

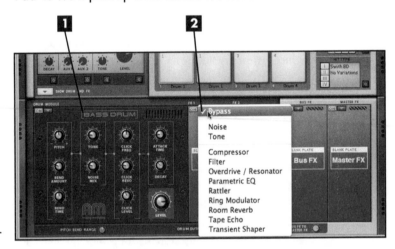

1 Using the small down arrow in the Drum Module section, **select** the **Synth Bass Drum**.

2 In the FX1 area next to your drum module, **click** the **down arrow** near the On button and notice all the FX possibilities. Let me give you a brief description of each.

※ **Support modules.** You can use the Noise and Tone modules either as supplemental frequency generators to other drum modules or as standalone drum modules. They provide a great way to add more thickness to a snare using the Noise module or to simply generate a very quick synth percussion sound with Tone on its own. You can also use Tone to add an additional low-end or high-end frequency to a tom, kick, hi-hat, and so on.

❋ **Compressor.** The Compressor is great for balancing the levels of certain drums. But it's even better for giving certain drums definition and just making them seem bigger. The Compressor is simply a must for your kick drums, but you can also use it for snares, loops, and more when they seem to be too far in the back. Additionally, it never hurts to have a compressor on your Master FX slot, which affects every drum within Kong.

❋ **Filter.** Use the filter when you want to quickly eliminate certain frequencies within one drum that clash with other drums inside your Kong patch. Also, filters are great for loops! Drop a band-pass filter on a Nurse REX and then use the Compressor on FX 2. You'll be able to keep that nice groove but also hear it clearly without creating a lot of mud.

❋ **Overdrive/Resonator.** This is basically a mini Scream unit. If you need distortion, if you need resonance in a pinch, look no further. The Resonance section is a light version of the body section of the Scream unit as well.

❋ **Parametric EQ.** Use this for sculpting your drums when they are close but not quite fitting in. With the Parametric EQ, you can boost needed signals and shelve signals that really aren't helping.

❋ **Rattler.** You can use this to add more snare rattle and feel to the Physical Snare module or the Synth Snare module. But with additional experimentation, who knows what else you could come up with.

❋ **Ring Modulator.** If you like tinny, metallic noises in your music, or if you just want to make something natural sound otherworldly, the Ring Modulator can definitely assist you. I've also found that the Ring Modulator is quite nice for creating synthetic tabla-type sounds when used with the Tone Generator.

❋ **Room Reverb.** Sometimes you want that snare to be a bit bigger, with a longer decay and a slight hollowness. Sometimes you may need a little cushion in that kick. The Room Reverb does just what the name says—it adds reverb to your sound or your patch. It gives the drum mix dimension and makes it sound more real when used in small, thoughtful amounts.

❋ **Tape Echo.** Designed to emulate the old Roland Tape Echo FX modules, the Tape Echo not only supplies an echo to whatever it's assigned to, but it also has a wonderful filter enabled on it. The filter is for filtering out lows during each repetition of the echo. So, if you're running a muddy sound through the Tape Echo, it would be advisable to raise the Freq so that each echo is of a higher frequency and does not create mud in your mix. The Wobble knob adds a very slight modulation to the repetitions of the echo that is for emulating the Roland Space Echo as well. Apply for that warbly, dub effect.

What makes the Tape Echo seriously fun is using it for an effects loop. Raise the Feedback, hit a pad that is going through the Tape Echo, and then adjust the timing. You'll hear the rate increase of each echo in an ethereal, washed-out, magnetic collage that sounds dreamy and drug reminiscent. It's great for reggae, dub, and any other ethereal music.

❋ **Transient Shaper.** This handy FX module works similarly to the Compressor, but only in the sense that it is used to accentuate the attack and decay of a drum, giving it more definition.

Bus FX

Bus FX allows you to instantiate one FX module that can be used across all of your pads. This is great for creating a slight atmosphere where all of your drums can sit, and it also allows you to save valuable CPU. (Though who am I kidding? Reason is so light on CPU!)

To use the Bus FX:

1 Select an **FX module** in the Bus FX slot.

2 For each drum that you want to exhibit some of this effect, **raise** the **Bus FX knob** in the Drum Control panel. Note: You will need to click on the drum pad and then raise the knob for each drum that needs Bus FX, or else use the Quick Edit mode corresponding to this knob in the Drum Control Panel.

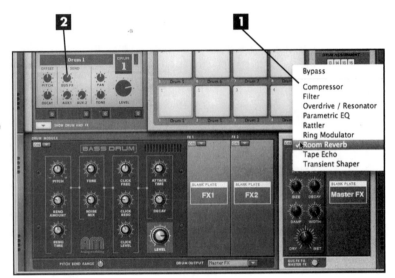

Master FX

Want to add some final polish to the total sound of your Kong kit? Then put a plug-in in the Master FX slot. You can choose any of the FX in Kong, though it is important to understand that all sounds coming from the main audio outs will be affected by this slot. I would suggest a compressor, EQ, or transient shaper—something that will give you some punch and not totally wash out your kit.

I suggest a compressor, transient shaper, or EQ if you are planning on a standard drum kit, and so on. However, if you are going to be using Kong for its other function, read on and disregard everything I just said!

Kong Using External FX

Kong not only has FX of its own; it can also use external Reason FX processors.

If you turn Kong around, using the Tab button with the Show Drum and FX button pressed in (yellow), you'll notice a small schematic that houses an audio input, an output, and inputs for an external FX loop.

Let's try setting up Kong with an external FX processor. This will be great information to know when you want to use an RV-7000 or any of the other Reason FX within Kong:

1 With Kong turned around and with the Show Drum and FX button pressed, **create** an **RV-7000** while holding Shift.

2 **Route** the **RV-7000 audio inputs** to the Breakout Output jack on Kong and **route** the **RV-7000 output jack** on Kong to the Breakout Input jack.

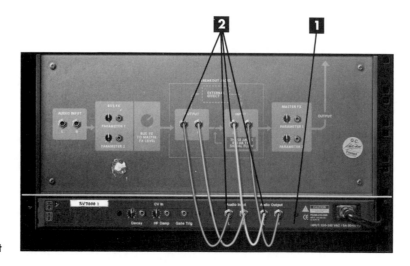

3 **Press** the **Tab button** and **select Pad 1**.

4 **Raise** the **Bus FX level** in the Drum Control Panel.

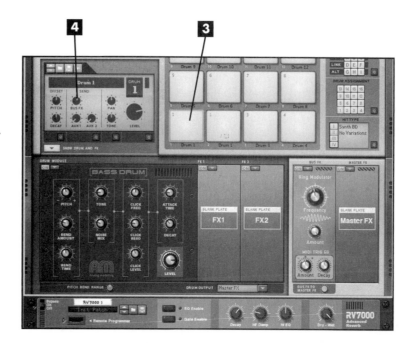

Now that Pad 1 has Bus FX routed externally, the FX module instantiated within the actual FX Module slot will work together with the RV-7000. Using an external FX processor and a Kong module together can yield some sonically interesting and sometimes astounding FX. Try experimenting!

Kong as an FX Processor

Believe it or not, you can actually use Kong as an FX processor as well. When you press Tab and then click the Show Drum and FX button and reveal the Drum Module area at the base of Kong, you'll notice an audio input. When you connect an instrument or audio input into these ports, you can now run this signal freely through not only the Bus FX, but also the Master FX. It's two FX processors for the price of one!

Conclusion

Hopefully, your eyes are now open to how incredibly powerful the mighty Kong is. Not only is it a mega drum module with more flexibility than one knows what to do with, but it's also a very powerful FX module!

} Index

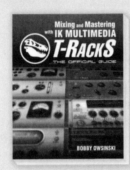

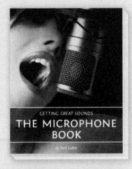